Hannah Boie

Civilian Power

Hannah Boie

CIVILIAN POWER

An Analysis
of Euro-Mediterranean Relations

LIT

To Bertram and Johannes

D 188

Bibliographic information published by the Deutsche Nationalbibliothek
The Deutsche Nationalbibliothek lists this publication in the Deutsche
Nationalbibliografie; detailed bibliographic data are available in the Internet at
http://dnb.d-nb.de.

ISBN 978-3-643-10590-5
Zugl.: FU Berlin, Univ., Diss., 2009

A catalogue record for this book is available from the British Library

©LIT VERLAG Dr. W. Hopf Berlin 2010
Fresnostr. 2   D-48159 Münster
Tel. +49 (0) 2 51-620 320   Fax +49 (0) 2 51-922 60 99
e-Mail: lit@lit-verlag.de   http://www.lit-verlag.de

Distribution:
In Germany: LIT Verlag Fresnostr. 2, D-48159 Münster
Tel. +49 (0) 2 51-620 32 22, Fax +49 (0) 2 51-922 60 99, e-Mail: vertrieb@lit-verlag.de
In Austria: Medienlogistik Pichler-ÖBZ, e-mail: mlo@medien-logistik.at
In Switzerland: B + M Buch- und Medienvertrieb, e-mail: order@buch-medien.ch

In the UK: Global Book Marketing, e-mail: mo@centralbooks.com

In North America by:

Transaction Publishers
New Brunswick (U.S.A.) and London (U.K.)

Transaction Publishers
Rutgers University
35 Berrue Circle
Piscataway, NJ 08854

Phone: +1 (732) 445 - 2280
Fax: + 1 (732) 445 - 3138
for orders (U. S. only):
toll free (888) 999 - 6778
e-mail: orders@transactionpub.com

Acknowledgements

I am indebted to many people whose assistance was invaluable for the successful completion of this dissertation. In the following lines some of them are gratefully acknowledged. However, I am aware of the fact that there are many more - among them the people of the Tel Aviv University campus, where this dissertation was written - and that these words cannot express the gratitude and respect I feel for all of those.

I would like to thank the people who provided scientific and financial support to make this work possible. My advisors Prof. Dr. Sven Chojnacki (Freie Universität Berlin) and Prof. Dr. Joseph Kostiner (Tel Aviv University) have guided me through the research and have provided precious advise. The Friedrich-Ebert-Stiftung (FES) and the Deutscher Akademischer Austauschdienst (DAAD) have made this research possible granting me scholarships.

Furthermore, my research was facilitated by an internship in the European Parliament office of Dr. Klaus Hänsch in Brussels. I have conducted interviews with EU officials in Brussels, Cairo and Tel Aviv, as well as with the Israeli Mission to the European Union. I thank all my interview partners and all others who provided information and gave me important insights in their work and in the concrete realization of Euro-Mediterranean relations. Without their friendly cooperation and indispensable help this dissertation work would not have gained the results it eventually came up with.

I especially thank all those who have always given generously and reliably of their support, encouragement, and true friendship. They include Chen Alon, Erich von Arnstein, Carolin Banzhaf, Christiane Bauer, Jens-Michael Bopp, Naomi Brenner, Ronny Fried, Isabelle Gras, Maya Gur, Kamel Hazbon, Gundula Klein, Alexander Legel, Christian Mohr, Robert Nachum, Tilman Nagel, Rita Rosenblit, Asaf Tsanany, and Constanze Woltag. A special note of gratitude belongs to my family. Their firm support and love is something I shall cherish always.

Contents

X

Abbreviations

AA	Association Agreement(s)
AC	Action Plan(s
CSBM	Confidence and Security-Building Measures
CR	Country Report(s)
CSP	Country Strategy Paper(s)
CFSP	Common Foreign and Security Policy
CIHRS	Cairo Institute for Human Rights Studies
CSDP	Common Security and Defense Policy
DG RELEX	Directorate-General for External Relations
EC	European Commission
EIB	European Investment Bank
EIDHR	European Initiative for Democracy and Human Rights
EMAA	Euro-Mediterranean Association Agreement(s)
EMHRN	Euro-Mediterranean Human Rights Network
EMP	Euro-Mediterranean Partnership
EMPA	Euro-Mediterranean Parliamentary Assembly
ENP	European Neighbourhood Policy
ENPI	European Neighbourhood and Partnership Instrument
EP	European Parliament
EPC	European Political Cooperation
ESDP	European Security and Defense Policy
EU	European Union
EuropeAid	European Commission's cooperation office that manages EU external aid programs
INTERREG	European Union program aiming to stimulate inter-regional cooperation within the EU
MEDA	European Union assistance program for the Mediterranean countries

MPC	Mediterranean Partner Country/ies
NATO	North Atlantic Treaty Organization
NIP	National Indicative Programme
PHARE	European Union assistance program for the Central European candidate countries
PR	Progress Report(s)
RIP	Regional Indicative Programme
TACIS	European Union technical assistance program for the Commonwealth of Independent States
UN	United Nations
UNDP	United Nations Development Program
UNDR	Universal Declaration on Human Rights
OSCE	Organization for Security and Cooperation in Europe

1   Introduction

Power as a concept has occupied the minds of people, societies and states at least since the beginning of Western political historiography, when Thucydides wrote in his *History of the Peloponnesian War* that "the strong do what they have the power to do and the weak accept what they have to accept" (Thucydides 1972: 402). Power has indeed been associated with force for most of history. On the other hand, common wisdom has also developed over the centuries, which claims that "the pen is mightier than the sword[1]," or that "knowledge is power[2]." Looking at history and the rich body of political theory on power, one can easily follow Max Weber (1919), who pointed out that power is one of the central elements, or even *the* central element, of politics and political science (see Weber 1958). This study, accordingly, deals with power as a major concept of political theory and of political reality. For the sake of a clearer research focus, it stays away from age-old questions of power in warfare, but concentrates instead on questions of civilian power. Non-civilian (military) forms of power are thus excluded from the study.[3] Instead, we are interested in how non-military power works in specific relationships.

To gain insights into civilian power, we have thus chosen a typical example of civilian power policies: the relationship between the European Union (EU) and two Mediterranean countries in the

---

[1]   This saying was coined by Edward Bulwer-Lytton in 1839.

[2]   This saying was coined by Francis Bacon in 1597. For a modern and more refined version of a confrontation of power and violence, see Arendt 1970. In her essay "On Violence" she develops her notion that power and violence are indeed opposites.

[3]   Non-civilian forms of power are excluded from the study only for the sake of a focused research. This does not imply that we consider these forms less relevant or less interesting. By contrast, Joseph S. Nye is right when he calls for an integration of different, i.e. civilian and military power strategies into a single strategy of "smart power" (see Nye 2007: 172). His concept is rather meant to give impetuses for policy strategies than to add to academic research on power. As this study attempts to contribute to an academic dialogue rather than to a dialogue on concrete foreign policy strategies, it will only deal with non-military issues.

framework of the Euro-Mediterranean Partnership (EMP) and the European Neighbourhood[4] Policy (ENP). The EU itself has widely been called a typical civilian power and the EMP and the ENP especially are regarded as prime examples of civilian power policy. Different scholars have suggested that the EU plays the decisive role in the EMP/ENP power game. It has been said, for example, that the EMP has consolidated Europe's hegemony in the region (see Attinà 2003), while others have viewed the EU as caught between expressions of post-colonialism and the manners of neo-colonialism (see Adler/Crawford 2006). Even more, some authors are of the opinion that the EU behaves similar to the Romans regarding their *mare nostrum* (see Demmelhuber 2006) and accuse the EU of imperial behavior (see Doty 1996).

These widespread opinions evoke the question of whether the EU really is the only, or at least the dominant actor in the relationship. And even further: how does power work at all in this civilian relationship? And how could its manifestation be traced back in units that are smaller and more understandable than the broad hypothesis of one dominant actor? A closer look at this relationship is therefore interesting and might develop a clearer understanding of how civilian power works in this specific case.

1.1   Research objective

The *aim of the study* is thus to gain a refined understanding of the appearance of civilian power in two concrete cases of Euro-Mediterranean policies. Taking a closer look at underlying power structures, and the open and hidden exercise of power in these two concrete cases, might reveal insights about how civilian power works.

---

[4]   The study at hand uses American orthography. However, in direct quotations as well as referring to specific EU programs, the British (European) spelling is used.

2

The study is conducted in the hope that such insights might lead to broader knowledge about the way civilian power appears—on the other hand, due to the delicate way in which power sometimes reveals itself, its manifestations in these specific cases may be subtle or indeed barely visible.

In order to examine the way civilian power appears in the specific relationship and to develop a more refined and precise conception of how it works, a case study has been conducted. Relations between the European Union and Israel, as well as relations between the European Union and Egypt, are analyzed in the framework of the Euro-Mediterranean Partnership, also called Barcelona-Process, and the European Neighbourhood Policy. This analysis is conducted within the framework of *four main types of power* that have been identified by recent scholarly work and represent the latest state of research (see Barnett/Duvall 2005). These are deeply rooted in the literature and in the ongoing scientific debates and therefore may serve as a guideline along which European-Israel/Egyptian relations are explored. Characterized as *compulsory, institutional, structural,* and *productive* power, these types embrace the main schools of thought in power research that have been discussed to the present day. This fourfold characterization of power will be adjusted to the fields of international civilian relations.

To guide the study, the following *basic questions* have been chosen:

1) How, i.e., by which of the four types of power, is the civilian power between the EU and Israel/Egypt in the examined case characterized?
2) Which of the types do(es) not appear at all in the examined case?
3) Does the appearance of the four types differ between the two examined cases?
4) On what, in particular, does the appearance of the four types of power depend?

These basic questions serve as guidelines for the selection of data required to conduct the research. They are set up according to the research objective and highlight the contributions the study will try to make to the research of civilian power. Hereby, the study attempts to make two primary theoretical contributions, one to political theory and one to the research of international relations. Its main pursued contributions to research in power theory are the following: First of all, it is based on the fourfold characteristic of power that includes the main ways in which power may occur. By including different forms of power, the perception of power on which it is based is much broader than the definitions of prevalent schools. By taking different forms of power into account, the study keeps from neglecting expressions of power that are harder to notice. The study takes these four types as a starting point and refines them in two ways: First, it makes them feasible for a study that is located within international relations (and not sociology or psychology). Secondly, it filters them in order to arrive at an understanding of a specifically civilian form of power (as opposed to military forms). This approach serves as the theoretical basis of the case study.

The study also aims to contribute to research on international relations. In European-Middle Eastern relations, power is not exercised in a military way, and its forms are subtle and hard to grasp. Therefore, power in civilian international constellations is widely unexplored. This is especially true for the analysis of European-Middle Eastern relations. Neither the European foreign policy per se nor its Middle Eastern forms has been examined in the sole light of power aspects. This is due to a widespread misunderstanding: The European Union and its policies are regularly described as civilian. For many schools, "civilian" goes together with "peaceful"—and "powerless." By concentrating on cooperation and dialogue in relationships, they tend to forget that power is also a (perhaps even determining) part of these peaceful forms of relationships. This is also true for European foreign policy. As Europe is mostly described as a typically civilian actor, questions of power have been neglected in research on European foreign relations. Ironically, there has been a whole debate concerning the character of the European Union as a so-called civilian power. The civilian nature of the "civilian power EU" (and its possible transformation into military forms) has been discussed and typologized. "Civilian power EU" has been used to describe the EU as a civilian actor. In the same sense one could speak of a superpower or a regional power—meaning states or international actors. Therefore, only the word "civilian" has been examined for the EU, but not the word "power." It is simply not understood in the basic sense of "exercise of power"—rather, only in the sense of "actor." Moreover, parts of the discussion of the EU as a civilian power have concentrated on analyzing its capability as a norm-sender (see Johansson-Nogués 2006: 1).[5] This approach does not take into account that power has more than one side. It does not only depend on the EU as a norm (or whatever else)-sender, but also on the readiness of the other side to receive the sent messages, to accept or to reject them—and to send its own messages.

The study at hand brings power back into this context and also takes into account its characteristics as a relation. It therefore tries to make a contribution to the understanding of power in international contexts, referring to it in terms of relation as well as of civilian character. The study therefore has two goals: first, to lead to new insights into how civilian power appears in a specific case, taking into account notions of power as a relationship; second, to enrich research of European foreign policy in the Middle East, which until now has barely been examined from the aspect of power.

---

[5]   Elisabeth Johansson-Nogués has commented that norm-receivers are seldom taken into account, and has chosen to apply regime theory in order to examine the EU's promotion of civil society. She does not examine this promotion under the focus of power, though.

1.2 Basic challenges: how to explore civilian power?

While developing the setup of this research, it became clear that every scholar dealing with the fields of power is confronted with *two major challenges*. First of all, up to the present time, no generally agreed-upon theory or concept of power exists. Instead, power continues to be a highly controversial subject. This is especially true for civilian forms of power. Secondly, up to the present time, no method has been developed that could be used to measure power structures in different fields.

1.2.1 The lack of a consistent theory of power

Researchers in the fields of power are confronted with a severe lack of knowledge concerning their subject. Robert Bierstedt has suggested that few "problems in sociology are more perplexing than the problem of social power. In the entire lexicon of social concepts none is more troublesome than the concept of power. We may say about it in general only what St. Augustine said about time, that we all know perfectly well what it is—until someone asks us" (Bierstedt 1950: 730).

Debates on power have circled around a number of questions. There have been long disputes about potential versus actualized power, about the legitimacy and consensus of norms as a basis for describing power; and about problems of agency (see Green 1998: 610). Up to the present time, however, no definition of power exists on which a majority of scholars would agree. This means that one cannot speak of gaps in an existing theory—rather, there are many explanations, definitions and fragments of definitions on single issues of power.

Connected to the lack of a definition of power is the lack of a commonly agreed-upon theory of power upon which one could build further research. Instead, there are different lines of research that have been conducted during the last centuries. They are not uniform, but rather concentrate on different aspects of power and are not necessarily connected explicitly to the fields of international relations. This is especially surprising if one considers the central meaning that power has in the fields of political science and—more importantly—in the human activity that the social sciences try to depict.

One major reason for this situation may be that power is very difficult to measure. More than being a central subject of political sciences, power is also a typical one, because it is highly complex and will not be grasped by simple models. Moreover, power is a critical topic for most actors in political and everyday life. It may take very different forms, is not exercised openly in many cases, and in most cases is treated as a taboo. It touches social realities and the position of every individual in society, as well as of every state in international politics. In most cases, dealing with power means dealing with interests, with interdependencies, with inequalities, and sometimes also with injustice. Therefore, it is a topic that is as delicate as it is relevant to our lives. Every study dealing with power will most probably be confronted with obstacles in its investigation. It is thus very hard to explore power and to reach conclusions that would explain the matter even in part, not to mention as a whole.

1.2.2   The lack of a consistent method of measuring power

The measurement of power has been one of the biggest challenges in political theory. It has been assumed that political science should find an index to measure power as much as economic sciences have their currencies for measuring economic transactions (see Merritt/Zinnes 1988: 142). Up to the present, however, no generally agreed-upon method has been developed with which power could be measured. In this context, David A. Baldwin even speaks of "The Measurement Problem" (Baldwin 2002: 181), and Frederick Frey claims that definitions of power have been developed in a way that makes them easier to operationalize and measure later on, instead of in a way that deals with present complex concepts of power (see Frey 1989: 7 et seq).

Researchers have been trying to "rank nation-states from the most to the least powerful" (Merritt/Zinnes 1988: 141), mostly equating power with certain kinds of resources. Especially in realist research, power has been defined as military. The question of "who has more military resources" has led many analysts to statements concerning the power distribution among states. The comparisons of the different military potentials lead to the assumption that the state with the larger and better-developed military means is the more powerful one. Another single-variable indicator that has become popular among researches is national income (see, for example, Art/Waltz 1983; Davis 1954; Knorr 1956; Organski 1958; Organski/Kugler 1980; Osgood/Tucker 1967; Sprout/Sprout 1962; 1965; Wright 1955).[6] Other single-variable indicators that have been regarded as signs of power were calculated for single states and then compared. These are, for example, demographic indices, natural resources, GNP and economic strength. Such indicators have been criticized for oversimplification and for not taking account of important parts of a country's possible power facets (see Baldwin 2002: 181). The question that came up was how one could measure more than one of these resources, for example, military *and* economic *and* natural resources—and then compare them? Citing James Lee Ray and Ayse Vural, Baldwin uses the illustrative example of sports. He points out that looking for the number-one athlete by comparing "a golfer, a swimmer, an archer, a runner and a weightlifter" (Baldwin 2002: 181; see Lukes 2007: 86; Ray/Vural 1986) will not lead to a reasonable answer. And comparing an athlete who masters more than one sport to another who excels in different disciplines will not be enlightening either.

---

[6]   Organski developed a theory of power transition which argues that conflicts are most likely when power transition takes place.

Nevertheless, there have been attempts to combine different power figures and to assemble a list suggesting the number one figure in the world of power (see Singer/Diehl 1990). The most famous measurement of power is the Correlates of War Project and its differentiations. In an attempt to gain systematic insights into international conflicts, J. David Singer and his associate Melvin Small began in 1963 to collect the most complete and precise figures possible for all wars since 1815. They listed the number of deaths, the durations of the wars, and the number of participants (see Small/Singer 1982; Singer/Small 1972). Up to the present, the data collection of Singer/Small is one of the most comprehensive quantitative studies on war. As Singer and Small concentrated on the results of war, its possible causes only became of interest later on. Among the most famous studies in this context are those of Leng and Singer (1988) on "militarized interstate crises" and of Maoz (1982), who takes the Correlates of War Project as a basis and examines serious interstate disputes. Gochman and Maoz (1984) collected data on "militarized interstate disputes." Leng and Singer added a behavioral component to the Correlates of War Project and tried to grasp the events that lead to the militarized crisis and its development. Gochman and Maoz also adhered to the Correlates of War data in order to find out "objectives, motives and methods of states" (Gochman/Maoz 1984: 615) in conflicts (which, according to the authors, remain the same even if technology has changed). Moreover, Gochman and Leng developed a new dataset dealing with sub-war conflicts connected to the Behavioral Correlates of War project. They also inquired about the reasons for war when researching why some militarized conflicts escalate to wars and some do not (see Gochman/Leng 1988). At present, these early approaches to systemizing wars have been differentiated and refined significantly further and developed into typologies of violence and wars (see Chojnacki 2004; 2008).

Assuming that power is reflected in certain indicators of states, Singer and other scholars started collecting data on these figures. According to Singer, power is expressed in "demographic, industrial, and military indicators of national capabilities" (Singer 1988: 116). He explains that each dimension is based on two subdimensions: the demographic dimension, for example, is composed of the total state population and of the number of people living in urban areas. Therefore, an element of the development of the population is assumed to be included. The industrial dimension consists of industrial energy consumption and steel production. And the military dimension is made up of the size of armed forces and the military expenditures over the past five years (see Singer 1982: 206; ibid. 1988: 117).

Without going into details, it becomes clear that there have been ambitious and comprehensive attempts to understand power. However, "even if realists generally conceptualize power in terms of material resources and embrace the view that war-fighting ability is the essence of state power, they have not reached a consensus on the appropriate criteria for measuring power" (Schmidt 2007: 62). More than that, many of these studies share one basic dilemma: they regard power as a material state possession, as the state's *"capacity to influence"* (Singer 1963: 420) or as an attribute of actors that is comparable and can lead to an estimation of the relative power of each actor (see Wolfinger 1971a). These assumptions do not take into account that power takes place in relationships and therefore can hardly be summed up by dimensions like the ones described above. Moreover, these studies only see power in the context of (military) crisis and war. The basic assumption of the Correlates of War Project and its behavioral specifications is that power is the causation of crisis and military conflicts. It does not examine power in the context of peaceful relationships, however, and therefore does not take into account other basic elements of power.

1.3 Confronting the challenges

1.3.1 Confronting the lack of a definition of power

As scholars have been able neither to come to an agreement on single issues of power nor to create a unified and comprehensive theory of power, there is no well-established typology or even theory that one could test, no contradictory theories that one could consider against each other, and no shoots of a typology or theory that one could further develop and refine, or explore on another level, or in another context than has previously been done. Therefore, the study at hand needs to be explorative. The study is rooted in the literature on power and tries to take the heterogeneity and broadness of the matter into account. It is built on the four major types of power that Michael Barnett and Raymond Duvall have summarized and conceptualized in a taxonomy derived from the great number of different scientific notions on power, including the main scientific paradigms of power research that have been developed in the literature of the last century. Their conceptualization of power is similar to the so-called four-faces approach of power that has been developed and discussed during the last decades and gained recognition (see Clegg 1989; Digeser 1992; Hay 1997; Hayward 2000). The four-faces approach, too, combines the various lines of power research and tries to understand power in a schematic way. It tries to find answers to the four following questions: "Under the first face of power the central question is, 'Who, if anyone, is exercising power?' Under the second face, 'What issues have been mobilized off the agenda and by whom?' Under the radical conception, 'Whose objective interests are being harmed?' Under the fourth face of power the critical issue is, 'What kind of subject is being produced?'" (Digeser 1992: 980; see Barnett/Duvall 2005: 8). This four-faced approach was developed during a yearlong critical examination of existing concepts, their gaps and contradictions. Responding to the lack of systematic, sharp, and analytical criteria to distinguish between the four faces, Barnett and Duvall have developed a more schematic and analytical approach. As their approach is the most current, elaborated and well-conceived taxonomy of power one can find at the moment, it is used as a basis in the study at hand. The four types developed by Barnett and Duvall serve as a starting point for the study with the aim of figuring out whether a further differentiation of this existing quadripartite classification can take place.

Coming up with refined statements of the four types of power in two cases would contribute to the power debate especially as the basics of the field are still lacking.

1.3.2 Confronting the lack of a power measurement

This research follows an idea of power that is more multifaceted than approaches that equate power with military means. As has been pointed out before, different aspects of power are taken into consideration in order to do justice to the matter's complexity. Power is not regarded as a possession that one could count up. Rather, it is regarded as a relationship between actors. Indeed, this relationship may be influenced by the actors' strength, which originates from its military, economic, demographic or natural resources. In the context of this study, a comparison of such figures will not take place, though. Instead, power structures will be looked at in detail and under consideration of some basic specifications developed by different scholars to show that power is a multidimensional matter (see Dahl 1968: 407; Harsanyi 1962; Tedeschi/Bonoma 1972: 8 et seq.). Up to the present time, there has been no agreement about which specifications are needed to describe power. However, many scholars share the opinion that one has to take into account scope and domain as two basic dimensions. If one states that A has power, the first question will be: Over what does he have power? Dealing with the "over" means referring to scope and domain (see Nagel 1975: 14). Scope describes the alteration of B's behavior due to A's influence in a certain field, i.e. "the behavior, response, attitude, belief, or choice influenced" (ibid.). This alteration may be different according to the fields of relationship between A and B. A's influence in a military issue may be less than in an economic one, for example,. Domain refers to B, who is subject to A's power. It is "the actor or set of actors influenced—an individual, group, collectivity, organization, nation, or whatever" (ibid.). Measuring A's power therefore has to take into consideration how many Bs A influences and how big they are (see Baldwin 2002: 178; Dahl 1963; Deutsch 1978; Frey 1971; Lasswell/Kaplan 1950).[7] Baldwin goes so far to say that rather "than trying to identify a single overall international power structure, scholars should strive to identify multiple structures of power in different issue areas. Admittedly, such research will not try to provide answers to the question of 'Who's number one in the game of international poker?' But simply redirecting attention away from that kind of question would, in itself, constitute progress in international power analysis" (Baldwin 2002: 188). Consequently, scope and domain will serve as two basic dimensions in the study at hand to make sure that the basic conditions of analyzing power relationships are met.

1.4   The limits of the study: a building-block approach

The study will deal only with non-military power, in this work called civilian power. It will examine two typical cases of civilian power and compare them. That means that the phenomenon is not analyzed via a single case or a no-variance study but as a comparison in a traced-back way, in order to gain insights concerning a possible variance in the

---

[7]   The concept of scope and setting in which the power relationship takes place was first laid out by Harold D. Lasswell and Abraham Kaplan in their book *Power and Society* (1950).

depending variables. Further studies will need to be conducted in the future to test the arguments attained by this study against new cases and to develop arguments about other parts of civilian power that cannot be examined in the context of this work. It is clear that the components of the greater typological theory being developed in this study depend on the examined case studies. Other cases will either prove the achieved findings or characterize new types that did not occur in the cases under consideration. Logically, inductively building a differentiation, a typology or a typological theory is an open-ended process, as one always needs to expect that there are cases of types or of subtypes that have not been examined yet. More than that, theories are always only "versions of the world" (Flick 2007: 100; see Goodman 1978) that reflect the researcher's perception of her environment and have to undergo revision, assessment and reconstruction over a time and by a number of researchers. Therefore the study is part of a so-called *building-block* approach. It is in many respects one piece of a theoretical structure still under construction.

First of all, power will not be examined as a whole, but only in its civilian form and with regard to the different occurrences of this form. Secondly, this examination is limited in the range of its content: it is founded on the example of the relationship between the European Union and two other countries, and only in a specific field of the relationship. Moreover, the study is composed as a snapshot of a specified period, but not as a before-after design. This goes along with the typical problem of every case study: A case may "multiply in a given piece of research: What the case is may change both in the hands of the researcher (during the course of the research and when the results are presented) and in the hands of the researcher's audiences" (Ragin 1992: 8).

Studies are also imaginable concerning other, non-civilian types of power, concerning civilian power actors other than the European Union, concerning other cases of the exercise of civilian power (for example, between the European Union and other states than the ones

14

chosen in this study) and concerning other specific fields of content than the ones examined here. Also, a second or a third snapshot of the cases examined after a certain period of time could be useful for theory development. And even inside its own range of content and time, the study is only a first step on the way to a more comprehensive differentiation because it cannot make comprehensive and closing statements about the four types of power analyzed. Necessarily designed as a building-block study, differential and typological theorizing cannot reveal how many of the discovered mechanisms exist. It deals with the entirety of a phenomenon and not with a limited sample. Therefore, it is not possible to say how many cases of a (sub)type exist—and how many (sub)types are still undiscovered. For the research of civilian power, this methodological constraint does not matter, though. It is not important how many times a type of civilian power occurs, but rather what characterizes its appearance and its mode of action. In order to be able to arrive at a further differentiation, the study has chosen a property space that is especially informative for an analysis of civilian power: the European Foreign policy in the Middle East presents a (perhaps currently even *the*) typical instance of the exercise of civilian power.

Given these facts, the study at hand must be seen as only a singular and very basic element on the long way to the establishment of a more comprehensive typology and theory building, during which the same phenomenon should be studied again at different times and places and in different settings (see Denzin 1989). It serves as a starting point for the development of further differentiation of the four types of (civilian) power and provides case study options for approaching power. Further studies could add other blocks to the development of a typology or a theory of civilian power by building on these results, and devise them in new contexts or from a different angle. It is important to note that further blocks should use the same methods of measuring power in order to gain results that can be integrated with the results of this study.

2 Methods

As stated above, a revealing study in the fields of (civilian) power needs to meet two basic conditions: These are, first of all, determination of scope and domain, and secondly, consideration of the fact that power is relational.

In order to allow for both considerations, a case study design has been chosen for the study at hand. The four types of (civilian) power will be analyzed on this basis. This promises insights into structures of power that would be missed in a less specified study or in an attempt to create a ranking of actors according to their alleged power.

In order to reach scientific results, the case study design must be set up in an organized way that allows for further comparative studies. In this context, scope and domain go along with the arrangement of the case study. They indicate which cases have been chosen for the study and justify these choices. Consequently, the case study design will be presented first, followed by the presentation of scope and domain, i.e. the explanation of which cases have been chosen and why.

2.1 Case study design: a structured focused comparison as a tool for analyzing civilian power

Even though the study at hand will result in basic considerations rather than a civilian power typology, for the sake of theoretical consistency we have chosen an approach that has been approved in previous efforts of theory development. The approach's aim is to contribute to the development of typologies, or even a theory in coming studies.[1] In

---

[1] As stated above, this study tries to refine the knowledge we have on civilian power further. Therefore, "typology building" is used here as a method only—and is referred to as such. The aim of the study is differentiation building rather than typology building, but it uses this approved method as well as the terms coined in the literature for it.

studying how deterrence works, Alexander L. George and Richard Smoke put emphasis on yielding knowledge in an explicitly scientific way that would be organized systematically and lead to conclusions beyond the examined cases (see George/Smoke 1974). Hereby, they created a new method of using case studies for scientific research. Before, case studies had been severely criticized for not being sufficiently analytical and theory-driven. Instead, most of the early case studies relied on historical descriptions of single events. Without doubt, some of these drew interesting findings or suggested new ways of interpreting historical events. They did not, however, contribute to theory development, as they did not examine events from a more focused and analytical angle. Moreover, these kinds of descriptions only examined events in their specific context. They did not compare cases and therefore could not come to a generalizable conclusion that would be right for more than one case. This criticism was also aimed at case studies concerning deterrence. George and Smoke state that different case studies on deterrence reflect the richness in which the phenomenon occurs. They therefore provide insights that merely statistical methods could not generate. They do not contribute to theory development, however, as the cases are not comparable, even though all of the case studies use similar decision-making approaches (see ibid.: 93).

In reaction to the criticism regarding case studies, George and Smoke developed a more scientific approach to case studies that is of great use for theory development. They attempted to maintain the diversity that case studies reflect, but analyzed this rich material in a cumulative way. The method they developed was one of structured, focused comparison (see ibid.: 95). Sidney Verba, who suggested examining different factors across many cases, formulated its basic idea. As these factors remain the same for the analysis of every single case, cases become comparable: "The 'uniqueness' of the explanation for any particular case arises from the fact that the combination of relevant factors that accounts for a nation's pattern of politics will be different from the combination in other cases, and the relative importance of various factors will differ from case to case. But the 'unique' explanation of a particular case can rest on general hypotheses" (Verba 1967: 114). The method combines the advantages of statistical approaches as well as of the former, unstructured type of case studies. It is close to statistical approaches as it bases its conclusions on a number of different cases and compares them. Moreover, it tests only a limited number of hypotheses or questions in a specified field. Therefore, it may achieve structured results close to those that may be gained by statistical research. In contrast to statistical research, it is able to capture the complexity and diversity of reality and shed light on facets of a phenomenon that a mere statistical approach would have overlooked. The method does not only contribute to theory building (as is its main aim, of course), but also provides a deeper understanding of the examined cases. This is especially true for cases which are yet undiscovered or require a new perspective (see Eisenhardt 2002: 31). Due to its close linkage to empirical insights, theory development based on case studies is therefore appreciated for its strengths, such as novelty, empirical validity[2], and testability (see ibid.: 32). Making use of the method of structured, focused comparison, a number of studies have been published. These deal with different fields of research such as international relations, comparative politics or internal politics (see, for example, Duyvesteyn 2002; Evans/Nelson 1989; Mitchell 2005). However, each tries to come to scientific results by asking the same questions in the different examined cases and examining the variation that occurs between the cases.

In recent years, additional theoretical insights about case studies and how to conduct them have further contributed to conducting case studies along a focused and structured way (see, for example, Miles/Huberman 1984; 2002; Ritchie/Spencer 2002). In the tradition of early differentiations of case studies by Lijphard (1971) and Eckstein (1975), Charles C. Ragin has asked the very basic question

---

[2] For the question of validity in qualitative research, see Maxwell 2002.

about what a case is at all (see Ragin 1992) and has come up with a four-folded conceptualization of how cases can be understood. He suggests differentiating between empirical versus theoretical understandings of cases as well as between specific versus general case constructs (see ibid.: 8 et seq.). The first differentiation points to the debate (see, for example, Miles/Huberman 1984; 2002; Ritchie/Spencer 2002) over whether empirically verifiable cases exist and can thus become the basis of a case study, or whether cases are rather theoretical constructs. If cases are regarded in the latter, i.e. in the nominalist sense, they are seen as the consequences of theories (see ibid.: 8). Regarding cases in a generic sense means referring to established units, such as societies, families, or individuals. On the contrary, specific case categories are developed over the course of the research itself. If one combines these four approaches, one will find four different answers for the question of what a case is: If one takes a specific and empirical approach, Ragin claims that "cases are found" (ibid: 9; see Harper 1992). On the contrary, "cases are made" (Ragin 1992: 9; see Wieviorka 1992) if they are regarded as specific theoretical constructs. If a general approach is chosen for a study, then "cases are objects" (Ragin 1992: 9; see Vaughan 1992) when they are regarded as empirical units. Finally, "cases are conventions" (Ragin 1992: 9; see Platt 1992) when they are perceived as theoretical constructs. Recently, another, more detailed typology has been promoted by Jack S. Levy. He differentiates according to the purposes followed by a case study: is it inductive, does it generate hypotheses, does it test them, or does it probe plausibility? (See Levy 2008.)

Even though different scholars have come up with these rather clear and theoretically exciting schemes of different types of case studies, Ragin and Levy point out that many studies may use cases in more than one approach because research often uses both theoretical and empirical analysis and thus relies on the chosen case(s) in more than one way (see Ragin 1992: 11, Levy 2008). More than that, case studies should not be regarded as an inferior tool that is useful only in the very early phase of research. It rather makes sense to use research strategies in an inclusive and pluralistic way (see Yin 2003: 3). Case studies—as much as other means of research, for example, experiments—can be explorative as well as descriptive or explanatory (see ibid. 1981).

In Ragin's sense, the study at hand also uses the case design in more than one approach. Basically, civilian power structures in the EMP and the ENP are regarded as an empirical fact in a specified way. Analyzing them, may however lead to new cases, i.e. to theoretically developed constructs of civilian power and its sub-forms. The study at hand will probably not be able to come up with such new cases. However, it does attempt to uncover civilian power structures in a specific relationship, and thus makes it possible to build further study on these new categories or perceptions, which may also function as cases themselves. As much as Yin is right concerning the different functions that case studies can fulfill, in the study at hand it is used in a rather traditional, i.e. explorative sense. This is due to the fact that the way civilian power works is a rather undiscovered field.

To enable the development of new cases, it is especially important to conduct research in the structured and focused way described above. Like every method used in political science, however, the method of structured, focused comparison has its limitations. "Unlike the statistical-correlative approach to multiple cases, it does not and cannot determine the relative frequency with which any given conjunction of independent and dependent variables occurs, since it does not employ" (George/Smoke 1974: 96). As only a limited, or even small number of cases can be examined in detail, neither statistically proven prediction, nor the degree of verification offered by quantitative research designs can be contrived. There is therefore a high risk that case study theory building will only describe a very particular phenomenon and that a level of generality will not be reached (see Eisenhardt 2002: 30). It is true that fresh and interesting models have been developed through structured case studies, but they are mostly limited to specific phenomena. Great theories of international relations have not been developed through case studies, though (see ibid.). Nevertheless, case studies can be parts of a greater puzzle. They can function as stones in building a longer way. One may also predict outcomes by relying on thoroughly examined case studies. Furthermore, using case studies as a research tool does not necessarily mean negating statistical measurement methods. For example, with the cooperation of different researchers, case studies could also be conducted in large numbers. George and Smoke point as well to the fact that case studies can provide the researcher with a result that may be of greater importance than a high degree of statistical verification: "a significantly greater degree of relevance to real policy problems" (George/Smoke 1974: 97). As the research design and its hypothesis do not need to fit into the corset of statistic measurability, case study design may choose ways besides the measurement mainstream and thus lead to unexpected results that are close to relevant policy questions. Moreover, variables do not need to be chosen by their measurability. Instead, the case as a whole is examined and compared to other cases. The method of structured and focused comparison is consequently of great value if we want to understand why cases are the way they are and which circumstances and structures lead to their specific appearance.

The structured and focused approach will help to avoid a non-cumulative and therefore non-scientific case study on power. It will assist in gaining knowledge in an orderly way that will enable coming studies with the same focus to build upon its structure.[3] This study will not be able to explore the complete picture of civilian power. It could, however, provide insights for further case studies in civilian power. As power is a highly complex phenomenon that has not been understood in its whole until today, a statistical approach might possibly overlook facets that determine the character of civilian power. Consequently, a method dealing with the analysis of power needs to be more

---

[3] For a discussion of the principle of repetition in case study design, i.e. the relation between the analyzed case and other cases, see Feagin/Orum/Sjoberg 1991. For a strong support of single case studies, see Flyvbjerg 2006.

explorative and less predetermined. Case studies that are built up in an analytical way could lead to more revealing findings and contribute to an innovative way of differentiating existing types of power. As the same questions are asked and the same hypotheses tested in every case, one may compare the outcomes of the cases. In follow-up studies, the findings may then be generalized and applied to a broader theoretical context. If one examines cases that are regarded as typical for the phenomenon in question, one will expect that these cases will have the same or at least highly similar outcomes. If this proves to be true, it is possible to state that A leads to B. If hypotheses tested in cases of the same type have different outcomes, though, one may also conclude something meaningful from this: it must be asked which factors lead to different outcomes. Identifying these factors may lead to a further differentiation of types of the phenomenon. Using a structured, focused comparison is thus of great use and may lead to fresh insights into the matter of civilian power.

2.2   Choosing the cases

This research uses structured, focused comparison in order to generate knowledge about civilian power and try to refine the existing body of knowledge. In doing so, it takes the following steps:

First, the four basic types in which (civilian) power may occur are characterized and specified concerning their civilian components and made amenable to the fields of international relations. According to these four basic types, we set up questions and hypotheses concerning the appearance of civilian power.

Second, we select two cases of civilian power. These cases (i.e. two countries) of the same type (i.e. with the same policy programs) have been chosen to provide a comparable analysis. According to the methodological approach, they are considered particularly *typical* as

well as politically especially important, i. e. *sensitive*.[4] The first
criterion of selection is based on the assumption that especially typical
cases have a higher probability of reflecting the majority of cases. The
field of research is here revealed internally and from its center (see
Flick 2007: 130). In the research at hand, political importance is also
relevant because it includes the EU's policies and thus contributes to
the criterion of typicality.

2.2.1 The cases: scope and domain

In the case of civilian power, *scope* can be determined in various
ways, depending on the aim of the study. If one tries to define the
European Union's civilian power, it becomes obvious that this power
is different depending on the issue one looks at. One may assume, for
example, that the EU is militarily a more powerful actor than Middle
Eastern countries. If one looks at the development of worldwide
religious opinions, however, then the Middle East may be the more
powerful actor. Its influence on Moslems and on political movements
connected to religious beliefs seems to be a lot stronger than Europe's
ability to exercise influence in this area. At first glance, one might also
find arguments for European superiority over the Middle East when it
comes to economic power. If one further differentiates, though, one
will have to deal with the question of oil—a factor that shows
European dependency and Arab superiority concerning its distribution.

And even if one does not compare the power of two or more actors,
but rather the power of one actor in different fields, one will
understand why the determination of scope is of fundamental
importance for every study in the fields of power. Europe's ability to
exercise power may be strong in the fields of economy, but relatively
weak in military dimensions. Or: it may be strong in military

---

[4] For a list of suggestions on how to select cases, see for example, Flick 2007: 130;
Patton 2002.

dimensions, but relatively weak if one takes population growth as a criterion for power and compares which population grows more rapidly. These assumptions can neither be proven nor refuted here; it is important to note, though, how different the power of an actor may be depending on the fields in which it is exercised.

The same is true concerning the *domain* of power. How many actors are subject to European power on a specific field? For example, Europe could be very influential concerning the determination of public opinion in the Middle East, but less so in China. Here, also, a historical component comes in. The French influence in many African countries and the Maghreb stems from its past as a colonial power. It is far less able to exercise power towards countries that were British colonies, though.

The examples highlighted above show that *scope as well as domain* need to be defined in a frame that is as small as necessary and as big as possible. One needs to find the size for a study that is assessable and will generate significant results at the same time. The example of respective European influence in China and the Middle East shows that the regions chosen are still too big to be compared, so that a meaningful statement cannot be made. Accordingly, *domain and scope have been determined for this study as follows*:

Two Middle Eastern countries have been chosen as a domain, and only one field of contents will be examined concerning the scope. Israel and Egypt serve as an example because they embody key positions for political and social development in the Middle East. Stability and peace in the region depend strongly on these countries. One has to note that in order to maintain clear sight in the Middle Eastern scenery, we have chosen to study an Arab state and the Jewish state (and not two Arab states or only Israel). As a scope the EMP and the ENP have been chosen. The fact that both countries, Israel and Egypt, are part of the same European policy programs, i.e. the EMP and the ENP, allows for an analysis of how civilian power takes place in each of the relationships and for a comparison of the relationship. As both countries are part of exactly the same programs, one might expect that these policies are carried out similarly and follow the same rules. That means that if differences between these two cases do appear, we might be able to gain insights in how civilian power works and what it depends on in the examined policy programs. In the following, the choice of Egypt, Israel, and the EU`s Middle Eastern policy will be explained in detail:

Egypt's importance in the Middle East becomes obvious if one has a closer look at its position in the region: since its peace agreement with Israel, the West regards Egypt as one of the few reliable partners in the Arab World. Its example is meant to show other Arab countries that peace with Israel is possible, and that it pays. Egypt has also been active as a mediator between Israelis and Palestinians. Moreover, Mubarak's government continues to strike down the Moslem Brotherhood, an Islamic movement that enjoys great popularity in Egypt and in the Arab world but is seen as dangerous in the Western world. Egypt is said to be one of the most open Arab countries, and perhaps on its way to democratization. Therefore, the USA and Europe have a great interest in promoting Egyptian strength in the region and its not unfriendly attitude towards the West. As the EU regards Egypt as a strategic player in the region, it is among the main beneficiaries of community assistance among Mediterranean partners. The EU as a whole (as a Community, with its member states and European Investment Bank (EIB)) is the second largest donor to Egypt (see EC SEC (2005) 287/3/COM (2005) 72 final). From 2000 to 2006, a total of 594 million euros was committed to Egypt under the MEDA II national programme (see EC/Egypt 2007: 15).

It is not only the West that tries to establish and maintain good relations to Egypt. Also in the Arab world, Egypt is widely regarded as the leading cultural and political Arab country. The Arab League is located in Cairo, and a number of Egyptians assume key positions in such international bodies as the United Nations (UN). The center of

Sunni religion, the Al Azhar Mosque, attracts Sunni Moslems from all over the world to come and to study Islam. Not to be forgotten is the great prestige of Egyptian history, which is seen as a symbol of Arab greatness. Egyptian culture today is (together with Lebanese culture) the most popular in the Arabic world. Singers like Um Kulthum as well as modern TV programs have gained great importance in modern Arabic culture.

Also *Israel* plays a regional key role. Maybe even more than Egypt, it is of greatest interest to Europe and to the US, as it is of basic significance regarding the political and social movements in the regions and even worldwide. The ongoing conflict between Israel and the Palestinians keeps the atmosphere in the region heated and causes sociopolitical movements across the globe. After decades of war between Israel and its Arab neighbors, world policy is also determined by each state's position towards the conflict parties. Moreover, the West fears spillover conflicts into its own territories. Israel also takes a prominent place in the argument between promoters of democracy and others, as it is the only democratic country in the Middle East. Therefore, different sides use its position in order to strengthen their ideological arguments. Not to be forgotten is Israel's significance as a Jewish state that Western countries, especially Germany and the United States, seek to support in part for that reason.

As has been said, the *European Union*'s respective relationships with Israel and Egypt have been chosen as examples due to the fact that the European Union can be called a typical civilian actor, and also because the European Neighbourhood Policy towards the Middle East presents a prime example for the exercise of civilian power. European policy towards the Middle East is especially expressed through the Barcelona Process that was established in 1995. It is designed as a holistic program for the entire Middle Eastern region, without adequately taking into account the fundamental differences between the various Middle Eastern countries. Basically, the European Middle East policy is designed according to the three main chapters of the

26

Barcelona Process: the Political and Security Chapter; the Economic and Financial Chapter; and the Social, Cultural and Human Chapter. Moreover, in 2004, the European Neighbourhood Policy was developed. Even though it applies to the whole region (and also to Eastern European countries),[5] it works through bilateral agreements, so-called Action Plans (AC). It is meant to be the bilateral completion of the regional EMP. As both Israel and Egypt are part of the same political program, the EMP and the ENP offer an ideal framework for the comparison of both cases.

In order to obtain an assessable frame for the study, only a part of *the EMP and the ENP* can be analyzed regarding their power structures. Therefore, the study does not only concentrate on the EU and two Middle Eastern countries, but also further specifies the field of contents of the case study. The EMP and the ENP represent the framework of the study. Out of the different policies they comprise, the study focuses on the policies that are described in the third chapter of the EMP and are also part of the ENP, i.e. the EU's respective relationships with Israel and Egypt in the fields of social, cultural and human issues. This concept is so important to the makers of European Policy that it even obtained its own chapter in the Barcelona Process. It has even been claimed that "when all the policies, programmes, declarations and action plans are pared down to their essential nucleus, the Barcelona Process is really about bringing people and cultures together through partnership and dialogue. Dialogue between cultures is essentially a dialogue between people, not between anonymous cultural entities" (Leffler 2005: 62 et seq.). In contrast to the fields of economic cooperation, however, the element of power is especially veiled in this chapter. Interests are not as open here as in dealing with economic questions. Instead, the accentuation of a social, cultural and human chapter of the Barcelona Process creates the impression of a partnership among equals that will lead to a more humane and fair

---

[5]   The ENP applies to Algeria, Armenia, Azerbaijan, Belarus, Egypt, Georgia, Israel, Jordan, Lebanon, Libya, Moldova, Morocco, the Palestinian Authority, Syria, Tunisia and Ukraine.

situation. Unveiling the exercise of power in this field, therefore, is of special interest and promises fresh understandings concerning the appearance of civilian power. Consequently, the promotion of civil society groups in Israel and in Egypt by the European Union[6] has been chosen as the specified object of research. In order to gain a complete picture that does not neglect important cross connections, the security and political dialogue in the EMP/ENP framework are also taken into account if necessary for the focus of the study. This is especially relevant as EU security strategies include civil society promotion and democratization and therefore interlink with the social, cultural and human issues (see Haddadi 2006).

We have also set a further confinement concerning the *timeframe of the research*. In this context, Frederick Frey puts forth an objection to the assertion "that the conception of a power structure is invalid because it assumes a static distribution of power. In a trivial sense this is true. The power structure does depict a fixed set of relations for a given time period. But in a deeper sense it is false. The analyst describing the power structure must establish criteria for concluding that a power relation existed between two actors during the period. If the period is too long, so that significant change in power relations occurred during it, he is likely to have a hard time developing such criteria. At one point X will have influenced Y, but at another point no

---

[6]   The EU uses the term "civil society" in a rather unspecific, broad sense. In the ENP as well as in the Action Plans there are no definitions at all, so that one can only sense a "generally positive and progressive role to civil society, indicating a rather uncritical, or, more correctly, imprecise use of the term" (Simoni 2007: 153). In the MEDA Regulation, for example, it is referred to as "local authorities, rural and village groups, mutual-aid associations, trade unions, the media and organisations supporting business" (EC No 2698/2000: 8). Academically, this is not a satisfying definition. Especially in the 1990s and in connection to issues of good governance, there has been a discussion about how to define civil society (see, for example, Benington 1996; Bliss 2003; Carothers 1999/2000; Diamond 1994; Hirst 1997; Howell/Pearce 2001; Seligman 1995; White 1996). Nevertheless, this thesis will not deal with scientifically satisfying definitions of civil society, as these are less relevant in this context. Rather, it will take the EU's perception as a basis because it examines the EU's concepts and projects that are based on this broad notion of civil society.

such influence will be found. The conscientious researcher will then either indicate this fact in describing the power structure or, more likely, reduce the length of the period to obtain more stability in the power relations described. Thus, a situation of change will be depicted by several power structures. The periods can be as short as necessary to accommodate the data. In fact, the existence of the change and its precise nature is most suitably revealed by thinking in terms of power structures. Moreover, if one wishes to become more sophisticated, probabilistic representations of power relations, notions of dynamic structures, moving equilibria, and the like are available for even more adept handling of change" (Frey 1971: 1101). The timespan chosen therefore needs to be homogenous enough to show certain stability in the relationship. At the same time, it needs to be broad enough to show more than a snapshot and to come up with enough material to be evaluated in order to gain results that cover more than a very specified and limited situation. Therefore, for this study a fixed and firm framework was chosen in the form of the EMP and the ENP. That means that the timespan between the launching of the Barcelona Process in November 1995 and November 2007 will be evaluated. This timeframe accounts for the current and ongoing European policy towards the Middle East. It includes the EMP as well as the ENP. Both the EMP and the ENP offer stability in their strategies and approaches. At the same time, they have been running long enough to show power structures beyond the moment. More than that, they provide the documents needed for a reliable analysis, which a shorter timespan would not be able to provide. The chosen timeframe supplies the necessary homogeneity and stability needed for a power study as well as for an image that is more than a snapshot of the situation. It covers a typical civilian power context and is as up-to-date as possible. It promises a relatively clear picture concerning the policies in the given field that will allow for conclusions about how civilian power appears in the examined context.

The research is thus focused as regards content, but also concerning its time concentration. The method is structured in that it asks the same questions and sets up the same hypotheses in both of the chosen case examples. It collects the same data for both cases and analyzes them in the same way. Thus, it will be possible to compare the exercise of civilian power in the relationship between the EU and Egypt to the exercise of civilian power in the relationship between the EU and Israel analytically and in a structured manner. The comparison between both cases will shed light on the question of whether there are differences in the appearance of civilian power, and, if yes, what are the intervening factors that lead to these differences.

To further clarify scope and domain of the case study, *certain aspects were excluded*: The study does not explicitly deal with the Israeli-Arab conflict, and therefore will not involve itself in ongoing issues between Israel and its Arab neighbors. Also the relationship between Israel and Egypt is not part of the study. Furthermore, one must note that the study does not deal with internal structures and processes of the EU, Israel or Egypt. It may be true that there are internal arguments between DG External Relations, DG Commerce and DG Development and that the European Parliament (EP) has often fulfilled the function of a watchdog in human rights matters with an anti-Israel bias (see van Dam 2006). The Council is sometimes said to be of a double-faced identity, as values and historical references may clash with commercial and geopolitical interests (see Bartels 2004: 369; Johansson-Nogués 2006: 8 et seq.). Also, different interests of the EU member states play a role in formulating a European policy towards the Middle East. Scandinavian countries usually have a more values-oriented approach than European states that border the Mediterranean Sea. Moreover, history imposes different policies on different countries, i.e. Germany and France (see Gerstenfeld 2006; Gordon 1998: 32ff; Rummel/Wiedemann 1997: 13; Schmid 2007).[7] Naturally, Israel and Egypt as national states also have complex internal processes of coordination and decision-making. It is clear that political systems that generate and receive power are also part of a

---

[7]   For an overview of these and related questions see Nathanson/Stetter 2007.

greater context, i.e. a regional, sociopolitical, temporal and spatial environment, and that any relationship is embedded in multiple other relationships. For the sake of simplicity and feasibility, however, this study deals neither with internal processes nor with the influence of a greater environment. Instead, it only regards the outcome of internal processes in a relationship that is specified temporally, spatially, and concerning contents, i.e. the agreements made with partner states and the measures taken.

2.2.2 Taking power as a relation into the account of the comparison

Approaches that mostly examined power from the aspect of resources were among the first systematic examinations of power in the 20th century. These were questioned by a second group of scholars (see, for example, Barry 1976; Cartwright 1965; Dahl 1957; Frey 1971; Nagel 1975; Oppenheim 1981; Simon 1957; Tedeschi/Bonoma 1972). The groundbreaking book in this field, *Power and Society* (1950), was written by Harold Lasswell and Abraham Kaplan. Lasswell and Kaplan regard power as relational, i.e. taking place within structures. In their eyes, power takes place in interpersonal relations and therefore is not a pure property (see Lasswell/Kaplan 1950: 75 et seq.). This approach caused a "revolution in power analysis" (Baldwin 2002: 178). Due to its great persuasiveness and its importance in subsequent studies of power, it can hardly be neglected when studying power today. In this context, Frederick Frey points out that in general, "all discussions of power distributions, dispersed inequalities of power, even democracy and dictatorship, imply thinking in terms of power structures. Sociometry, systems of analysis, and many core notions of political science are predicated on such a concept. Like the nonissue, the notion of power structures is basic and workable, though difficult and needing further exploration" (Frey 1971: 1101)

This study also assumes that power is relational. It takes different actors and parts of their relationships (i.e. in the EMP/ENP framework) into account. Thus, the study goes further—but also turns out more complicated and harder to explore than a study that concentrates solely on one actor and its exercise of power. It will not be able to cover the European Union's respective relationships with Israel and Egypt in their complexity and the constant transformations to which they succumb. It does not evaluate the complete EMP and the ENP and does not come to general statements concerning the question of who ranks higher on the power scale.

Instead, the present study tries to analyze the relationship impartially and attempts not to present the EU a priori as the alleged stronger actor that may exercise power in its policies over the other actors. Consequently, the study does not examine the foreign policy of the European Union in the Middle East or the Barcelona Process as a European means of dealing with the challenges of the Middle East. Rather, it claims that power takes place within the relationship *between* the EU and the Middle Eastern countries. The common term "European Neighbourhood Policy" presumes that EU-Middle Eastern power relations are more bilateral by calling the actors "neighbors." However, the term in effect implies that the EU is the primary actor determining its policies regarding its "neighbors." Other definitions speak of a *dialogue* between partners, trying to avoid statements about a more powerful actor. Most of these definitions are based on the assumption that the EU is the more powerful actor in general, but cloak this assumption for the sake of political convenience. Therefore, they do not reveal their convictions, but speak in a euphemistic way of a partnership between equals. Nevertheless, they contain the assumption that the EU is the more powerful actor in the ranking of power because they assume that it disposes of more (or better) military means, that its economies are stronger, and perhaps even that its democratic forms of government and its secular way of life are more valid.

To do justice to the relational aspect of power, it has to be differentiated according to fields in which the relationship takes place and according to the actors involved. Therefore, we will attempt to look at the EU's respective relationships with Israel and Egypt in terms of actors that may influence each other and exercise power towards each other. The notion that power is expressed in relationships (and less in the attributes one actor may have) will be facilitated by two approaches:

1) The types of *institutional, structural, and productive power* can take relational aspects of power into account. Therefore, power is not regarded as a possession or as an attribute of A, but rather measured in terms of its relationship to B. Accordingly, though one may begin with the assumption that the EU exercises a certain policy, one will take B (in this case, Israel and Egypt) into account as partners and aim at describing power as manifested in the relation between the EU and these two states.

2) For the study, two specific relationships (EU-Israel and EU-Egypt) have been chosen, by whose means power will be analyzed. Accordingly, power is not treated as an abstract (or even absolute) capacity of the EU, but as a part of *specific relationships*.

Nevertheless, the terms "Euro-Mediterreanan Partnership" and "European Neighbourhood Policy" will be used, because they are the official terms for the policies of the Euro-Mediterranean relationship.

2.3   Comparing the cases: within-case analysis

The method of structured, focused comparison chooses a limited number of cases according to the research objective, and compares them. The most common way of comparing cases is a so-called controlled comparison[8] in which typical examples of the phenomenon in question are compared to one another. These cases resemble each other in every aspect but one; therefore, one can find statements concerning independent and dependent variables and their behavior in different cases. This comparison applies the logic of an experiment and promises insightful results. In reality, however, it is hard or even impossible to find instances of a phenomenon that differ in one aspect only. It may even be the case that only one instance of a phenomenon exists—and it may still be worthwhile to conduct a study of this phenomenon. The exploration of the phenomenon of civilian power faces the same challenges. Case studies provide the key to understanding how it works—one will not find two cases of civilian power, though, that are characterized by exactly the same factors except for one.

In response to this problem, there have been a number of efforts to deal with the strict requirements of controlled comparison.[9] None of these approaches, however, manages to meet the criteria of controlled comparison, so that further methodological development is based on an unstable starting position. Gary King, Robert Keohane and Sidney Verba have developed an alternative in their famous book "Designing Social Inquiry." They try to solve the problem by not considering intervening variables at all. Instead, they merely concentrate on independent and dependent variables and therefore avoid having to deal with the strict criteria of controlled comparison (see King/Keohane/Verba 1994).

---

[8]   The term "controlled comparison" was coined by Fred Eggan (1954). Other studies speak of "comparable-cases" using the term of Arend Lijphart's study: "The Comparable-Case Strategy in Comparative Research" (1975). Though both terms deal with the same matter, the first term hints more clearly at the specificity of the comparison, and will therefore be used in the following.

[9]   The most famous of these efforts are Mill's method (1843) (see Mill 2002) and its continuation as qualitative comparative analysis (see Ragin 1987), counterfactual analysis (see Tetlock/Belkin 1996), and before-after comparisons (see Lijphart 1971; 1975).

As an alternative method, Alexander L. George and Andrew Bennett have promoted within-case analysis (see George/Bennett 2005). In contrast to such attempts as the controlled comparison, it does not concentrate on comparing the performance of variables in different cases. Instead, it tries to follow the causal path in a small number of cases or even in a single case. Within-case analysis may be applied in its form as process-tracing or as congruence analysis. The congruence approach depends on a preexisting theory, according to which the outcome of a case is predicted. Afterwards, the value of the independent and dependent variables of the case is measured and compared to the predicted value. If the congruence is high, the possibility of causality is corroborated. As a developed theory does not always exist, process-tracing may be used as another method of within-case analysis. It is a means to explore processes on a micro-level and in fine detail and provides a way to understand why a phenomenon works in the special way it does. In contrast to the method King, Keohane and Verba have proposed, it takes a close look at intervening variables. Within-case analysis is compatible with the method of structured, focused comparison. It allows comparing cases without having to use the hard-to-meet criteria of controlled comparison. Moreover, it may be used for the development of typological theories.

This study will use within-case analysis to overcome the problems of controlled comparison. It chooses two cases of the phenomenon of civilian power—the EU's respective relationships with Egypt and Israel. Both cases are typical for the object of investigation. They are part of the same political programs—the Euro-Mediterranean Partnership and the European Neighbourhood Policy—and subject to their aims and instruments; both are located in the same regional area and face the problems of the region. However, there are differences between Egypt and Israel due to their different cultures, systems of government, positions in the region and religion. One cannot claim that both cases differ in only one aspect. In contrast, it is hard to estimate in which and in how many aspects they differ. The same would also be true if one chose different countries than these. Despite the holistic approach of the Barcelona Process, the Middle East is by no means a homogenous region. Even if one chose two Arab countries, a number of severe differences in culture, systems of government, regional positions and religion would occur.[10] The requirements of controlled comparison cannot be met in this case. Therefore, a different approach has to be followed. Instead of attempting to find two cases that differ only in one factor, two cases have been researched that promise interesting and real insights in how power appears. Both Egypt and Israel are key actors in the Middle East. Their strategic importance has been recognized by the United States and by the European Union. Both of these Western actors try to keep their fingers in the Middle Eastern pie, especially via Egypt and Israel, and actively try to influence them in different ways. They therefore present a good example for analyzing the exercise of civilian power.

As the requirements of controlled comparison are impossible to meet in the fields of civilian power analysis, within-case analysis will be used to conduct the study. Instead of basing the study on assumptions that cannot be met in empirical study, within-case analysis will attempt to understand how power works by looking at phenomena in detail and in gradations. This does not mean that the cases will not be compared. Both cases are typical examples for the exercise of civilian power; therefore one can compare them and could expect outcomes that are similar to each other. The comparison will not take place, however, merely according to a concentration on variables. Instead, it will be much broader and take settings and backgrounds into account. As two cases that are similar in every respect but one cannot be found in the fields of civilian power, it is probable that more than one factor has an causal impact on the outcome. Within-case analysis, especially process-tracing, will help to reveal which facets of the imperfectly

---

[10]   For comprehensive analyses on state formation and on (the development of) religious gaps and cleavages in Arab societies, for example, in Saudi-Arabia, see Khoury/Kostiner 1990; Kostiner 1993; 2008.

matched cases are causal for the outcome (see ibid.: 214). As a developed theory that one could build upon does not yet exist in the fields of civilian power, the study cannot rely on the congruence approach and will use process-tracing instead. In order to reach fruitful results for a differentiation of civilian power, it is bound up with typological theorizing.

2.4 Typological theorizing as a means to set up a differentiation of civilian power

In its attempt to inductively develop a picture of civilian power, its facets and its causes,[11] the study will try to gain statements that are as general as well as rich in detail. Typological theorizing offers an adequate tool for this aim. It offers—as Smoke and George have nicely put it—"the promise of cumulation without losing sensitivity to context" (George/Bennett 2005: 149). Especially in combination with the inductive form of process-tracing as a tool of within-case analysis, it helps to generate general theoretical statements that take mechanisms and processes on the micro-level into account. Therefore, it contributes to general as well as to particular explanations of a phenomenon. It is limited insofar as it only gains statements about specific mechanisms and is not necessarily able to say whether these mechanisms will be the same in different cases. "At the same time, typological theorizing attempts to outline the conditions under which a particular causal mechanism has a defined effect, and the differing effects it has in different contexts, by modeling recurrent combinations

---

[11]   Some advocates of rational choice theory argue that one cannot produce causal chains in an inductive way, but only by deriving them from general theories. Edgar Kiser and Michael Hechter claim that, "[to] justifiably infer causality, all possible spurious causes of Y must be ruled out. Since there is no opportunity to manipulate causal factors in nonexperimental data, drawing causal inferences from these data raises much greater problems" (Kiser/Hechter 1991: 4). According to them, this is especially true for historical data, as it is impossible to manipulate or control historical cases (see ibid.: 5; 23).

and interactions of mechanisms" (ibid.). Typological theory is "a theory that specifies independent variables, delineates them into their categories for which the researcher will measure the case and their outcomes, and provides not only hypotheses on how these variables operate individually, but also contingent generalizations on how and under what conditions they behave in specified conjunctions or configurations to produce effects on specified dependent variables" (ibid.: 235). These configurations of variables are the differentiations or types that are to be created. Differentiations and types may be characterized by specific conditions under which they occur or by different paths that lead to certain outcomes. Building up typological theories means analyzing these conditions and following these paths in order to create types of the phenomenon—or at least to find out more about already existing types. In case studies, typological theorizing will discover the specific types occurring in the examined example. Beyond that, it will generalize its findings of the specific type by stressing the causal chains and the specific conditions and outcomes that lead to the case in question. Therefore, statements concerning types that do not occur in the analyzed case, i.e. potential types, may also be made.

Typological theories are to be divided from typologies. Developing "ideal types" of a specific phenomenon has been a topic of scientific debate that dates back to Max Weber's (1922) famous distinction of types, especially of types of legitimate domination (see Weber 1968: Vol.1, Chapter I; III). Paul Lazarsfeld, Allen Barton and Louis Guttman have had a major influence on the methodological development in this field. Lazarsfeld starts with a typology using substruction, i.e. the reconstruction of a property space from a set of types, and reduction, i.e. the condensation of a property space. By filtering the underlying dimensions of a given set of types, he reaches a property space (see Barton 1955; Lazarsfeld/Barton 1951). As Guttman does not act on a typology, his approach is less specific than Lazarsfeld's and Barton's. He uses facet theory for property-space reduction via smallest space analysis and multidimensional scalogram analysis (see Guttman 1954/55).[12] Even though there is a debate about how to divide typologies from typological theories (see, for example, Achen/Snidal 1989: 157 et seq.; Bailey 1994; Diesing 1971; Stinchcombe 1968: 44 et seq.), one may say that typologies are less ambitious than typological theories (see Haas 1990: 6 et seq.). Their aim is to show which basic types of a certain phenomenon exist. They do not specify causal pathways, do not necessarily test hypotheses, and do not come up with findings concerning connections between independent and dependent variables. Therefore, they do not build up theory but may facilitate it, as they accomplish basic work for further theorizing.

This research project will not be able to develop a complete theory and even not a typology of civilian power with all its potential and actual facets. It takes four types of civilian power as a basis for further research with the aim of specifying and delineating them. It therefore builds on scientific work already accomplished and aims at inductively developing the four established types towards a more comprehensive typological scaffolding. As this study cannot hope to create a typology but only differentiations of existing types, it also cannot come up with generalizations beyond the case examined. Instead, it will examine the types only in a limited case example and will try to find statements of how power works in the specific case. It is uncertain, however, if this will work out. To avoid all inflated declarations it has to be emphasized that the study at hand can only cover a minimal part of reality. Even though the researcher will try to offer a differentiated argument and hopes to be able to further refine the existing fourfold concept of power, it is unclear if this is what the study will be able to come up with. Its results are open and unpredictable, especially because the field of civilian power is still relatively undiscovered. Results may as well be as simple as the statement that a further refinement of existing concepts of power

---

[12]   For a comparison of these two approaches and further distinctions, see Bailey 1972.

failed and that a different method of research must be undertaken in coming studies.

2.5   Integrating typology/differentiation building and within-case analysis in power research

As has been said, the study at hand will not come up with a typology, but only with a precondition for creating a typology, namely with differentiation building. It is nevertheless possible and helpful to use the same methods as for creating a typology. Typology building (as well as typological theorizing) presents one possibility of integrating cross-case comparison with within-case analysis. First of all, typological theorizing facilitates the selection of cases that suit the development of a specific typology or theory and their comparison. In addition, process-tracing as a method of within-case analysis can be used in order to take a close look at cases. Comparison is a tool that tries to find out why variables differ among cases. In contrast, process-tracing follows every single step that has led to a certain outcome. It forms hypotheses that predict causal chains in every single element. These elements do not have to occur in a statistically relevant number. What is important is, for what reasons and under which conditions they occur and how they are causally linked. An integration of typological theorizing and process-tracing therefore offers a great chance for typology development and for prior differentiation building. It promises the refinement of established types and the exposure of new ones or of subtypes. Comparing cases according to typological aspects will lead to results that can be generalized carefully and form the starting point for typology or theory building. Within-case analysis will help to understand what exactly characterizes a type and how it works in detail, i.e. the measurement of variables. It is an ideal tool for typology and theory formation and its development, and may be applied on the macro- as well as on the micro-level of a phenomenon of interest. This has been recognized by a number of scientists and applied in various studies (see, for example, Bueno de Mesquita/Stokman 1994; Ray 1995; Skocpol 1979).

Process-tracing basically means following causal paths that lead to a certain outcome of a case. It examines what happens between the independent variable and the outcome of the dependent one. By tracing back the processes that lead to a certain outcome, it will be able to identify causal mechanisms, interactions, and new relevant variables. Process-tracing is a highly explorative tool as it tries to discover, almost as in detective work, how a certain outcome emerged. It will seek the parameters of the relationship between the independent A and the dependent B (who can also exchange roles), as well as the ways in which A addresses B in the context of B's identity. Following the process that potentially led to a certain outcome generates an understanding of how different forms of power determine the character of a relationship. It is possible that more than one factor caused a particular kind of interaction. Especially in such highly delicate areas as that occupied by power, it is also probable that causal pathways will be concealed or that different causal pathways will lead to the same or a similar outcome of a dependent variable. Process-tracing is sensitive to this possibility of multiple causality, or equifinality, and will take into account different possibilities of causal chains that could lead to a certain outcome (see George/Bennett 2005: 63, 215). As process-tracing examines a fresh case, it can offer a sophisticated picture and capture the complexity of social life as closely as possible. The more cases will be examined concerning their outcomes and the processes that lead to these outcomes, the clearer the understanding of a phenomenon and its peculiarity will get. Putting these results together will lead to the creation of a differentiation, and, proceeding further, to a typology and, finally, to a typological theory (see ibid.: 207).

Civilian power is a highly undiscovered field, so that an investigative tool like process-tracing promises a great deal for the researcher. It will come up with a number of observations discovered as it tracks events. What is more, it can link these events and make clear which interactions take place. Therefore, for each case more than a mere observation of events takes place. Instead, intervening factors are followed in an approach to discover their causal relationship and their interactions. Consequently, the level of indefiniteness is reduced.

The usage of typological theorizing as well as of process tracing also has an effect on possible mistakes a research design may have. First of all, the cases only reflect a limited sample of what the phenomenon in question, i.e. civilian power, may be. It is likely to miss some facets of the phenomenon. Moreover, it is hard to set up all relevant variables in a first research design and most probably one will overlook some variables and their interactions. Careful and painstaking process-tracing can limit these problems. If relevant variables are missed in the original design, within-case analysis in combination with cross-case comparison may call attention to neglected variables, overlooked interactions between them, or spurious explanations. It is sensitive to equifinality and will find out if one or more causal paths lead to a certain outcome. Identifying more than one causally significant variable or path can be the starting point for the further inductive development of a typology. This is a major advantage compared to large-N statistical studies, which often follow only one path without taking into account that there may be more causes for the outcome. Furthermore, evaluating compared cases in detail by the means of process-tracing will help to find out whether variables differ between the cases because of real differences between the cases or due to other reasons (see ibid.: 254).

The study at hand will use typological theorizing in order to come up with a first differentiation of civilian power. In order to limit the potential problems of typology building described above, it combines typological theorizing with cross-case comparison and process-tracing. In an approach of differentiation building, it chooses two especially informative cases of the accordant property-space. The study is built on the latest debates on power, which come to the conclusion that there are four basic types of power: compulsory, institutional, structural, and productive power. In order to gain structured and cumulative cognition concerning the exercised type of power and its causes and effects (i.e., the relational aspect between actors A and B), the method of case comparison is applied as well as process-tracing. For each case, it will have to be asked how and under what conditions compulsory, institutional, structural, and productive power were exercised. A detailed process-tracing analysis will lead to theoretical statements concerning the four types of power. Moreover, in future studies, process-tracing could identify new coherences and lead to the opening of new power types or subtypes, as well as break the four types of civilian power down into subtypes.

As power is a highly complex phenomenon, it will not be possible to follow its path in the form of a historical linear narrative. Instead, an analytical form of process-tracing,[13] which will be channeled into theoretical forms, is necessary. The analytical categories along which the study is adjusted are chosen according to the four types of power. Every type will be followed in its occurrence and mode of action for the specific case. Consequently, the analysis will be selective and specific about the relevant elements of each type but not about the complete process.

The analytical form of process-tracing will be supported by a comparison between the two chosen cases. A comparison is more variable-orientated than mere process-tracing would be. Therefore, it can draw attention to possible variances of a type between the cases. A concentration on only one case would overlook these possible variances and therefore neglect important facets. In order to find out what generates possible differences, a broader approach is needed which will clarify why the outcome is what it is, which intervening variables are crucial, and which interactions take place between

---

[13]   Possible forms of process-tracing are: the detailed narrative, the use of hypotheses and generalization, the analytical explanation, and the more general explanation (see George/Bennett 2005: 210 et seq.).

variables. Process-tracing as an analytical explanation cannot help in this case, as it establishes an analytical grid and forces the elements of the case into it. However, such a predetermined scheme will not allow the inclusion of certain facets that have not been thought of before. The tool of process-tracing also faces limits if it proves impossible to come up with an uninterrupted causal chain leading to a certain outcome. This may be especially problematic for a study on power, as important elements of the chain may be concealed or not amenable to research. Moreover, the great amounts of information required for a complete understanding of civilian power can hardly be acquired completely. Therefore, one will not be able to identify a linear causal chain. Moreover, power as a phenomenon is too complex and multilayered to be captured in a linear way. Instead, the study will have to take a number of conditions, facets and pathways into account.

In order to deal with possible limitations that may occur, the study at hand is couched in the method of structured focused comparison. A less detailed form of process-tracing is needed to have a look at the general conditions in which power takes place. For this purpose, process-tracing in its form as a more general explanation will be used. This kind of process-tracing does not look at every element and does not highlight historical linear steps of the process chain, but rather moves up the ladder of generality (see George/Bennett 2005: 212; Skocpol 1979: 38, 43). It will not examine every single step, but rather have a look at the macro-level in which power is exercised, i.e. it will have a look at the picture as a whole by taking the setting of the EMP and the ENP into account. Thus, it points towards analyzing the specific conditions under which civilian power appears without leaving out decisive causes of the non-linear process. This may lead to the exploration of missing intervening variables that have not have been thought of before. Process-tracing is thus used as a valuable instrument for understanding the details of rich and complex events, but it is not the only tool that is methodically relied on. Instead, process-tracing is seen as a complementary tool that will help to make up for the limitations of cross-case analysis—and the other way round.

44

2.6 Data requirements

Assessing power structures requires information on all actors involved. As not every interaction is documented and thus cannot be captured, this study relies on certain core elements of the relationship. These are the fields of the social, cultural and human partnership of the EMP. Political and security aspects are included only if necessary in order to attain a complete picture of power structures in the cultural and social fields. Economic and financial questions are excluded because these are multi-layered and complex enough that they should be dealt with in an extra study. This setup is comparable to the first and third baskets of the Barcelona aims. Besides the main contents of the EMP, the main aims of the fields named above, i.e. political, security, social and cultural aspects of the ENP, are also included.

On the operational level of European-Middle Eastern relations, i.e. concerning the programs on the ground, a further restriction has been made in order to attain a manageable framework of research. There has been a clear focus on the promotion of civil society groups— which is one of the main parts of the third basket of the Barcelona aims. For Egypt, groups that promote human rights and issues related to democratic standards were of special interest; while for Israel, peace movements were in the center of the research. This is due to the fact that there are different political emphases and efforts in the two countries. In Israel, the promotion of peace on a grassroots level is of great importance, whereas Egypt is not directly concerned with the Israel-Palestinian conflict and maintains peace with Israel besides. Instead, questions of human rights and democratic standards are of much greater importance in Egyptian society and under its authoritarian regime than they are in Israel's democracy.

The EMP and the ENP represent the framework for Euro-Mediterranean relations. Accordingly, one cannot help but consider central elements of the relationship. The EMP and ENP framework is broad enough to include the major topics in which power structures could take place and therefore to allow for process-tracing, i.e. not to miss out on important variables and to discover possible connections between variables. Also, more subtle types of power, such as structural or productive power, require a broader framework in order to be discovered, as they cannot be detected in direct and specific actions. On the other hand, the EMP/ENP framework is limited enough to lead to realistic results in the structure of the study. Last but not least, this framework is well documented, so that one can rely on it as a trustworthy source.

As pointed out above, neighboring fields of content, especially political and security aspects, have been taken into account if they were relevant to the findings in the fields of research. Thus, the focus of the study was clear, but also open to neighboring topics. This openness was not intended in the very beginning of conducting the study, but was taken into account consciously during the deeper development of the research. It became clear that power, a highly complex topic, has remained in great part unexplored up to the present day. To fathom it, one needs to allow a certain openness in the fields of content and in underlying data. This is the only way to discover connections one did not think of before, to reveal hidden connections and dependencies between different fields of content, and to deal with delicate topics during field research. This openness comes at the costs of scientific purity, but promises a deeper insight into and understanding of the matter itself.

This approach is consequently reflected in a certain heterogeneity of the data used, and it is clear that due to the mimetic process to which qualitative research is subject (see Gebauer/Wulf 1995), the results of the study will reflect this fact. The study is conducted on the basis of three types of data. These are, first of all, key documents of the EMP and the ENP. In many cases, however, power is not clearly reflected in documents. It is often hidden intentionally, as revealing it might disarm it and could easily lead to the opposite of the intended effects and aims. As the topic is gravely volatile for the actors involved, it is often visible only through indirect expressions. Consequently, in addition to analyzing EMP/ENP documents, we have sought a more subtle form of gaining information. Besides relying on the analysis of documents, the research also analyzes the 2005 "Barcelona+10" conference, which was meant to celebrate the EMP's tenth birthday, and employs the instrument of expert interviews in order to obtain information that is hidden and does not occur openly in the official EMP/ENP documents. This will allow for a thorough analysis of the subject.

2.6.1 EMP/ENP documents and Barcelona+10

Documents reflect the set-up of the relationship. Considered as "fields, frames and networks of action" (Prior 2003: 2), they reveal the basic parameters, terms, and conditions of how the partners have decided to deal with each other. They show as well how rights and duties are distributed in the relationship: which and whose interests find more room than others'. This is especially illuminating for the analysis of compulsory and institutional power. Therefore, running as well as episodic records have been taken into account in this study.

The *running records* that are analyzed in the study comprise the key elements of both the EMP and the ENP. For the EMP these are the Association Agreements (AA) with Israel and Egypt, as well as key documents in the fields of human rights, democracy promotion and the third basket of the EMP in general. Related documents, such as documents on security and political dialogue, are also taken into account. In the framework of the ENP, the main documents are ENP Country Reports (CR), Action Plans, Country Strategy Papers (CSP), and Progress Reports (PR). They are the basis of the ENP and therefore reflect the (power) relationship between the EU and the Mediterranean Partner Countries (MPC). (It must be noted that a Progress Report for Egypt had not yet been published while the study was being written. This is due to the fact that the Action Plan for Egypt was only adopted in March 2007.) We have also included documents that accompanied the establishment and development of the EMP and the ENP in the examined fields, as they reveal the underlying principles of these programs. Both the planning level and the operational level have been taken into account. Therefore, general documents covering the relevant parts of the EMP and the ENP are considered and analyzed, as well as documents that are connected to the programs on the ground, i.e. the promotion of civil society groups in Israel and Egypt.

Secondly, we have taken into account the preparation and the management of the 2005 Barcelona+10 conference. As this conference was held to mark the ten-year anniversary of the EMP, it reflects the relationship that has emerged from the EMP and the ENP cooperation since the beginning of the program. The inclusion of material from and analysis of a conference adds another element to the picture. Surveying a conference allows an observation of indirect channels of the exercise of power, such as agenda setting, the absence of certain invitees to the conference, and various other political gestures that are not captured in the documents and interviews published by the involved actors. This analysis is mainly based on academic and newspaper articles, i.e. on *episodic records*, about this conference, so that it also takes the form of document analysis.

The study also had to face the *typical problems* of document analysis: the access to EMP and ENP documents was not easy. Even though documents were not lost or unavailable, it was hard to get all the EMP and ENP documents relevant for the case study. What especially served as a gate opener was an internship in the European Parliament in Brussels where the research of documents was possible, as well as the interviews conducted in which some interviewees were kind enough to hand out information material. As with the interview (see next chapter), the EU Delegation in Egypt was rather protective of information, though, hinting at the tense situation in which the agreements with the Egyptian counterpart were made. Nevertheless, in the end all necessary documents could be acquired and analyzed in the framework of the case study.

A greater, and less practical, challenge with document analysis lies in how far documents are reliable—and in how far explicit content goes together with implicit meaning in the document (see Flick 2007: 252). For the running records, as well as for the episodic records used for the study, the four criteria that were developed by Scott (see Scott 1990: 6) and that have found recognition (see Flick 2007: 248) have been taken into account: documents should be authentic, credible, representative and comprehensible. Here, as has been described, only selected documents that are relevant for the cases of research are used. Even though they are comprehensible, authentic and credible, it is significant to consider that absolutely neutral documents do not exist. It is thus significant to consider the political background in which documents are published: it is the EU that publishes these documents and sets the framework for the EMP and the ENP. By contrast, the Action Plans are jointly agreed upon documents that both sides have signed and therefore also reflect the partner's aims to a certain degree. Even though it is not the same document type that is published regularly, but follow-up reports, or complementary reports dealing with related topics, one can speak of running records (see Lee 2000) in the cases analyzed. In the episodic documents dealing with the Barcelona conference only, opinions will be less, or at least differently, biased than in reports published by the EU only, so that these documents present a different view and add a new perspective. In every case, however, one must not forget that documents are always constructed realities, and not only standardized, regularly published artifacts (see Wolff 2004).

Even more problematic was the way of analyzing the documents, i.e. the question Mayring has famously put in terms of what one actually wants to get out of them (see Mayring 2008). An analysis according to key words was impossible as "power" is hidden and as a key word did naturally not appear in the documents. Breaking it down into assessable key words was also impossible because, first of all, the concept of civilian power is too complicated to be put into key words; second, the documents were too heterogeneous; and third, the topic of research was still too unexplored to make it possible to find the right key words in advance. Confronted with these problems, it was decided to combine means of a qualitative, summarizing content analysis (see Bauer 2000) with more interpretative methods (see Glaser/Strauss 1967; Strauss/Corbin 1998): the four basic types of power were established as analytical units according to which the texts were read and filtered. Thus, for each of the four types, as well as for each of the four types in a certain case, statements were arrived at after the analysis of the documents. In line with a summarizing content analysis, the material was reduced by bundling the documents' main statements. Overlapping statements or notions that came up repeatedly in the documents were skipped. Finally, each was subsumed under one of the four types of power. This is admittedly a less ambiguous way than (computer-supported) document analysis according to key words or thorough coding would have been. It does fit the research objective, though, and goes hand in hand with a traced-back within-case analysis, as it is less precast. It also suits the study at hand because a larger number of documents was taken into account that often comprised similar information and thus had to be handled in a reductive approach. Moreover, due to the nature of the documents and their publishers, the documents contained mostly politically correct statements, and not necessarily openly communicated intentions. Thus an interpretative approach was used in an attempt to understand the documents and press the data gained into the form of concepts, i.e. into the form of at least one of the power types. A more categorized, and possibly methodically clearer analysis would not have been able to consider this. In order to be able to reach into the depths of the documents, interpretative means were needed, and a lack of methodical clarity was therefore taken into account.

2.6.2 Expert interviews

Internal policy aims and strategies, internal planning, and the efforts taken to reach one's interests are usually hard to find in written documents. Also, the personal appraisals of people involved and nuances in their statements are mostly not visible in literature and documents. They also can hardly be fathomed through a standardized questionnaire, as this interview form is too pre-established and fixed to allow for new insights. It would deprive the researcher of the chance to gain true insider knowledge of which he was not aware and to understand nuances of statements. The best form for interviews in a rather unexplored field is an open approach, which has been especially been promoted by the psychologists Brigitte Scheele and Norbert Groeben (see Groeben 1990; Scheele/Greoben 1988). This means that an adequate instrument to encounter the challenge of power research is *guideline-oriented, semi-structured expert interviews* (see Flick 1992). Accordingly, interviews were focused and flexible at the same time. They were prepared in advance according to thematic blocks and questions that could be verified, specified, exchanged and complemented during the interview itself. This allowed the conditions necessary to achieve the required sensitivity as well as to make the necessary inquiries.

Expert interviews were conducted with representatives of the EMP/ENP on all three sides, i.e. at the EU, in Egypt and in Israel. The planning level as well as the operational level was taken into account. On the planning level, we conducted interviews with three responsible EU officials in Brussels, as well as with the Israeli official at his Mission to the European Union. Despite intense efforts from the researcher's side, the Egyptian Mission to the EU refused to give any information. The European officials were Dr. Christian Berger, representative of the EC's Crisis Management and Conflict Prevention Unit (DG Relex), previously the Political Advisor on the Near East with the European Commission's External Relations Directorate General/South Mediterranean and Middle East; and Ms. Nina

Obermaier, representative of the EC's Israel desk. The interviewee from the Israeli side was Mr. Sagi Karni, spokesman for the Israeli Mission to the EU.

On the operational level, interviews were conducted with the EU officials from the European Delegations to Israel and to Egypt. In Israel, this was Ms. Alexandra Meir, who is responsible for the EU Partnership for Peace Programme. In Cairo, the interview was conducted with Mr. Nicola Bellomo, who is the EU's counselor for human rights and non-governmental organizations there. All interviews were conducted between December 2006 and December 2007.

Interviews were conducted in a face-to-face-form with Mr. Berger (EU/Brussels) and with the EU officials in Israel and Egypt, Ms. Meir (EU/Tel Aviv) and Mr. Bellomo (EU/Cairo). The interviews with Ms. Obermaier (EU/Brussels) and Mr. Karni (Israeli Mission/Brussels) were conducted over the telephone. This was due to security and planning restrictions from the sides of these institutions. Interviewing the abovenamed officials guarantees the inclusion of all sides of the relationship (the EU, Israel and Egypt), and the consideration of all players in the game of power structures, on the planning level as well as on the operational level.

Conducting these semi-standardized interviews, a number of *challenges* came up. First of all, it was difficult even to get in touch with the interviewees and obtain the necessary information. Because power is such a delicate matter, several preliminary efforts were undertaken. They were not only meant to gain a profound and acute insight into policy structures and the relationship between actors, but also to build up trust in order to receive the necessary information. Thanks to work conducted previously in Egypt, contacts were already established there, so that the European Commission's Delegation to Egypt in Cairo could be approached rather easily. The study was written at Tel Aviv University, so that the necessary connections were also established in order to get in touch with the EC's Delegation to Israel, located in Tel Aviv. An internship in the European Parliament in Brussels served as a door opener in order to gain access to interview partners, as well as to documents.

Secondly, even though questions were not confrontational as Flick suggests to use for this type of interview (see Flick 2007: 160), they were *sensitive* to the interviewee: despite the careful preparation and the procurement of the necessary electronic equipment, in none of the interviews was permission given to record the conversation. Neither direct citations nor the course of conversation was permitted to be published. The results and insights that came out of the interviews will therefore be presented in an indirect way. The chapters in part V of this study which describe the ongoing civil society programs in Israel and Egypt are based on the interviews and provide the information gained by talking to Mrs. Meir and Mr. Bellomo. Also the sections in part VI, which trace results back to the political context and attempt to provide more detailed insights and a deeper understanding, include information as well as feelings for the situation and the relationship between the actors gained during the interviews. The chapter dealing with productive power is built especially on the interviews, as productive power is difficult to trace in documents. Besides the restriction from both sides, here, already a first difference between the Israeli and the Egyptian case was clearly reflected: whereas the EU's Delegation office in Israel handed out a great amount of information material and allowed open, and also critical insights in ongoing projects, the Delegation in Egypt was extremely careful with information and did not provide many details.

Third, and maybe most important, the study encountered a *typical problem of semi-standardized interviews*. Because of its explorative approach and the openness of questions, the interviewees' answers were sometimes surprising and even brought up new issues that we hadn't considered before. On the other hand, different questions turned out to be irrelevant. As a consequence, adaptations had to be made in the course of the research: during the first interview with Mrs. Meir in Tel Aviv, it already turned out that certain thematic, hypothesis-driven blocks, which had been prepared in advance and that were based on the previously studied literature, did not meet with the reality of the interviewee. Instead, other thematic blocks were discussed longer and were enriched by new information that we hadn't thought of before. After the interviewer had overcome her first surprise in the aftermath of the interview, this clash between the preparation of the interview and the encountered reality led to a rethinking of the literary work and of the hypothesis building done before. In consequence, the four forms of power that had been worked out before were questioned through the lens of the new information gained—and of the lack of information in certain fields that had been (wrongly) assumed to be significant in advance. This led to a rethinking of how each of the four types of power could be characterized, and finally, found its expression in the reformulation of the hypotheses. In a follow-up phone call with Mrs. Meir, the newly adjusted thematic blocks were considered and the information now necessary for the new focus of the study was requested.

Based on the experience of this first interview, the second interview with Mr. Bellomo in Egypt was conducted with the newly worked out thematic question block based on the modified hypotheses. This was due to the assumption that both cases were of the same type due to their roots in the same political programs, i.e. the EMP and the ENP. Nevertheless, the second interview also differed from what had been expected. It did meet with the theoretical considerations worked out before on the basis of literature and on the basis of the first interview. It was surprising, however, in terms of how the political programs were carried out and especially in terms of how different this process was compared to the first, Euro-Israeli case. It had been planned in advance that Israeli and Egyptian officials should have been interviewed on the operational level, i.e. in their function as counterparts to the EU in their respective countries. During the interview with Mrs. Meir in Israel, it turned out that there were no such counterparts on the Israeli side. In Egypt, however, counterparts were involved, but the EU did not want to hand out their contact data, pointing to the delicateness of the talks between the EU and the Egyptian counterparts. Consequently, this plan lost its necessity during the course of the study. This is already a first hint at the results of the study.

3　The state of power research

3.1　The main understandings of power

Power is not simply one of many issues in political science, but rather a key concept. With its roots in the Latin word *posse*, i.e. *to be able to* or *can*, it is perhaps even the most fundamental concept of political science. Assuming that power tells us about characteristics of political systems and societies, philosophers and scholars have been trying to understand its essence and its role at least since the times of Socrates. At the same time, it is one of the most controversial and most difficult topics that political science deals with (see Gilpin 1981: 13). For centuries, there has been intensive research concerning the power of societies and states, based mostly on Machiavelli's and Hobbes' assumption that the thirst for power is never satisfied. Scholars have asked how to organize power inside societies and how to exercise leadership. Questions have included those of how to preserve liberty of the individual, how to prevent the abuse of power, and how to organize power, for example, in matters of establishing organization and bureaucracy inside a state. When dealing with power, the question also arises of how and if the term "power" can and should be delineated against related concepts. For many centuries, distinguishing between power and other facets of influence was not of key interest to researchers. Aristotle, and after him many more, did not bother to differentiate between power, influence, authority, and rule because these may have fallen under categories of common sense. Outside of Hobbes, differentiation in this field was not undertaken for a long time. Even Machiavelli, who introduced a major change from classical-normative to modern-empirical theory, used the terms *imperio, forza, potente*, and *autorità* interchangeably (see Dahl 1968: 406).

In the research of international relations, however, philosophy and theories of power have been neglected for a long time. In particular, the "systematic empirical study of power relations is remarkably new" (ibid.: 414). This also goes along with attempts to differentiate between the related forms of power (see Berenskoetter 2007). Different scholars have tried to distinguish between terms like power, persuasion, influence, authority, control, coercion, force, deterrence, compellence, inducement and others (see Baldwin 2002: 177). If one looks at this rich literature on power and its differentiations, one might come up with an organization of the material according to four basic understandings of power: these are 1) power as a potential, 2) power as an influence, 3) power as a resource, and 4) power as authority, or rule.

3.1.1 Power as a potential

Describing power as a potential is one of the most basic understandings of power. It is rooted in the historical and even etymological development of the concept by making a difference between *potestas* and *potentia*. *Potestas* refers to "power over," also called domination or *Herrschaft*. On the other hand, *potentia* is the "power to" in Spinoza's sense, i.e. *Macht* as a capability, an opportunity, or the faculty of transforming a potential into actuality. Or, in other words: "While *potestas* is the power through which the world is governed, *potentia* is the power through which the world is made" (Ringmar 2007: 195). When talking about power as a potential, it is important to note how *potentia* and *potestas* are connected: "'Power to' is best understood as a precondition for 'power over'—*potestas* requires *potentia*—no one can be powerful who is not first empowered. Yet the opposite is not the case: *potentia* does not require *potestas*. You can have the power to do something without necessarily having power over others" (ibid.: 196). When talking about power as a potential, we mostly refer to power as *potentia*. It describes power as a means of survival in a hostile environment. This concept has a basis in

Machiavelli's writings and has led to modern political realism. In his *Discorsi* (1531), Machiavelli states: "...for it does not appear to men that they possess securely what a man has unless he acquires something else new" (Machiavelli 1996: 19). Hobbes (1651), who together with Machiavelli represents thinkers of political ideas in the transition of the Middle Ages to modern times (see Schölderle 2002), is clearer in his definition than Machiavelli. He speaks of a "perpetual and restless desire of Power after power, that ceaseth only in Death" (Hobbes 1996: 70). Likewise, Spinoza (1677) suggests that "the natural right of every man is determined not by sound reason, but by his desire and his power" (Spinoza 1989: 236). Men would therefore try to "get for himself by any means, by force, deceit, entreaty, or in any other way he best can" (ibid.). In more recent times, George E.G. Catlin writes about "the Political Man with the Desire for Power" (Catlin 1964: 215).

The perception of power as a potential has also found its way into the fields of international politics. In the eighteenth century, the few states that were able to exercise their foreign policies militarily were called Great Powers (see Simonds/Emeny 1935). In the context of the two world wars, scholars dealt with ideas of *Machtpolitik*, or power politics (see Carr 1946; Morgenthau 1960; Sprout/Sprout 1945; Spykman 1942; Wight 1946; Wright 1955), and argued for a *balance of power* (see Claude 1965; Gulick 1955; Haas 1953; Morgenthau 1960). In the second half of the 20th century, the Cold War brought matters of power to the center of academic considerations. Realist scholars such as Carr, Morgenthau, Mearsheimer, Waltz and Gilpin developed a concept of power that has determined the study of international relations ever since (see Carr 1946; Gilpin 1981; Mearsheimer 1994/95; Morgenthau 1960; Waltz 1979). This concept is connected to the assumptions of the 18th century and to thoughts of *Machtpolitik* and assumes that sovereign states attempt to pursue their aims with their own power resources in order to survive in a dangerous environment of hostility and threats. Preserving and furthering national interests, which depend on a state's capabilities, is the ultimate goal in an anarchic international system. The struggle for power is a basic characteristic of human nature and will not cease on an international level as long as nation-states exist in a international system that is threatening the survival of each state. This fight for power can take the form of either collaboration or of competition, depending on whether states' national interests coincide or clash (see Morgenthau 1960). Also, in the recent context of the debate concerning the EU as a normative power, realists have made their point by claiming that the EU's member states remain dominant actors that use the EU as a pawn in their power interests (see Hyde-Price 2006).

3.1.2   Power as influence

As influence, power has been specially treated in sociological and cybernetic[1] approaches. Based on Max Weber's[2] prominent sociological theories (see Weber 1968), these concepts mainly assume that power means the ability to direct social relations also against opposition, and thus represent one of the very few concepts in power research that has found widespread reception. Referring to this assumption and diagnosing a crisis of theory building in political science, Karl W. Deutsch has developed his system-theoretical approach in the fields of cybernetics and communication theory. Based on the assumption of a dynamic model of society that depends on communication, he comes up with a multi-causal analysis of social

---

[1]   Cybernetics—which linguistically has the same roots as the word "government"—tries to understand how systems are run through the processing of data, i.e. how processes in closed, circular systems work. They are especially applied in exact sciences, but also have been applied to sociology, especially in analyzing group dynamics (see, for example, Birnbaum 1988). For details on cybernetic system analysis see, for example, Jenner 1994; Stevenson/Sebo 1976. For cybernetic debates of how political culture and power are connected see Yolles 2005.

[2]   The Weberian approach will be dealt with in more detail later, as it includes elements of force and is thus closely connected to the type of compulsory power.

processes that is meant to be universally applicable (see Deutsch 1963). He describes the political system as a system of communication in society, which is characterized by self-governance and by the ability to learn, and which is responsible for reaching the aims of the society as a whole (see Albert/Walter 2005: 100). Functioning as the internal intelligence of society, it is the place where power comes in: it has not only the power to silence alternative aims, interests, and preferences but can also produce and change social commitments (see Deutsch 1963: 243). Governing is thus taken as "less a problem of power and somewhat more as a problem of steering" (ibid: XXVII). In addition, Niklas Luhman sees power as part of a closed social system. These social systems, which are neither people nor actions, but communication, differ clearly from their external environment. This goes along with the constructivist assumption that understanding is not possible beyond the context of the system itself. The main operations taking place in the social system are a process of communications, which are tied to one another. In this process of communication, power takes place by threatening and selecting the flow of communication. It thus helps to make the system functional (see Luhmann 1984; 1997).

Besides these main paths of regarding power as an influence, there has been a debate about how power and influence could be divided as concepts. In 1939, Herbert Goldhamer and Edward Shils came up with distinctions between three basic forms of power, namely: force, i.e. physical influence exercised on a subordinate; domination, i.e. explicitly expressed influence; and manipulation, i.e. non-explicit influence (see Goldhamer/Shils 1939: 171 et seq.). In contrast, Harold D. Lasswell and Abraham Kaplan subsumed power into a bigger framework, namely of influence (see Lasswell/Kaplan 1950: 77). In more recent research, Bachrach and Baratz have developed another differentiation. In their study of decision-making, they distance themselves from Lasswell and Kaplan by saying that influence is not a higher category than power but that power needs to be distinguished from authority, influence, manipulation, and force without sub- or super classification (see Bachrach/Baratz 1963). Similarly, William Connolly lists different phenomena of power, giving different examples describing situations of persuasion, manipulation, coercion, anticipatory surrender, deterrence and force, and conditioning. This list differs from the catalog arrived at by Bachrach and Baratz, but with them—excepting only persuasion—he considers all of these forms of power and does not subsume power into one of them or the other way around. Brian Fay also distinguishes between power, force, coercion, manipulation and leadership. Both Connolly and Fay point out that the processes that lead to a specific influence may differ from one another (see Fay 1987: 120 et seq.). Connolly's main criterion of distinguishing between the different forms of power is the question of responsibility. In each distinct form of power, responsibility is shifted to the side of the stronger actor A, who initiates these pressures. Furthermore, Connolly points to moral considerations in order to distinguish between the different forms of power. For example, morality-based criteria allow manipulation, but not persuasion, to represent a form of power. As persuasion is not as morally problematic as manipulation, only the latter can be counted as a form of power. Connolly describes all forms of power as "presumptively wrong acts" (Connolly 1993: 95) that can only partly be justified for good reasons. He goes so far as to say that the one who possesses power needs to justify his position of power, which limits others. That is why, according to Connolly, the bearer of power will likely deny or hide his power. This is also true the other way around: describing someone as powerful is tantamount to accusing him (see ibid.: 88ff.; 94f; 97).

Klaus Eugen Knorr also suggests a distinction between influence and power. According to him, power is only relevant in interstate relations that are conflictive, whereas cooperation between states is subject only to influence (see Knorr 1975: 3). Knorr defines power as either coercive influence or direct force. In the case that influence is non-coercive, it is not to be called power (see ibid.: 4). This kind of non-power influence mainly occurs when negotiating exchanges of goods with symmetrical values. Therefore it regularly characterizes "positive nonzero sum game[s]" (ibid.: 311). These kinds of interstate relations may include hidden power. If A, for example, receives a so-declared present from B, but B expects to get something in return, power is involved. Knorr claims, however, that there are cases of support without any stipulation. A could provide B with financial aid for the pure aim of helping B develop his economy. Other examples are A's proposal to establish a customs union with B and C, or A's mediation of a conflict between B and C (see ibid.: 311). To distinguish here between influence and power hardly seems realistic, though. It is hard to imagine a case in which A provides help to B without expecting anything in return and in which B does not feel obliged to A afterwards. Even if A does not expect to get goods in exchange, he follows a strategy in supporting B. For instance, he might intend to spread his values. The same is true for cases of conflict mediation. It may be in A's interest to prevent spillover effects into his own territory or to gain a worldwide reputation as a conflict mediator which he will be able to use again afterwards. Customs unions are an even more complex case of mutual influence in which every actor does not only expect to gain benefits but also tries to form the union according to his personal setup and interests. To differentiate between power and non-coercive influence, therefore, hardly enlightens the conceptualization of power.

3.1.3 Power as a resource

Neo-realists especially have regarded power as a resource. In contrast to Morgenthau's realism, which argues with anthropological assumptions but includes elements of *Realpolitik,* neo-realism has its foundations in Kenneth Waltz's structural considerations and tries to be more theoretically founded than realism is (see James 1995: 181). Neo-realism, or structural realism, assumes that nation-states act in an international environment of anarchy that does not have a hierarchy or an authority that would govern or enforce rules. In this environment of disorder, resources of power serve as criteria for structuring social relationships. It is the nation-states that use resources in order to achieve their aims and to preserve their interests. Power thus is not an end in itself, but is used as a means to achieve the basic need of every state, i.e. security (see Waltz 1979). As in realism, the power of a state is often assumed to be connected to the size of its territory, its wealth, manpower and military capacities (see Gulick 1955: 24 et seq.). States are imagined to be independent actors following mostly conflicting policies in order to maintain or to enforce their worldwide role. This assumption is also the basis for the previously discussed Correlates of War project initiated by David J. Singer, which attempts to study war and its causes by using quantitative indicators. A more defensive version of neo-realism has been coined by Joseph M. Crieco. He supports the realist theory of Morgenthau and Waltz, believing that "relative capabilities between and among states have played and will continue an important role in influencing the risk of war" (Grieco 2007: 80), but demands a more careful research of the meaning of polarity and how it influences the possibilities of war and peace (see ibid.: 81). He also argues that states should try to keep to their status quo rather than trying to enlarge their influence. The attempt to gain more power in the international system would pose a threat to the other state-actors and lead to the pooling of other states to not allow the aspiring state to rise up in the system, leading the fragile equilibrium of power among the states into danger (see ibid.: 1988a; 1988b; 1990; 1993).

Neo-realism has had difficulties, however, in explaining sustained cooperation, relative gains, and exceptional forms of cooperation such as the EU (see Collard-Wexler 2006). In the 1980s, neo-realist approaches were therefore questioned by institutionalism and regime-theory with the more optimistic assumption that states interact in a regularly peaceful way, characterized by rule-led international cooperation (see, for example, Keohane/Nye (1977) 2001; Krupnick

1996: 150; Mitrany 1975).[3] In a more recent debate on power (see Barnett/Duvall 2005), it has been acknowledged that institutionalism or regime theory may have a point in their criticism of realism. It has been argued, however, that institutionalism neglects the question of which role power plays in institutions. In this regard, realism rightly stresses that power matters and that states remain central actors in the international area (see Hurrell 2005: 48). Institutionalism underestimates the fact that institutions are not just means to solve conflicts peacefully and promote democracy worldwide. Rather, they are places where power is exercised, and they are actors that exercise power themselves. The position of weaker states is clearly determined according to the agenda setting and demands of stronger states inside international organizations. International organizations may also become powerful actors themselves in putting pressure on single states. That means that conflict resolution is not a power-free zone as long as it is provided by international institutions. Thus, also international institutions could be resources of power. In addition, the promotion of so-called common values, like human rights, could be seen as an exercise of power.

Both of the two main schools in international theory thus neglect important parts of power. At the same time, the controversy between realism and institutionalism has limited the creation of new ideas about power because other schools of thought have not been sufficiently heard.[4] Baldwin has summarized this problem, stating that "the importance of military force has been exaggerated; the role of non-military forms of power has been underestimated; and the field of

---

[3] For the foundations of the interdependence-theory, see, for example, Cooper 1968; Keohane/Nye 1972; 2001. For the foundations of liberal neo-institutionalism, see, for example, Axelrod 1984; Caporaso 1992; Katzenstein/Keohane/Krasner 1998; Keck 1994; Keohane 1986; March/Olsen 1989; Scharpf 2000. For the foundations of regime-theory, see, for example, Hasenclever/Mayer/Rittberger 1997; Keohane 1989; Kohler-Koch 1989; Müller 1995; Rittberger 1990; Young 1986; Zürn 1997.
[4] See Sterling-Folker/Shinko 2007 for suggestions on how to bridge the divide.

international relations has been impoverished by its insulation from studies of power in other realms" (Baldwin 2002: 184).

3.1.4 Power as authority, or rule

Understandings of power as authority, or as rule, are closely connected to criticism of an unequal distribution of power. It is therefore mostly sociological and Marxist approaches that deal with power as authority. In this context, the most famous distinctions of power and related concepts may be Max Weber's. He defines the essence of politics as the distribution of power. Similarly, Lasswell and Kaplan even use the broad statement that "the political progress is the shaping, distribution, and exercise of power" (Lasswell/Kaplan 1950: 75). Johan Galtung has tied into this understanding of power. His peace research is based on the notion that "*resources* are unevenly distributed, as when income distributions are heavily skewed, literarcy/education unevenly distributed, medical services existent in some districts and for some groups only, and so on. Above all the *power to decide over the distribution of resources* is unevenly distributed. The situation is aggravated further if the persons low on income are also low in education, low on health, and low on power—as is frequently the case because these rank dimensions tend to be heavily correlated due to the way they are tied together in the social structure" (Galtung 2005: 26).

More than pointing to an unequal distribution of power, Weber then distinguishes between domination and authority (as well as political leadership), suggesting the use of "domination" in a narrower sense than "power," that is to signify *"authoritarian power of command"* (Weber 1968: 946). He concludes that, "[looked] upon from the other end, this situation will be called *obedience*" (ibid). This distinction is one of the few that have gained significant acceptance in power research. Similarly, William Connolly distinguishes the different forms of power from authority. Power and authority can even be contrary, in his opinion, even though authority can also legitimize power and function as its source (see Connolly 1993: 197ff). His differentiation is based on Hannah Arendt, who distinguishes between power, strength, force, authority, and violence (see Arendt 1970: 43 et seq.). For Arendt, power differs from strength, as strength is "the property inherent in an object or person and belongs to its character, which may prove itself in relation to other things or persons, but is essentially independent of them. The strength of even the strongest individual can always be overpowered by the many..." (ibid.: 44). This already hints at Arendt's structural understanding of power, i.e., it depends on multiple actors and agents. For Arendt, force is merely energy exercised by physical or social movements, authority is always related to a specific person, and violence has an instrumental character, similar to strength. Power, however, depends on the ability to act as a group (see ibid.).[5]

Similar to these attempts to further define power as authority or to distinguish between both of them, Bruce Lincoln, Dennis Wrong, as well as Hans Gerth and C. Wright Mills have established the debate. As it shows again how multi-faceted opinions in these matters are, it will be shortly summarized in the following. Bruce Lincoln does not distinguish authority from power but rather from persuasion, which is described as belonging to the "realm of words and the mind" (Lincoln 1994: 4), and force, as belonging to the realm of "deeds and the body" (ibid.). For Lincoln, authority is "related to coercion and persuasion in symmetrical ways. Both of these exist as capacities or potentialities implicit within authority, but are actualized only when those who claim authority sense that they have begun to lose the trust of those

---

[5]   Similarly, Talcott Parsons differentiates between force, as the most intrinsically effective of all means of coercion, and power (see Parsons 1967: 309). He claims that power involves legitimization and defines power as a "generalized capacity to secure the performance of binding obligations by units in a system of collective organization when the obligations are legitimized with reference to their bearing on collective goals and where in case of recalcitrance there is a presumption of enforcement by negative situational sanctions—whatever the actual agency of that enforcement" (ibid.: 308).

over whom they seek to exercise it. In a state of latency or occulation, persuasion and coercion alike are constitutive parts of authority, but once actualized and rendered explicit they signal—indeed, they are at least temporarily—its negation" (ibid.: 6). Yet another option of dealing with power as authority, or rule, is suggested by Dennis Wrong, who does not regard power and authority as two opposing terms on the same conceptual level, but rather subsumes authority into power, as he regards it—along with force, manipulation, and persuasion—as a form of power (see Wrong 1980: chapter 2; 3). On this basis he develops a typology of these ideal types, admitting that there may be combinations and interrelations between them (see ibid.: chapter 4). For him, force is mainly related to physical or biological means. Manipulation, in contrast, is a "deliberate and successful effort to influence the response of another where the desired response has not been explicitly communicated to the other" (ibid.: 28). Even persuasion is a means of power, according to Wrong, as it constitutes an intended effect on someone else's behavior. It basically receives its strength through the presentation of arguments (see ibid.: 32, 35). Wrong considers the concept of authority broad enough to form subtypes: coercive, legitimate, competent, and personal authority, as well as authority by inducement (see ibid: chapter 2). Similarly, Hans Gerth and C. Wright Mills distinguish between power and authority. For them, authority means legitimated power. Whereas power may be based on numerous motives from fear to indifference, authority acts on voluntary obedience (see Gerth/Mills 1953: 195) and could thus be differentiated again as Wrong has suggested.

In most recent research, Michael Barnett and Martha Finnemore propose that both authority and power are social constructions. In contrast to power, authority can only exist when other actors recognize it. Power, however, may also appear without being recognized. Moreover, authority gives weight to an actor's statements. His voice will be heard and respected and his influence will be bigger than that of an actor without authority. It is important to note that authority does not only persuade people to behave in a special way, but also has a normative component. In many ways, actors perceive the opinion of an authoritarian actor as right and follow it, believing in his wisdom. Even if they decide not to agree, or to follow another authority, they will respect the opinion of the authority (see Barnett/Finnemore 2005: 170). In contrast, the opinion of a powerful but non-authoritarian actor will not always be treated with respect, and may sometimes even be rejected and treated with hatred.

3.1.5   Recent understandings of power

During the 1990s, the debate concentrated on other concepts, such as security (see, for example, Krause/Williams 1996; 1997). In recent years, it turned back to the question of power, with a special focus on the US's status as a so-called superpower. Joseph Nye undertook one of the latest well-known attempts at defining power. In 1990, he coined the term *soft power*, which had already been brought up in slightly different ways by Foucault (1995), Bourdieu (1993), and Gramsci (1971), and has been further differentiated in the latest debates. It deals with a non-military exercise of influence, especially from an American viewpoint, defining soft power as "the ability to get what you want through attraction rather than coercion or payments. It arises from the attractiveness of a country's culture, political ideals, and policies" (Nye 2004: x).

Today's term "soft power" has its roots in Robert Keohane's and Joseph Nye's study "Power and Interdependence" from 1977 (see Keohane/Nye 2001). The authors act on the assumption that the actors in the international, multipolar system are intertwined and depend on each other. They are affected differently by these interdependencies, though. Keohane and Nye use the categories "vulnerability" and "sensibility" to define how deeply each is affected. Whereas vulnerability points especially to a state's dependency on natural resources, sensibility has a less concrete character. Keohane and Nye distinguish between *power of resources* and *power over outcomes* with the first term saying less about the de facto influence an actor has than the second term. With this approach Keohane and Nye initiated a more differentiated analysis of structures and power relations than many schools had produced before. At the same time, their approach was exposed to manifold criticism, as it was perceived as not operationable. Moreover, it was criticized for not taking into account previous schools and lines of argumentation of power analysis (see Lemke 2000: 31).

This is also true for Nye's analysis of soft power. As Nye was an Assistant Secretary of Defense in the Clinton administration, it is not surprising that his description of soft power is relatively concrete and has found readers beyond academic circles. Even though Nye claims that it "is time for academic research to go beyond sterile debates" (Nye 2007: 172), this approach has rather led to a simplification and to a political pocketing of his idea. More than that, his concept of soft power is not rooted in the literature on power and therefore does not tie into the academic discussion on power.[6] Instead, it develops assumedly new categories that overlap with already well-known features. This is enlightening for ongoing political discussions, but does not lead to significantly new insights on power in an academic context.[7] Moreover, it has been criticized that Nye does not specify

---

[6]   In this context, the following anecdote has become well-known: when Joseph S. Nye asked Donald Rumsfeld about the concept of *soft power*, Rumsfeld replied that he didn't know what soft power is. On the other hand, when Nye was asked for his opinion on Steven Luke's concept of power, he answered that he was not aware of this concept when he conceived of soft power in 1989 (see Ringmar 2007: 2003).

[7]   Steven Lukes has pointed to the fact that Nye as well as Foucault fail to come up with a distinction "between the exercise of power as indoctrination and the promotion of policies, procedures and arrangements that render people more free (in Spinoza's phrase to live according to the dictates of their nature and judgment" (Lukes 2007: 97). Lukes therefore suggests that, no matter whether we follow Foucault's subject-centered or Nye's agent-centered view, we are not allowed to exclude subjects or agents in total, but rather have to concentrate on the question of how exactly agents succeed in winning the hearts and minds of the subjects to their influence (see ibid.).

what makes someone or something attractive to someone else, i.e. how attraction works (see Bially Mattern 2007: 98). He also does not make clear why universal values are the right ones or how they are acquired (see ibid.: 101). Most important, criticism is pointed at the question of whether soft power is as soft as it sounds, or whether its softness is not rather a moral illusion. Janice Bially Mattern thus suggests the encouragement of "some critical rethinking about its ethical value" (ibid.: 117). [8]

Soft power and civilian power are often mixed up. As civilian power, soft power is often understood as the spreading of one's culture and values in a peaceful way. For both concepts, it is also true that some authors completely neglect the aspect of power in the terms "soft power" or "civilian power" and speak of a community of values that is defined by common values and shared ways of life. They define soft power as a shared notion between actors about democracy, peace, integration, human rights and multilateralism (see Gratius 2007: 1)— and completely forget to take into account that power is not a shared concept of life, but includes the notion of influencing others, even if it is in a soft form.

The confusion between soft power and civilian power happens first of all because Nye does not root his ideas in the previous academic discussion. More than that, it derives from the lack of a clear definition of civilian power. Soft power deals with issues that can be found in institutional, structural and productive power. More than that, attempts to describe the EU and its influence are neither valorizations of Nyeian soft power in contrast to hard power, nor concepts of weakness as Robert Kagan (see Kagan 2002) understands it. The various descriptions, sometimes also under the labels of *quiet, middle, emancipatory, post-national, ideological,* and lately *normative power*

---

[8]   Nye has countered this criticism by saying that he does regard soft power as neither good nor bad and treats it as a descriptive rather than a normative concept. He does see the point, though, that its reception has been linked to ethical-normative considerations (see Nye 2007: 169).

are rather efforts to deal with a new kind of an actor and its power that is still in the making (see Adler/Crawford 2006: 9 et seq.; Diez/Manners: 2007; Galtung 1973: 37; Manners 2002; Nicolaïdis/Nicolaïdis 2006: 347). In particular, the question of whether and to what extent the EU could be an "ethical power" (Aggestam 2008) was subject to research. The concept of an ethical power encompasses not only civilian, but also military power, as well as material and social forms of power (see ibid.: 2).[9] Similarly, Tim Dunne depicts an EU that does not have to decide between military and civilian means, but could develop both while taking its often-cited values into account (see Dunne 2008: 15). Others point to the importance of European domestic affairs when it comes to formulating a foreign policy and demand that any European foreign policy has to take relations with European Moslem populations into account while becoming an ethical or at least a value-based power (see Aggestam/Hill 2008). Lately, Mary Kaldor et al. have promoted the term human security to combine ESDP conflict prevention, crisis management and civil-military cooperation. They suggest that human security was a more dynamic concept than normative or civilian power were in their attempt to categorize the EU's foreign policy (see Kaldor/Martin/Selchow 2008). The concept of human security has been criticized as "naïve and ideological" (Matlary 2008: 142) for its basic assumption that armies should and could protect and preserve rather than fight the enemy.

All of these concepts, though sometimes overlapping or even contradictory, have a normative approach in common. They do not only research power as a factum, but rather look for "good" forms of power in an attempt to characterize the EU as such—or to help turn it into such (see Diez/Manners 2007: 175). Even though some of these concepts claim to be based on Duchêne's concept of civilian power

---

[9]   For a realist opinion on Europe as an ethical power see Hyde-Price 2008. For a critique of the term "ethical power" and the call for its replacement by a more concrete and better-defined concept of European foreign responsibilities see Mayer 2008.

(see ibid.: 177), a significant difference must be made: civilian power is simply regarded as non-military in the study at hand. This does not imply a judgment concerning the ethical quality of the power in question. The study at hand also does not focus on European foreign policy, as most of these approaches do, but rather takes it as a case example to come up with insights into how civilian power works. That means that the treatment of civilian power here will tie more closely to the literature on power itself, rather than to Europe as a power, i.e. an actor and its foreign policy.

Ironically, none of the past or ongoing discussions has brought us a widely accepted definition of the term power. Its identification remains a matter of dispute and controversy (see Waltz 1986: 333). In 1957, Robert A. Dahl stated in his famous essay "The Concept of Power" that "we are not likely to produce—certainly not for some considerable time to come—anything like a single, consistent, coherent 'Theory of Power.' We are much more likely to produce a variety of theories of limited scope, each of which employs some definition of power that is useful in the context of the particular piece of research or theory but different in important respects from the definitions of other studies. Thus we may never get through the swamp. But it looks as if we might someday get around it" (Dahl 1957: 202). This day, however, has not yet come. With this in mind, this study has to be understood as an attempt to contribute to the discussion of power. It cannot, however, provide the golden solution to the lack of a single definition and theory. Instead, it will concentrate on civilian power and try to gain limited insights in order to contribute to further discussions.

3.1.6 Consequences for the research

Upon consideration of these selected writings on power, it becomes clear that there are certain similarities between existing differentiations of power terms, but that there is no general agreement between them, and no all-embracing explanation or differentiation that would succeed in convincing a majority of academics. The terms rather remain fuzzy, and most approaches neglect important aspects of power. Or, as Stanley Benn puts it, the "meanings of 'power', 'influence', 'control', and 'domination' are uncertain, shifting and overlapping. Although two of these words may be interchangeable in one context, in another context one of these words may refer to a genus and another to a species, or one may refer to a cause and another to an effect" (Benn 1967: 424). Most commonly, definitions of power are set up through the examination of direct coercive relations between actors. They do not recognize, for example, that the non-coercive spread of values might have much stronger effects than military action. Dahl, who is especially concerned with the question of how to find out who has more power and who has less, points to the fact that every research will have to consider specific requirements and therefore is singular in a way. He concludes that "the particular definition one chooses will evidently have to merge from considerations of the substance and objectives of a specific piece of research, and not from general theoretical considerations" (Dahl 1957: 207). Power comparability is not the main interest of this study. Nevertheless, this research has no other chance but to choose a certain framework that, while not conclusive, will fit the specific interest of this research. Here, not only coercion but also more subtle forms of power are taken into account. In order to comprise all of its aspects, we will not differentiate between "power" and its possible sisters. Instead, power itself will be understood in a broad generic sense in order to include notions of influence, authority, and other such forms. Without doubt, differentiations between these terms are useful and should be developed. This is not the aim of the following discussion, though. If not otherwise indicated and as long as terms are not part of a quotation, they will be treated as commensurable with one another (see Baldwin 2002: 177; Dahl 1957: 202).

3.2 The state of research concerning the European Union as a civilian power

One of the basic assumptions of this study is that the EU is a typical civilian power that can serve as a prime example for an analysis of how civilian power works. The following, will discuss first the development of the concept of a civilian power, then the most important features of the civilian power EU, in order to explain why its foreign policy is primarily civilian and consequently why the EU may serve as a key example for a study on civilian power.

3.2.1 The development of the concept of a civilian power

In the beginning of the 1970s, during a worldwide political phase of détente, François Duchêne first brought up the model of the civilian power Europe. Under the influence of the Cold War, he assumes that Europe is threatened by Soviet communism on the one side and retains an integrated American ally on the other side. This American ally takes its European protégés less into consideration than it did before. Moreover, he believes that Europe is economically strong enough to be a partner rather than a minor actor. Therefore, Europe represents a unity that needs to create a common defense system as well as an ideology that is able to face the confrontations (see Duchêne 1973: 13, 15). According to Duchêne, Europe is a new power in world politics. The key question is, however, what this new power stands for. From the beginning of the creation of a European Union, there have been two arguments why the idea of a European Union was promoted. These lines have their basics in the various reasons and ideologies that made people support the creation of the Union as well as the idea of the integration itself.

First of all, the main vision of the European integration that found its expression in the Schuman Declaration of May 9, 1950, was to create peace between former enemies and to spread the idea of a peaceful and respectful coexistence and partnership inside Europe as well as beyond the European borders. This means the triumph of the liberal rule of law and of an attitude of mutual respect and even friendship.

Secondly, from the very beginning, the European Union was an instrument of power politics for different actors. Jean Monnet claimed that only a powerful Union could be an adequate counterpart for cooperation with the American superpower in the West and for a peace with the Soviet superpower in the East. Other politicians rather based their idea of a powerful European Union on their national traditions as (formerly) powerful actors in world politics. They rather saw the European Union as a means to support their national ambitions in a broader framework (see ibid: 18).

Today, as the EU unites almost all European countries, has a common currency in many of its member states and even tries to take further steps towards a common Foreign and Security Policy (CFSP), the question of the character of this actor as a power comes up more urgently. What is this union and what does it stand for in a power framework? Even though the European unification was many steps behind its current situation during Duchêne's considerations, already in the beginning of the 1970s he inquired about the aim of a EU that was increasingly unifying politically. Hereby, he described three basic options for a European power: first of all, the creation of a national European state with the adequate military options; second, a neutral Europe; and finally, the conception of Europe as a process.

The first idea is based on the assumption that a European Union that is strong in world trade and represents most Europeans could become an actor similar to the national superpowers of the previous centuries. Its economic capacities and the common interests in developing those of the European Union member states already make it a power bloc (see Hill 1990: 35). For such a power, military potential would be a basic characteristic. Duchêne believes that Europe is weakened due to its lack of conventional military and especially of nuclear military means.

This may be an assumption of the Cold War, but it has regained relevance lately due to US, Russian, Iranian and North Korean efforts in the fields of (nuclear) armament and deterrence. Duchêne claims that Europe could only pursue a credible and forceful foreign policy if it possesses nuclear means to underline its seriousness. Moreover, the European dependence on US military protection needs to be paid back economically. In the longer term this could lead to the European wish to get rid of American dominance and become a military (and nuclear) superpower itself (see Duchêne 1973: 21). Duchêne himself calls the option of the EU becoming a nuclear superpower improbable. Though political circumstances have changed, this does not seem to be more realistic in today's constellations. Moreover, the notion of a European nuclear superpower is rather unpopular among European peoples. Many Germans oppose it for historical reasons, and other European nations are also opposed to this idea—be it for national, democracy-based or left-wing reasons.

Duchêne concludes aptly and significantly that there is no realistic chance that the EU will be a superpower that is based on traditional means of power politics. All it could try to be is a one of the major powers, and it will not be able to exercise its influence using traditional means. Under such circumstances, any European foreign policy that tries to gain influence abroad will be a mere policy of economics or of prestige. The first one would be too silent, the second one too loud and too much based on empty phrases to be able to lead to success in a crisis or against real opposition (see ibid.: 25, et seq.).

As there is no basis for a European nationalism that would dispose of the necessary military means, Duchêne next considers the option of a neutral European community. This means that Europe would try not to get involved in political conflicts. The historical basis and political support for such an option are rather weak, though. One could imagine neutrality in the Swiss sense of armed neutrality. This would not work out due to the lack of military (nuclear) means. An unarmed neutral power that is so big in size, population and economic strength as the

European Union is also hard to imagine. Such a Union would have to depend on the guarantee of the American superpower and would not be able to increase its coherence. Therefore, neutrality presents an unrealistic option that would lead to disintegration rather than to an (internally) strong European Union (see ibid.: 26 et seq.).

The third option would be to understand Europe as a process. This means the establishment of a common and shared approach between Europeans in order to make up for the lack of common military means and to deal with the challenges of an interdependent and globalized world. Due to the transnational character of these challenges, nation states are no longer able to deal alone with the problems that concern their nations, such as worldwide diseases, human trafficking, pollution and climate change. This is especially true for European countries that share a number of challenges, such as immigration and the integration of migrants, questions of trade and its regulation with non-European countries—and making their voice heard in world politics. Common European policies in these fields would be the only way to maintain Europe's capacity to act under the current circumstances and to avoid a loss of security and property.

A European policy that would try to find a common way in an interdependent world that is explicitly not based on military potential but on civilian means of power, like economics and diplomacy, would, according to Duchêne, reflect postwar Europeanness in its typical way. That means that the idea of a European Union was created in an atmosphere of war-weariness, conciliation and peace building that could be exemplary for Europeans and their politics. These attitudes and new values are not only typical for post-war Europe; they are also a conscious attitude that no longer supports military-based power politics. Duchêne claims that postwar Europe's civilian power policy does not only reflect a lack of means but also the deliberate decision not to form a European Union with military (nuclear) means. He even speaks of a new level of political culture and the unique chance to demonstrate how civilian power politics could make a difference. To give it a real chance, the European Union should strengthen its approach toward base political agreements and processes on international law and contracts. This would be the door to make a non-military power policy efficient.

Duchêne claims that the civility of foreign policy represents the true character of the European Community. It may be questioned elsewhere whether this is true for a European Union that is trying to increasingly develop a common defense policy; it is true, though, that civilian foreign policy remains the typical European policy. This civilian character of foreign policy reflects typical European values, such as equality, justice, social values, and respect and tolerance towards others. If Europe wants to succeed with this kind of policy, it must spread it and its democratic values. Otherwise it could perish in a world of military superpowers (see ibid.: 35).

Not surprisingly, this notion was severely criticized at the end of the 1970s, with analysts saying that the EU did not have any "real," i.e. military power, and therefore did not have the qualities of an actor. In particular, Hedley Bull, of the English School of international relations theory, has coined this perception (see Bull 1982: 151). This criticism has been repudiated with reference to the fact that power is more than military means. With the new post-Cold War political constellations, Duchêne's assumptions have been said to be even more outdated. Nevertheless, the debate still rests on his insights when it comes to researching European foreign policy and the values that determine the EU in its international identity (see Whitman 1998: 12). It has been pointed out in particular that the EU should try to build up its credibility slowly and not risk it by trying to do things it is not able to do. This means it should stick to a civilian power policy, instead of trying to become a major actor in military defense or crisis management (see Lofthouse/Long 1996: 196). It has also been advised to continue researching the civilian power approach, as this seems to be an appropriate approach to look at the EU due to its great flexibility and the way it forms international relations as structures that are a construct as *sui generis* as the EU itself is often said to be (see Hill 1990: 54). Hanns W. Maull later described the term of a "civilian power" more precisely in the context of Germany and Japan, suggesting that a prototype of a civilian power accepts international cooperation as necessary, relies on non-military power above all and is willingly embedded in supranational structures (see Maull 1990/91: 92). In Maull's concept the element of power is still visible: according to him, a civilian power is aware of its interests and also tries to reach them. It does not necessarily reject the use of military means for ideological-normative reasons. On the contrary, military power may be a way (or at least the *ultima ratio*) to protect oneself and to achieve one's own interests. These interests are normative insofar as the promotion of civilianization is the major aim. Maull divides civilian powers from traditional actors according to the means and the content of their policies (see ibid. 1993: 537). Traditional great powers act in the Weberian sense of power: they pursue their aims against the will of others. The greater their control of their environment, the more powerful they are. On the other hand, civilian powers pursue their aims in an integrative framework and derive their own power also from this integrated whole.

3.2.2   The EU as a typical civilian power

Traditional concepts of state power are connected to Bodin's (1576) concept of sovereignty (see Bodin 1992). They are based on the historical notion that since the development of the modern state, power goes together with sovereignty. Foreign policy was the first bastion that the modern national states gained in their self-differentiation from the supranational powers of that time, the empire and to the papal empire. Foreign policy is the heart of each state's self-conception, forming the identities of states and giving them their character in demarcation against other actors. Due to the continuing dominance of national state foreign policy, the European Union has a hard time formulating and pursuing its own interests. The single European nation states have become relatively powerless in the sense of not being able to achieve their interests in the context of globalization—but they are also not yet willing or able to formulate a common foreign policy strategy in the framework of the EU.

Elie Barnavi has brought up the example of a power ladder: if the United States is at one end of this ladder and Somalia is at the other one, Europe is not at the ladder at all. Barnavi even doubts that it is an aim of the European Union to possess power and to exercise it. Referring to the Middle East, Barnavi believes that the European Union does not have any influence and that major decisions are not only taken without Europe, but even against it (see Barnavi 2006/07: 84 et seq.). Others claim that the EU's weight comes precisely from its particular characteristic of not being bellicose and of not having interests in gaining foreign territory (see Bahr: 94). Writers have also suggested that Europe may pursue a policy of justice—but consider this ridiculous in the context of power, as this (assumed) justice is not supported by military strength (see Sfeir 2006/07: 91). As the European Union is not a sovereign state and does not act like one, however, the classical concept of power on which Barnavi builds his argument can hardly be applied to it. At least in the context of power, the EU is an entity *sui generis*. Therefore, the term of a "civilian power" has become a key word in the analysis of the current European Foreign policy. Under realist perceptions, this creates the question of how such a Kantian concept of a civilian power may work in a world that remains a Hobbesian jungle (see Barnavi 2006/07: 87).

This goes together with other descriptions that claim that the Union is powerless in principle. The Member of the European Parliament and former French Minister responsible for European Affairs, Alain Lamassoure, claims, for instance, that in 1906 Europe was at odds with itself but dominated the world. By contrary, in 2006, Europe is as united as it has never been before—but the world is running its own course (see Lamassoure 2006/07: 47, 49). In a similar way, the

European Union is often said to be the fulfillment of Kant's dream of a perpetual peace. It has created peace on its territory and does not seem to face a direct military threat from other states. Shimon Peres made the famous statement during the signing of the Oslo Treaty that a state without enemies loses its foreign policy. In a traditional or realist perception, the European Union may be regarded as an actor that is not threatened by other states, and therefore lacks power and does not have a genuine foreign policy.

Moreover, the idea of a powerful Europe in its traditional sense is not very popular in Europe. Asked about the role of Europe in a multipolar world and a European conception of power, the former French Foreign Minister Hubert Védrine claimed that most Europeans would not see any necessity of making Europe a *puissance*, emphasizing that the EU would have to become *une force* in order to pursue its interests in the world (see Védrine 2006/07: 46). But it is doubtful whether Védrine has gathered a majority of Europeans behind his plea. As the referendums in France and the Netherlands and the current debate on a European constitution have shown, there is a widespread fear that the European Union could become a superpower and could even replace the national states. It is not (yet) supposed to develop the foreign policy and the power that a nation state may pursue.

3.2.3   Characteristics of the EU's civilian policy

According to the development of the term of civilian power, scholars have been trying to establish a catalogue of typical characteristics of a civilian power concept. The following criteria are mostly agreed upon:

Civilian powers are characterized by the fact that they do not exercise methods of classical power politics. That means that they do not use military power in order to pursue their interests (see Jünemann/Schörnig 2003: 106). Instead, they regard international relations as *mutual interdependences* and try to reach their aims in this interdependence-framework. They attempt to gain influence by setting up fixed *rules of the international game* to which every actor must keep. Therefore, civilian powers are typically characterized by their preference and promotion of *international legal systems* and *multilateral agreements* (see Telò 2006: 54). These international networks and legal systems reduce the possibility of military conflicts. Moreover, a comprehensive political and economic interweavement may promote a more equal distribution of resources and thus reduce the risk of conflicts about resources (see ibid.: 53). Moreover, military means present an *ultima ratio* only. Instead, *diplomatic and economic threats and incentives* are the major instruments upon which a civilian power's policies are based. Civilian powers also differ from traditional actors with regard to their aims: they want to achieve *stability* and therefore pursue a policy of *social justice and sustainability*. As they do not look for an enlargement of their territories but for aims that respect their partners, military means do not present an adequate option in any case (see Dembinski 2003: 75; Maull 1990/91; 1993: 536 et seq.). Instead, the *normative component*, also called ethical component (see Barbé/Johansson-Nogués 2008: 82), of the civilian power concept provides for the promotion of human rights and democratic values as well as for issues with worldwide relevance, such as environmental sustainability (see Lightfoot/Burchell 2005).[10]

It has been argued whether the EU meets these criteria and can therefore be called a civilian power (see Schlotter 2003). First of all, there is an obvious *primacy of diplomacy*. The EU does not only pursue intensive dialogues with a great number of states and international organizations, it does this in an organized way, for example, in the framework of its Neighborhood Policy. According to

---

[10]   Similar to and sometimes overlapping with the criteria developed for civilian power, Mary Kaldor et al have developed five principles of human security. These are human rights, legitimate political authority, multilateralism and a regional focus (see Glasius/Kaldor 2005; Kaldor 2007; Kaldor/Martin/Selchow 2007).

the European Union, this policy aims "to avoid new dividing lines between the enlarged EU and its neighbours to the east and on the southern and eastern shores of the Mediterranean" (EC 2007: http://ec.europa.eu/world/enp/index_en.htm).

Second, *multilateral arrangements* and the aim to *establish a further-reaching system of international law and legislation* are characteristic of European policy. The EU supports the United Nations and other international organizations in their attempt to create a more peaceful way of dealing with world problems. Also in acute crises, the EU regularly pushes for solutions in the framework of international agreements and by legitimizing resolutions of the UN-security council. Its aim is to create a world order with binding rules in order to make international relations more reliable and to create stability and greater security. The states in the EU's direct neighborhood are offered a comprehensive catalog of agreements and even of a legalization of the relationship. Thus cooperation between the EU and its close partners is established in a rather stable and firm way in the long run. The main incentive and future aim is always a membership in the EU or a close association (see Dembinski 2003: 78).

Moreover, the EU is a typical actor of civilian policy regarding the importance it attributes to *economic instruments* in its foreign policy (see Müller-Brandeck-Bocquet 2000). Economic incentives serve as a major instrument in achieving EU foreign policy aims. Political dialogue, closer association or even membership in the European Union are regularly linked to the achievement of economic goals or the fulfillment of agreements. Political aims like democratization or human rights are often pursued by linking economic cooperation or financial aid to their promotion in the partner states. Furthermore, trade agreements probably present the field in which European foreign policy follows its interests most strongly. The EU shapes the world by insisting on its trade advantages and heavily protecting its economies.

Fourth, and maybe most important, the EU is reputed for the moral issues it emphasizes in its foreign policy. It tries to spread *values and norms* that are regarded as typical for a civilian policy, as they are said to be highly altruistic (see Kirste/Maull 1996: 302). Morality in its general sense is probably a worldwide ideal. What may be characteristic for the European Union, though, is a commitment to democracy that has its roots in Greek antiquity. Democracy is the breeding ground for Western values such as freedom, equality, tolerance, and the capacity to compromise and to show solidarity (see Romilly 2006/07: 142, 147). These values are expressed in the European Union's self-perception and self-description, which appears in most official documents concerning the EU's aims and role in the world. Mostly, peace, cooperation and dialogue are mentioned as aims and means of European policies. The European Political Cooperation (EPC) has already referred to these values, and the Common Foreign and Security Policy, set up in the second pillar of the Maastricht Treaty, is also defined in a way that suits the criteria of civilian power established by Maull. Its objectives are "to safeguard the common values, fundamental interests, independence and integrity of the Union in conformity with the principles of the United Nations Charter; to strengthen the security of the Union in all ways; to preserve peace and strengthen international security, in accordance with the principles of the United Nations Charter, as well as the principles of the Helsinki Final Act and the objectives of the Paris Charter, including those on external borders; to promote international cooperation; to develop and consolidate democracy and the rule of law, and respect for human rights and fundamental freedoms" (Amsterdam Treaty: Article J.1). Moreover, even the European Security and Defense Policy (ESDP) finds its basis in typical objectives of a civilian power. The pursuit of democracy and human rights (see Schubert 2002) and the aim to establish a more peaceful, fair (see Lennon 2001) and secure world is said to be the essence of European policy. Even if this may contrast with its protectionist economic policy, its reputation of an altruistic power is widespread. Many Southern American and Arab countries see the EU also as a counterweight to the United States. They thereby

84

set their hopes on a more balanced policy, as they assume that the EU has a greater understanding for cultures and countries that the US does not support or even opposes. This may also be due to the fact that Europeans claim to act on an eye-to-eye basis of mutual respect and tolerance. In contrast, American policy is often regarded as ignorant of or even arrogant toward other cultures. This notion is highly ideological and is—as is every notion—a construction. Nevertheless, in its widespread existence, it influences international relations.

What characterizes the EU as a civilian power can especially be found in its policies towards the Middle East. Diplomacy and the regulation and legalization of relations and their embedding in agreements prevail. Economic questions are in the center of the relationship. "Military aspects were deliberately excluded from the EMP agenda. First of all due to a broader definition of security which focuses on political and socio-economic causes of instability rather than on 'hard' security issues, and secondly due to the inter-regional frictions, especially in the Middle East, that did not allow the tackling of hard security issues at the time when the EMP was established" (Jünemann 2003a: 39). The EMP therefore is a "model of civilian foreign relations" (ibid.).

3.2.4 Why does the EU pursue its civilian policy?

The question, why the EU may be called a civilian power or an actor that pursues a typical civilian policy, has been widely discussed. One of the most common explanations is, that the EU is a civilian power by mistake—because it has not managed to build up great common military capacities.[11]

---

[11] The European Defense Community, proposed in 1950 by René Pleven, failed in 1954 because the French National Assembly did not ratify it. Since then, European military instruments have been mainly integrated into the NATO framework. The Helsinki European Council in December 1999 was another major

According to Matthias Dembinski, one can derive six different explanations for the question of why civilian power occurs. These are a *rationalist*, an *institutions-related*, a *democracy theory-related*, a *normative*, a *constructivist* and a *liberal* explanation (see Dembinski 2002: 17 et seq.; ibid. 2003: 81 et seq.).

The *rationalist explanation* sees growing interdependence in international relations as the main reason for the use of civilian power. Supporters of this explanation claim that states or supranational actors take their decisions on a rational basis and try to maximize their benefit according to a cost-benefit analysis. In a world of mutual interdependence, non-military power holds more promise of reaching one's aims than the deployment of troops. Therefore, actors come to the conclusion that economic, ideological, political and cultural influence may lead them further than a military strike. The spread of their economic, political and cultural systems in interdependent structures will allow them to pursue their interests more easily and in a longer run than military options. It is unclear in how far this assumption depicts a trend in reality or is rather the result of theoretical considerations that are not necessarily reflected in world politics.

François Dûchene was among the first who raised this rationalist explanation in the context of his perception of civilian powers.

---

attempt to establish military forces: its target was to create a framework in which military forces could be deployed within sixty days and would be able to carry out the full range of tasks stated in Article 17 of the Treaty of the European Union. In 2004 the European Council discussed further steps and set up headline goals to be reached by 2010 in order to improve European military capacities. Its aim is to equip the Union with means for crisis management, like peace-keeping tasks, tasks of combat forces in crisis management and humanitarian and rescue tasks. In the same year, the European Council decided to establish an operational center (in 2007), a civilian-military cell (since 2005), a planning unit at SHAPE and a new element concerned with the relationship to NATO (since 2005). Yet, the efforts of recent years have not yet led to a military option comparable to the army of a state, and it remains unclear if this is a target at all.

Dealing with the balance of power and disarmament, Hedley Bull especially criticized his notion. Bull cited the example of the East-West conflict and claimed that the military silence between the Eastern and the Western blocs was not due to rational assumptions that made civilian means preferable over military instruments. Rather, nuclear bipolarity was the reason for the coldness of the war (see Bull 1961). It is hard to say whether military or civilian power is prevalent today. In the light of new armaments, especially in the Middle East, it seems doubtful that states operate on rational principles and thereby conclude that non-military means will help them to achieve their aims better than military options.

The explanation *related to institutions* claims that there is a link between institutional arrangements and the foreign policy of a state. It has been assumed that democracies tend to pursue peaceful relations among each other and are possibly more peaceful in their foreign policies in general.[12] No matter how one may assess this argument, it is clear that in democracies there are groups with special foreign policy interests that lobby actively and successfully for a non-peaceful foreign policy. These groups may be networks that are interested in supporting foreign wars for ideological, ethnic or religious reasons. More often, they are groups with economic interests, for example, the weapons industry. It is already doubtful whether the basic assumptions of this explanation are justified. As the EU cannot be compared to a state in its foreign policy, it is less vulnerable to the lobbying of security networks or the weapons industry. Until now, its foreign policy is simply not characterized by military actions, so that weapons

---

[12]   The question of whether there is a correlation between democracy and peace has been answered positively by of the empirical analyses which have come up with the result that democracies have not gone to war against each other since 1816 (see, for example, Bremer 1992; Ray 2000; Russett 1993; Levy 2002). Research on the monadic level analyzing the foreign policy of single states has come to a different result, suggesting that democracies are involved in conflicts to a similar degree as non-democracies are (see, for example, Henderson 2002; Reiter/Stam 2002). For critical evaluations see, for example, Aliboni/Guazzone 2004: 89 et seq.; Brock 2006; Brown/Lynn-Jones/Miller 1996; Chojnacki 2003; Daase 2006).

lobbying takes place rather in other constellations (see Dembinski 2003: 82 et seq.; Grande 1996).

The explanation that depends on *democracy theories* is partly based on the same assumptions. It also makes use of the argument that democracies are less likely to start wars among each other and possibly also against non-democracies. These theories claim that democracies internalize respect for human rights and lawful behavior and act towards other states as they have learned to behave internally. Moreover, the interests of the electorate and of internal pressure groups and networks may tend to work in favor of peaceful solutions. These assumptions face the same objections that confront peaceful-democracy theories. It is not clear why states should behave externally as they do internally (see Dixon 1994). The argument, that democracies are also more peaceful towards non-democracies has not been proven either, and there also have been assumptions that tensions may even increase between democracies and non-democracies (see Risse-Kappen 1995). Moreover, the EU is not a state and does not have the same internal dynamics that states have. It is not clear which internal movements should make it act in an especially civilian way towards other actors.

The *normative explanation* may be the most popular among researchers dealing with the EU as a civilian power. It reflects the hope that the EU might be a "special" actor, a new model created to ensure peace in Europe and to promote peace in the world. These expectations may be so high and normatively (over-)loaded because the European Union is still a relatively young actor that has not yet reached its final form. Already its foundation was accompanied by discussions filled with hopes and expectations, if not even euphoria in some circles (see Rosecrance 1998: 22). Therefore, rather normative aims have coined the vision of the political orientation of this actor. Moreover, due to its singular form, the EU is thought not to have the typical interests and options that a state may have. It even has been suggested that the EU is a normative power not due to what it does but due to what it is (see Manners 2002: 252) and because of changing perceptions in the international system of what is "normal" (see Manners 2008: 45). In this context, another attempt to define the EU as a power has been made: Federica Bicchi recommends distinguishing between a normative and a civilizing European power with a civilizing power lacking either inclusiveness or reflexivity or both (see Bicchi 2006a: 287).

As the EU itself regularly refers to its normative orientation, it is possible that this focus on a civilian policy does not only appear in the rhetoric of pro-EU groups, but that it also exists in the EU's self-perception. Nevertheless, this does not necessarily sa that the EU's de facto policy reflects this normative orientation. Even if it does, it is not clear where this orientation towards an explicitly civilian policy comes from (see Dembinski 2003: 83). This may well be true, but it does not explain why the EU should have developed its own special orientation and not another. After all, most states pursue their interests in a certain value framework. This does not mean, however, that they refrain from building their policies on military options.

One of the most interesting approaches is without doubt the *constructivist explanation*. Constructivist approaches assume that there is no national interest per se. Instead, there are norms and perceptions that are alterable and underlie changes because they are socially constructed—and not a given reality. According to different lines of constructivist theory, identities of states emerge in transactions with other actors in the international system. The construction of identities appears through processes of acting and communicating between the actors (see Risse 2007; Wendt 1999). Moreover, identities of states emerge through historical experiences and their reception. A society's internal debates and discussions, its political culture that is built over the years, contribute to the formation of a state's identity (see Katzenstein 1996). Moreover, the expectation and attitude in which other actors see the state and approach it, forms the state's identity and options of action.[13]

It is doubtful to what extent these constructivist assumptions can be transferred to the European Union. The EU is a rather singular actor with a very special history and internal processes that are hard to compare to any other form of actor. It is true that as an actor in the international system, the EU is subject to the processes which constructivist theory describes. It is not clear, though, whether constructivist processes lead to the specific civilian power orientation followed by the EU. This is especially hard to figure out, as European foreign policy is still defined by its members' notions and internal debates. In certain countries, a civilian power orientation may be found in the debates of society, science and politics. However, it is hard to say which countries' internal orientations are dominant in designing European foreign policy. The civilian power orientation is probably a lot stronger in Germany, for example, than it is in Great Britain or France. This may be explained by historical experiences, as stated above. There has not been decisive research on the question of how this phenomenon appears at the European policy level. This question is also linked to the ongoing discussion of whether there is a European public and, if yes, how it constitutes and articulates itself (see, for example, Steeg 2002, and in favor of this assumption Koopmans/Erbe 2004; Trenz 2004).

Matthias Dembinski comes up with a sixth possible explanation for the formation of a civilian power policy on the EU level. It is based on *liberal* theories and also takes constructivist references into account (see Dembinski 2003: 88 et seq.). Therefore, it combines two assumptions and claims that internal institutions are responsible for foreign policy conceptions as well as the interactions between the actors. Referring to Beate Kohler-Koch and Manfred G. Schmidt, Dembinski bases his argument on the notion that the EU can be compared to a consociate system, which makes its decisions neither by

---

[13]   These insights will be explored in detail later on in the context of productive power.

orders nor by majority decision. Instead, decisions are made on the basis of negotiations, preferably by reaching a consensus (see Dembinski 2003: 89; Kohler-Koch 1999; Schmidt 2000). This can be explained by the fact that the EU disposes of a rather fixed institutional structure that does not allow extreme changes. Developments can be reached only gradually and are embedded in a highly differentiated system of rules. Every actor has its specified tasks, so that decision-making paths are not generally open to drastic action. Major decisions are still in the hands of the national states, so that the principle of representation is decisive. The influence of the national states, their national cultures and processes of making decisions remains a major dimension in European foreign policy-making (see Börzel 2002).

Nevertheless, common norms are fixed in the treaties and rules of the European Union. Due to the path-dependence of the actors, decisions may be taken in spite of possibly differing opinions and interests of the actors and according to these norms. This influences the actors and may create a close-knit forum among states with similar norms and ideas in the long-term. Dembinski also points out that institutional dependencies restrict traditional resources of influence among the EU-partners, so that a structured and stabilized forum is created that depends on its ability to create common solutions—and not on the power of single national states (see Dembinski 2003: 91).

In this framework, solutions depend on trust among the partners. Intensive dialogue and openness may be facilitated by the system of rules in which decision-making takes place. Norms, ideas and approaches serve as the basic mission statements. According to these, the differing interests of the member states are aligned. Policy-making can be achieved by formulating aims subordinated to these basic norms without having to deal with the major policy orientation every time. Therefore, decisions are built on one another and rarely lead to major changes (see ibid.: 94). The civilian power policy is therefore rooted in these internal institutions and paths and the norms they are based on. They are practiced and internalized and lead to a specific civilian policy orientation over the years.

Dembinski suggests that the EU transports to its external partners these internalized paths of decision-making in a certain framework of norms. Its internal institutional setting is reflected in its affinity to multilateral frameworks and international rules and law. In addition, its policy of favoring dialogue with external partners can be explained by its internal procedures. Economic means allow the EU to follow its way because they agreements can be made step by step until a consensus is found. On the other hand, international crisis or challenges that require immediate and quick reactions and measurement present a problem to the EU. Its path-dependency is not made for fast decision-taking. This is especially true when the interests of one EU member state are involved in the crisis. Moreover, the EU lacks flexibility in severe, complicated and complex decisions, as in military conflicts. These internal procedural conditions therefore favor its civilian policy. Dembinski comes to a similar conclusion as do the explanations quoted above. He assumes that that the EU is a civilian power due to its institutional structure. Its orientation is based neither on an ideology nor on a rational cost-benefit analysis (see ibid.: 94).

3.3 Differentiating between the European Union as a civilian power actor and the power it exercises

It has been discussed that in contrast to the value-oriented objectives the EU claims to pursue, it does not necessarily act on an altruistic basis in reality, but rather like a national state pursuing its own interests. In particular, its positions on economics, above all concerning trade, are the ones of a national state that does not necessarily concern itself with ideals like justice or equality. For example, its protectionist positions do not leave room for the interests of development countries (see Dembinski 2003: 77). This view reflects a very narrow notion of a "civilian power." As has been described in the previous chapter, it claims that a "civilian power" is a "good actor" that pursues an altruistic ideology.

However, this conceptualization neglects the power-aspect of this actor of civilian power: the discussion concerning the so-called "civilian power EU" is trapped into the problem that the term "power" is used in the sense of an "actor" only and not in the sense of "influence." Moreover, the meaning of the term "power" is not understood in its sharp meaning but is softened normatively because of the concentration of the word "civilian." A civilian power is widely seen as "good" because it does not take military measure.[14] That a civilian actor nevertheless exercises power that may be even more influential than military means, hardly finds attention (see Manners 2006). This becomes obvious, for example, in the often-made confrontation between the model of a "peaceful civilian power Europe" and a "Europe that tries to play a role in world politics and follows its interests" (see Bailes 2008; Jünemann/Schörnig 2003: 102; Schlotter 2003: 7 et seq.). According to Jünemann, "a civilian power strives for harmonious and constructive relations with other countries, co-operates with international organizations or within international regimes and supports the authority of international law. To assert its national interests, a civilian power voluntarily restricts itself to the use of political and economic means" (Jünemann 2003a: 39 et seq.). Peter Schlotter even exposes confrontations between the policies of the EU that shows typical elements of a civilian power and those of many of its member states, whose foreign policies are based on traditional power policy (see Schlotter 2003: 13).

Another scholar asks whether the EU will become a "power block" due to the fact that the European Council decided in Helsinki in

---

[14]   A European Union that would exercise traditional military power in the Middle East and would try to turn the Mediterranean Sea into a *mare nostrum* has been warned of before (see Hager 1973: 264).

December 1999 to develop an EU crisis management capacity within the Common Foreign and Security Policy and to provide 60,000 soldiers for EU missions (see Dembinski 2003: 73). It is true that the decisions of Helsinki may have been a milestone in the history of European integration. The question raised concerning a potential "power block" EU is mistaken, however. Such notions reveal that many authors dealing with the "civilian power EU" are not aware that a civilian power is also an actor that exercises power. Confrontations like these neglect the fact that a civilian power is also an actor that may follow its interests, i.e. that a civilian actor exercises power. This leads to a biased focus in research concerning the European Union. Therefore, the disagreement among scholars concerning the legitimacy of the use of military means for humanitarian interventions[15] misses a crucial point: an actor can use civilian power even if it also uses military power. Even though the EU mainly exercises power that is civilian, it may also exercise power that is non-civilian, i.e. military.

This is also true for actors that are not typical civilian powers. Most scholars apply the notion "civilian power" to the EU but not to the United States, as the US policy relies much more on military means than the EU's. Even if US-led wars may have been examined more closely in recent years, one cannot neglect the great influence that the US exercises through political, economic and cultural means. That means that an actor that regularly relies on military means may also exercise civilian power. It is true, though, that the EU presents a better example for an actor exercising civilian power, as it exercises non-military power above all and thus meets the criteria of civilian power cited above far more. The debate about whether this is due to a lack of military means or whether it simply characterizes EU values (see Jünemann/Schörnig 2003: 101 ff.; Mawdsley 2003: 134 ff.; Schlotter 2003: 8 et seq.) is not relevant for this study: even if the EU will

---

[15]   Lofthouse and Long argue that for a civilianian power the use of military means is only legitimate in cases of self-defense, whereas Kirste and Maull support the deployment of weapons as an ultima ratio in humanitarian crises (see Kirste/Maull 1996: 303; Lofthouse/Long 1996).

become an actor that relies in its foreign policy on military means (see Jünemann 2003a), it will still continue exercising civilian power. There is no contradiction between a civilian policy that is built especially on the means of diplomacy, multilateral agreements and dialogue, and the exercise of power. Thus, the question of whether the EU is a civilian power, and whether it remains one despite the development of the ESDP, lacks ground. The EU exercises civilian power—even if, or *because,* it follows its self-interests. A fruitful characterization has been made by Henning Tewes in this context. He emphasizes that civilian power is concerned with the exercise of influence as a new form of governance in an era of increasing interdependence. Even though it tries to tame military force, it is not necessarily contradictory to force (see Tewes 2002: 11 et seq). This means that civilian power can exist in a non-military, but compulsory form. Maull also explicitly defines a civil power as an actor (see Maull 2007: 74).

The study at hand thus does not deal with the European Union as a civilian power in the sense of understanding the word "power" as an actor but in the sense of an agent that mainly exercises power that is civilian. Despite the manifold attempts of defining and characterizing power as well as dealing with the EU as a civilian power actor, it remains unclear what civilian power is as an influence. The coming chapter will therefore attempt to characterize power in the four basic types that have been developed in academic research and try to further sharpen their civilian and international characteristics.

4 Two basic dimensions of power

As the preceding chapters have shown, manifold efforts to explain the nature of power have already been made. The most current attempt, by Michael Barnett and Raymond Duvall, states that, "in general terms, power is the production, in and through social relations, of effects that shape the capacities of actors to determine their own circumstances and fate" (Barnett/Duvall 2005: 8). This definition takes previous discussions about power into account and incorporates its most important features. According to the definition, there are "two analytical dimensions that are the core of the general concept: the *kinds* of social relations through which power works; and the *specificity* of social relations through which effects on actors' capacities are produced" (ibid.: 9).

The first dimension, *kinds*, examines how power is expressed. It can be split into two parts. First of all, power can be "an attribute of particular actors and their interactions" (ibid.). Here, especially means to exercise power are important: whoever has the gun in his hands is more powerful than the unarmed one.

Secondly, "*kinds* of social relations" implies a "social process of constituting what actors are as social beings, that is their social identities and capacities" (ibid.). This means, for example, that one actor might dispose of more sophisticated knowledge, better means of influencing related actors, a more comfortable position in the social system, or just a better reputation than another actor.

The second dimension deals with the *specificity* of social relations, that is: how direct or diffuse are the social relations through which power works. *Direct* means that power can be executed openly and without processes lying in between. In the very moment that someone threatens someone else with his knife, he exercises power. By contrast, *diffuse* points to the fact that power is exercised through processes and constellations. For example, international institutions can be regarded as means to exercise power.

4.1 Power as an attribute versus power as a constitution

Power as an attribute describes what is mostly referred to as "power over." This basically means that one actor exercises control over another actor. It works through *behavioral relations* or *interactions*. Therefore, the one who is exposed to the power that another actor exercises will be affected in his actions, his conditions of being, or even in his existence itself. His ability to control his own circumstances will be limited by the power exercised by another actor. This theoretical approach to power mostly leads to the understanding that power is an attribute or action of the stronger actor. Mostly, it neglects the fact that power is more than a one-way exercise (see Barnett/Duvall 2005: 9 et seq.).

In contrast to the first approach, the second concept that looks at how power is expressed describes power as clearly social. Therefore, its analysis takes place in a broader framework that goes beyond looking at interactions. In this theoretical approach, power works in *social constitutions*. It manifests itself through *social relations*. These relations compose actors "as social beings with their respective capacities and interests" (ibid: 9). This means that the identity of actors is determined by social constellations.[1] Power is regarded as "power to": which actor has which abilities to act in which manner. This is due to his position in the social system, i.e. his social empowerment. This social position, respective to the options it provides for an actor to act and to influence his circumstances, is determined by the actor's self-perception and how others perceive him, two determinants that also influence each other. This second theoretical approach mostly looks at power only with regard to the creation of identities.

---

[1]   To demonstrate this fact, one might quote two novels by Max Frisch as a literary example: *Andorra* and *I'm not Stiller*. In both of them individuals fight with their own identities or develop new ones due to the power exercised by their social environment upon them.

Even though these approaches are represented by different scholars and schools, they are not necessarily contrary. Rather, are they complementary, as each covers different facets of power. They are even connected: if power works as a direct influence to which an actor is exposed, it can alter his behavior and even his self-understanding and self-esteem. Therefore, power as an interaction can have consequences for power that works through social constitutions. This is also true the other way round: If power determines the identity of actors as it works through social constitution, it also influences their behavior and therefore their interactions. Thus, whoever examines power in terms of interaction will discover effects concerning social identities—and whoever examines power in terms of social constitution will discover effects concerning interaction (see ibid.: 10 et seq.).

4.2   Direct versus diffuse exercise of power

The second analytical dimension of Barnett and Duvall's concept of power deals with relational specificity. Here, the first approach is to assume that power is exercised directly; that is, that there is some kind of link between two actors, A and B. This connection has mostly been thought of in terms of direct communication or interaction. It can also take place via A's laws, his policymaking, or his media; and A and B might not be two actors, but instead a group of people. Robert Dahl and his colleagues in the 50s and 60s are strict in their determination of the directness of power. According to Dahl, the distance between the two (or more) actors is short, even tangible (see Dahl 1957: 204). Any action causes an immediate consequence. As consequences appear prompt, it is rather easy to analyze power and its effects. Moreover, the relationship in which power takes place is specific, so that it is possible to identify the actors (see Bhaskar 1979; Dahl 1957: 204; Giddens 1984). As will be shown in the following chapters, scholars who regard power as compulsory or as structural tend to speak of such a direct link.

The second approach concerning the relational specificity of power states that power is wielded in indirect relations. In contrast to the first approach, power can work here also between actors that are not directly attached to each other. Socially diffuse relations, physical and temporal distances, do not prevent the exercise of power. Channels of power might be complex and convoluted. Even if there are intermediary actors, power can arrive from actor A to actor B. This includes various cases, such as power that is generated through language and discourse, that take place over time and distance (see Fairclough1989, ibid. 1992), as well as power that is exercised through institutions.

5   A fourfold conceptualization of power

These two main dimensions that have been explained above can be integrated into a taxonomy. Michael Barnett and Raymond Duvall have depicted the scheme that is then created. It describes four types of power that are generated by combining the two dimensions.

		Relational specificity	
		Direct	Diffuse
Power works through	Interactions of specific actors	Compulsory	Institutional
	Social relations of constitution	Structural	Productive

(Barnett/Duvall 2006).

In the following these four types will be dealt with in detail as they serve as the basis for the study. The foundational philosophers and writers on these topics and their input will be taken into account in order to root the study in the literature.

5.1   Compulsory power

In modern political theory, the concept of compulsory power can be traced back at least to Thomas Hobbes. Hobbes does not define power explicitly, but states in *Leviathan* (1651) that "the power of a man, to take it universally, is his present means to obtain some future apparent good" (Hobbes 1996: 62). In his opinion, in a *bellum omnium contra omnes*, everybody tries to exert his power over someone else. Only

100

transferring power to a sovereign can end this situation. A potential abuse of powers by this central authority has to be accepted for the benefit of peace. Hobbes understands power as a tool one possesses and therefore can transfer to someone else (see ibid.). With this notion he coined the understanding of power as compulsory that has influenced students of power until today.

Scholars who describe power as compulsory assume that it takes place in the interaction of defined actors. In these interactions, it is exerted directly by actor A over actor B. Probably the most famous definition of (compulsory) power stems from Max Weber (1922), who defines power as "the probability that one actor within a social relationship will be in a position to carry out his own will despite resistance, regardless of the basis on which his probability exists" (Weber 1968: 53). In his definition, power takes place in social relations. It is exercised directly and points to the fact that the weaker actor could try to resist the power he is exposed to. Richard Tawney developed a similar definition that gained fame, saying that "power may be defined as the capacity of an individual, or group of individuals, to modify the conduct of other individuals or groups in the manner which he desires, and to prevent his own conduct being modified in the manner in which he does not" (Tawney 1971: 159).

Linked to this conceptualization is Robert Dahl's description of power, which has greatly influenced power research in the last decades. His theoretical debate on power is one of the earliest in the fields of international relations as a university science, but still has not lost its importance.[1] Dahl also describes power as something that a stronger actor possesses and wields over the weaker actor. In comparison to Weber and Tawney, Robert Dahl's approach is more precise. His theory was partly meant as a critique of elite models, which he described as methodically weak and as ideology-based (see

---

[1]   For Dahl's most important texts on power see Dahl 1957; 1958; 1961; 1963; 1965; 1968; 1989.

Dahl 1958).[2] Developed during a time in which behaviorism was leading in political science, Dahl's theory is influenced by the methods of behaviorism (see Hayward 2000: 13 et seq.). An important part of his theory is based on empirical studies, especially on the analysis of politics in New Haven. Like Weber, Dahl states that "power is a relation among people" (Dahl 1957: 203). Dahl specifies that people are actors. These "may be individuals, groups, roles, offices, governments, nation-states, or other human aggregates" (ibid.). It is important to note that concepts of compulsory power mostly assume that power is dyadic and are based on the notion of the powerful versus the powerless actor (see Fay 1987: 117 et seq.).

In contrast to Weber's famous definition, Dahl does not consider the statement that "A has power over B" enlightening enough, and therefore adds four elements to the definition which need to be examined: the "*source, domain*, or *base*"; the "*means* or *instruments*"; the "*range* or *scope*"; and the "*amount* or *extent*" (ibid., italics mine) of power. These four elements have been dealt with in a large amount of literature (see, for example, Barry 1976; Deutsch 1978; Frey 1989; Lasswell/Kaplan 1950). Up to the present date, these have been some of the most important factors in the study of power. Moreover, *weight* and *costs* have been taken in consideration. *Weight* points to the size or percentage of an actor's chance to achieve his aims (see Baldwin 2002: 178; Deutsch 1978). *Costs* captures an actor's considerations of how expensive an exercise of power will be for him. If it is relatively cheap for him to exercise influence, his power will be relatively higher. Or: A commands more power if he induces B to do things that are rather costly for B (see Baldwin 2002: 178; Harsanyi 1962). Students of power who regard power in terms of networks have criticized these characteristics (see following chapters on structural and productive power). In the following analysis, Dahl's four elements will be referred to respectively as *base*, *means*, *scope*, and *amount*.

---

[2]   Dahl's critique was mainly directed at C. Wright Mills (see Mills 1956) and at Floyd Hunter (see Hunter 1953). A good overview on the debate is provided by David Ricci (see Ricci 1980).

5.1.1 Bases of power

To characterize a *base* of power, many—mainly realist—scholars would point to military resources. With or without an indication of a possibly broader definition of power, the majority of power studies have been conducted with a focus on military capabilities and a possible balance of these capabilities. Inis Claude, for example, defines power as "denot[ing] what is essentially military capability—the elements which contribute directly or indirectly to the capacity to coerce, kill, and destroy" (Claude 1965: 6). In his study, he points out that people have tried to kill each other since the time of Cain and Abel, and as such only considers military power (ibid.) to be important. Many scholars may harbor the intuition that power in the form of violence rules the world, so that they refer to power mainly in this regard (see Vasquez 1998). Even if scholars recognize non-military forms of power, research on military power takes a main place in their studies (see Knorr 1975: 45 et seq.). Dahl also mentions the "war potential of nations" (Dahl 1957: 203) in this context, but does not neglect the less obvious fact that the charm or charisma of a politician could also be a base of his power. Regarding states, however, he does not give a comparable example.

Most scholars who are dealing with power issues have concentrated on bases of power, continuing a discussion of whether the different actors possess these bases of power or whether they are manifested in their relationship. Bertrand Russell (1938) wrote one of the more preeminent and well-structured essays on the topic of power bases, which considers power as a property of an actor or a group (see Russell 1995). In spite of the discussion concerning the location of power bases, most scholars agree that power is based on controllable resources that are intentionally applied. In this context, Russell distinguishes between "direct physical power" (ibid.: 25), "rewards and punishments as inducements" (ibid.), and "influence on opinion, i.e. propaganda in its broadest sense" (ibid.). In praxis, these different forms of power can occur together. As an example, Russell proposes that "the law uses punishment, not only for the purpose of making undesired actions physically impossible, but also as an inducement" (ibid.: 26).

Moreover, Russell distinguishes between traditional power and newly acquired power. Each has a different basis of power. The former can rely on habits, customs, religion, and public opinion. Traditional power may be reached either by naked power or by revolutionary power. Naked power is mainly military and tries to rule by force. By contrast, revolutionary power has the ability to gain supporters with ideas, programs or feelings. Again, the division depends on the case. "In a democratic country, the power of government is not naked in relation to opposing political parties, but is naked in relation to a convinced anarchist" (ibid: 29).

Furthermore, individuals may come to power that is either based on heritage or on intellectualism and spirituality. Sons of kings and nobles have been granted power by birth. Their adequate behavior and the acceptance of this system by inferiors insure their power. In contrast to this passively acquired power, power can also be based on knowledge and the mystery with which it has historically gone hand in hand. The connection between knowledge and power has been discussed especially in the context of constructivism. Knowledge, defined as a "capacity that turns people into experts and courses of action into truthful, appropriate, efficient or rational policies" (Adler/Bernstein 2005: 295), may become the attribute of an actor. This knowledge, as much as the social world, is socially or intersubjectively constructed (see Guzzini 2007: 24 et seq.).[3] In this sense it can provide an actor with expertise that grants superiority over other actors. When knowledge is used directly to shape the behavior of other actors, it is without doubt a base of compulsory power (see

---

[3] As a representative of constructivism, Stefano Guzzini also points to the fact that there is a reflexive relationship between the social construction of knowledge and the construction of social reality. That means, that the construction of knowledge can affect the construction of social reality and vice versa (see Guzzini 2007: 25).

ibid.). Today, the spread of education and the demystification of special skills and knowledge by science have destabilized this base of power. The medium, the medicine man, and the mathematical expert are no longer what they used to be. Their bases of power have lost their uniqueness. It has declined, as certain kinds of knowledge are no longer unreachable and not incomprehensible for the majority of people (see Tawney 1971: 30 et seq.). Knowledge often goes along with symbols in order to make it visible. Whereas knowledge has lost its exclusiveness, symbols still remain a constructed base of power, as they instruct social understanding as well as social action (see Hassdorf 2007: 149).

Tawney also refers to different bases of power and speaks about religion, military strength, and exclusive forms of knowledge as possible sources of power. Like Russell, he explains that power depends on the effectiveness of its threats and on its exclusiveness. He sagely sums up that it is "thus both awful and fragile, and can dominate a continent, only in the end to be blown down by a whisper. To destroy it, nothing more is required than to be indifferent to its threats, and to prefer other goods to those, which it promises. Nothing less, however, is required also" (ibid.: 160). A special case of sources of power has been brought up by Peter M. Blau, who takes the Weberian definition as a starting point and broadens it. Unlike Lasswell and Kaplan, who claim that a decision involves severe sanctions and that power means taking part in making these decisions (see Lasswell/Kaplan 1950: 74 et seq.), Blau takes a more comprehensive stance. In his opinion, power is not only exerted by negative sanctions, like punishments or physical threat, but also by positive measures. It is not only the militarily strong actor who possesses power, but also the one who can promise awards (see Blau 1964: 116 et seq.). In international relations these could be money, economic support, development aid, or even the support of a country on the international stage, for example, concerning a contradictory topic in the United Nations Security Council.

In the last years, a considerable number of studies regarding non-military bases of power have been published. With an eye toward non-governmental organizations and civil society activities, bases of power have been described as highly symbolic. Many authors have been trying to explain how relatively small groups that do not dispose of military resources can exert power on whole states or on multinational companies (see, for example, Armstrong/Lloyd/Redmond 1996; Blondel 2004; Boli/Thomas 1997; Edwards/Hulme 1995; Lister 2000). Many international organizations, like Amnesty International, Greenpeace, or Human Rights Watch, have moral or normative bases of power that allow them to influence world politics. Moreover, non-state actors like international organizations may shape the behavior of other actors by financial means. The International Monetary Fond or the World Bank are prominent examples of institutions that set conditions for poor states by providing them (or refusing to provide them) with money. Laws and decrees may also prove sources of power for militarily weaker actors (see Johnstone 2005).

5.1.2   Means, scope, and amount of power

Means of power are instruments that allow an actor to use his power bases. Means could be the threat of a state's military potential. *Scope* of power refers to the fact that power takes place in relations. It describes the reactions of the actor exposed to power. Finally, *amount* of power tries to measure how probable it is that A will succeed in getting B to do what he wants. Here, a special case of power can occur: What happens if B is so opposed to A's will, that he does not just refuse to do what A wants—but even decides to do the opposite? In this context, Dahl speaks of "negative power" (Dahl 1957: 205).

Means and scope of power have also been referred to as putative and actualized power (see Knorr 1975: 9 et seq.). This crucial differentiation points to the fact that a state's superior military potential does not automatically lead to victory in a conflict. In realist thought, the major example of putative power is military strength. It is actualized either through wars, military threats, or the anticipated fear of other actors. One can assume that the third mechanism is the one that occurs most. It is probably already at work when state actors are determining their agenda. If a conflict has arisen, the government actors of the militarily weaker state may not speak about the fear of being defeated, but will in most cases try to avoid a military strike. In contrast, power that is actualized through threats occurs less; and power that finds its actualization in wars is even rarer—though it appears much more prominent (see ibid.).

In Dahl's opinion, and in the opinion of other theorists who regard power as compulsory, power can only be exercised when there is a time lag between A's actions and B's responses. Moreover, it needs a connection between A and B or at least an opportunity for such a connection (see Dahl 1957: 204). Here, Dahl's definition misses certain aspects of power relations: As is shown in the chapters regarding institutional or structural power, power can also be exerted even if there is no visible connection between A and B.

5.1.3   The intentionality of power

In the context of compulsory power, the question of intentionality in exercise of power has been discussed. In the 1950s and later, Dahl and other scholars of compulsory power claimed that power does not take place unintentionally, but is always exerted in a conscious way. For example, Dennis Wrong divides diffuse control from power by stating that power equals intended influence (see Wrong 1980: 3).[4] Russell even defines power as "the production of intended effects" (Russell 1995: 24).

---

[4]   He defines this further, though, by pointing to the fact that there may be „unintended byproducts of the action" (Wrong 1980: 5).

This assumption has been strongly criticized, and various students of power have tried to develop criteria to find out whether and to what extent power is connected to intention. Jack Nagel suggested investigating not intention, but rather preferences of actors (see Nagel 1975: 23 et seq.). Clarence Stone went even further and claimed that it was enough if the dominant actor was following his interests, no matter whether he was aware of their effects (see Stone 1980: 979). Bachrach and Baratz called the fact of unintentional power a "subtle form of domination; one in which those who actually dominate are not conscious of it themselves, simply because their position of dominance has never seriously been challenged" (Bachrach/Baratz 1962: 952). It could to be added that the reasons for unintentional power are not only settled on the side of the stronger actor A. Theoretically, it is possible to imagine that the actors A and B possess exactly the same bases of power. B, however, has such weak self-esteem or is so frightened of dealing with his environment in general that he treats A as the more powerful actor. Therefore, A becomes stronger de facto and exerts power on B—even if he does not intend to do so.

In 1975, Bachrach and Baratz again dealt with the question of unintended power and specified that power "is operative even when A *unconsciously* exercises it or when he is aware of exercising it and produces unintended effects" (ibid. 1975: 903). By contrast, William Connolly originated a concept in which each agent, i.e. each actor, is able to choose what he wants and is able to act accordingly. Every person is able to develop aims that are based on certain values and are carried out for specific reasons. Consequently, every human being has to be regarded as an agent with responsibility. Thus, the exercise of power can never be completely unintended but has to be seen—at least to a certain degree—as an action that actor A is responsible for (see Connolly 1993: 93 et seq.).

The question of whether the exercise of power is intentional is connected to that of whether the dominant actor A must benefit from

108

his exercise of power. The example of a crashing financier who causes great damage to his affiliates makes it clear that power may have negative effects for A but still represents his great influence over others (see Benn 1967: 426). In response to this connection and to Russell's claim of the intentionality of actor A in exercising power, Connolly points out that A could hurt himself by mistake while exercising power over B. Therefore, he rejects the necessity of benefit as a criterion (see Connolly 1993: 104).

This discussion continues to the present day. However, most students of power agree with the assumption that power can be unintentional, assuming that A does not always exercise power over B in an intentional way and keeping in mind the possibility that power could also be exerted over someone as a "side effect." It is possible to imagine that A puts B in an unfortunate position, for example, by firing him from his job. A may simply be trying to get rid of an unsuccessful worker—but this, however, does not only have consequences for B but also for his family. Barnett and Duvall cite the example of "collateral damage" (see Barnett/Duvall 2000: 14) in wartime—as much of a euphemism as "side effects." This describes the phenomenon of civilians being killed along with the army under attack. Moreover, it must be questioned whether collateral damage is really unintended. Even if it is not the aim or the wish of army A to kill civilians, it is always clear that this is what happens during a war. Nevertheless, it is probable that this form of power also can be exercised unintentionally.

It becomes obvious that concepts regarding power as compulsory point to important and even basic characteristics of power. Nevertheless, they also neglect aspects of power and therefore do not cover the whole picture. The coming chapters will try to reveal these missing facets of power by taking into account three more basic types of power.

5.2 Institutional power

Like compulsory power, institutional power works through the interactions of specific actors. These two types of power differ, however, concerning the specificity of the relations between these actors. Whereas compulsory power entails the direct control of one actor over the conditions and actions of others, institutional power is manifested as actors' control of others in indirect ways. Concepts of compulsory power act on the assumption that power is exerted directly. By contrast, institutional power is thought to take place in diffuse relations. A diffuse relationship implies that mediators between A and B exist. These mediators are formal or informal institutions and their formal and informal rules and means of action: A exerts power on B through these institutions. Even though this type of power is called institutional power, it may well be exercised through whole regimes, defined as "a set of rules which aim to regulate some specific activity of international interest" (Armstrong 1982: 119) or as "area of international life which is marked by some degree of orderliness and co-operation amongst states" (ibid.). In contrast to the concept of compulsory power, it is clear that A does not always intend to influence B in his existence, in whatever he does or does not do.

As A acts through institutions (or regimes), bases of power are here less important than they are in the concept of compulsory power. In most cases, these institutions are not the property of A but are determined by a number of actors. It is possible that some actors will be more dominant than others in the use of an institution. This does not mean, however, that they posses the institution. In the rare case that one single actor does possess an institution, the institution becomes a base of power and therefore has to be regarded in the sense of compulsory power. Mostly, institutions take care that not just one actor is dominant. Therefore, the constitutions of plural-actor institutions normally state the rules of co-action between the actors (see Barnett/Duvall 2005: 15 et seq.).

The institutions through which A acts can be military. The most famous example in this case is NATO. Mainly, however, they are non-military. It is also highly possible that these institutions will provide non-military as well as military means, and thus provide A with differing options of influencing B. The United Nations, for instance, offers a wide range of instruments, including diplomatic, financial and military options. Military options regularly play a minor role in most cases dealt with by the UN. Therefore, concepts of institutional power do not deal with military means as much as concepts of compulsory power do.

Moreover, the distance between A and B marks a main difference from the concept of compulsory power. This distance is always *social,* and can further be spatial or temporal (see ibid.: 16). *Spatially,* A exercises power over B by means of the institution. These means can be officially established agreements or rules as well as internalized process flows or habits that have been set up over time. A can also use structures established by the institution itself. If A is not powerful enough as a private actor to make B depend on him, he can achieve that power through structures of dependency provided by the institution. As such, A is not the owner of the institution, but can use its mechanisms (see ibid.: 16). As states try to use institutions according to their interests, a side effect occurs: the institution or organization is likely to lose its independence. It may become the pawn of the various actors who try to make it available for their interests. Thus, it is important for states to provide these organizations with a minimum of autonomy in order to make sure that they can fulfill their tasks. Only an organization that is (or appears) at least partly independent provides member states with the possibility to make their interests look legitimate in an international context. Therefore, even powerful states will avoid making an institution look completely dependant. Furthermore, only institutions that are supposed to be neutral have the means to act in conflict resolution.

Temporal distance refers to the phenomenon in which longstanding institutions set up constellations, relationships and dependencies between actors that cannot be overcome for a long period of time. A case in point is the United Nations. The composition of the Security Council and wide parts of the UN system reflect the international constellations and distribution of power prevailing after the Second World War. As the world's political landscape has since drastically shifted (the salient change being the end of the Cold War), new actors have become stronger and old powers have weakened. The world faces new dependencies, new challenges and conflicts. Nevertheless, it seems almost impossible to change the setup of the United Nations. Reforms have been discussed for many years, but it still looks improbable that real reform will be accomplished in the near future. The establishment of power structures in institutions effects not just the institution itself, but world politics as well. As actor A can use the institution in order to exert power over B, his position in the institution is fairly important. If the structure of the institution grants him special rights, he will profit from these for a long time—even if the organization was founded centuries ago. A will be able to use his intra-institutional position in order to strengthen his extra-institutional position in international relations.

Moreover, institutional power can be exercised through the control of knowledge. Considerable power lies in the position of deciding what should be regarded as true and what false. The actor in this position fixes public, even worldwide perception. In this context, Emanuel Adler and Steven Bernstein divide between knowledge and epistemes, describing knowledge as "the cumulative set of normative, ideological, technical, and scientific understanding" (Adler/Bernstein 2005: 295). Epistemes, by contrast, are background understandings that make us schematize the world (see Foucault 1971: 414). Consequentially, it seems that actors have understood the use of *agenda setting* as a prime instrument for the exercise of institutional power. Institutional constellations regularly allow the stronger actors to determine topics.

Bachrach and Baratz were among the first to refer to this facet of power. They published one of the first well-known critiques of Dahl's theory of power, in which they especially referred to Dahl's concept of *scope* of power, arguing that power can also cause invisible reactions. According to Bachrach and Baratz, non-participation does not necessarily stem from apathy or indifference but can also be a result of power. They argue that "the other side of the coin is *non*decision-making. When the dominant values, the accepted rules of the game, the existing power relations among groups, and the instruments of force, single or in combination, effectively prevent certain grievances from developing into full-fledged issues which call for decisions, it can be said that a nondecisions-making situation exists" (Bachrach/Baratz 1963: 641). Before them, Elmer Eric Schattschneider put this fact thus: "All forms of political organization have a bias in favor of the exploitation of some kinds of conflict and the suppression of others because *organization is the mobilization of bias*. Some issues are organized into politics while others are organized out" (Schattschneider 1960: 71). Thus, the dominant actor can simply avoid issues on the agenda that could challenge him, choosing rather to maintain the status quo (see Bachrach/Baratz 1963: 632). This second face of power (see ibid. 1962) had been neglected by pluralists and was described in a counter-argument as irrelevant to the discussion, as it is difficult or even impossible to find an appropriate method to research and measure it. Even though Bachrach and Baratz tried to deal with the research of non-decisions empirically (see ibid. 1970), their approach has been criticized for not being operational. It has especially been pointed out that it is hard to divide nondecisions from mere apathy (see Wolfinger 1971a: 1078).[5] In any case, Bachrach and Baratz opened a new way of looking at power that goes beyond the compulsory approach.

When considering institutional power in the context of agenda setting, it is useful to divide between formal and informal agenda setting (see

---

[5]   For the following debate see Frey (1971) and Wolfinger (1971b).

Pollack 1997: 121 et seq.). Formal agenda setting means the official right awarded to a body to determine the issues discussed. Informal agenda setting, by contrast, reflects the ability of a strong actor to set topics and influence opinions, not through his formal power but rather through his inherent authority. Informal agenda setting will work best for leaders in policy networks or in situations of imperfect information and general uncertainty. In this case, "power means the authority to validate the knowledge on which an episteme is based" (Adler/Bernstein 2005: 298).[6] In many cases, institutions are able to shape actions as well as understandings and perceptions. This can take place indirectly and over spatial and or historical distance. International organizations will be able, for instant, to crucially influence general opinions and decision-making processes. Already during an earlier stage of decision-making, they can exercise power through channels of informal contact. Thus, issues and decisions can already be avoided before they can be put on the agenda.

Moreover, organizations have the capacity to classify issues, to put emphasis on some topics at the expense of others, and to work on definitions of problems. They organize information in a way that forms perceptions long before decisions are made. Prominent examples are the definition of "terrorism" versus "resistance" in the Israeli-Palestinian conflict, or the development of classifications concerning environmental standards. It makes a difference if military conflicts are defined as "wars" or as "genocides", and whether individuals and groups receive recognition as "refugees" (see Barnett/Finnemore 2005: 178).

Whoever sets agendas, be they formal or informal, can influence not only decisions that are taken—but also those that are not taken. For A, it may even be possible to prevent the discussion of undesirable topics. Through his rights or through his influence, he can designate what

---

[6]   In contrast to this, knowledge as an attribute refers to compulsory power. Productive power is exercised, when epistemes construct a social reality (see Adler/Bernstein 2005: 298).

appears on the agenda. Therefore, he can choose topics that are important for him, and prevent the discussion of topics that are in B's interest. Thus, A can determine B's circumstances crucially by the mere means of agenda setting in a relevant institution, even if B is socially distant from him.

Some authors have pointed to constraints that develop from within political institutions. These are not only the exclusion and inclusion of topics from or in the agenda, but also internal rules, customs and habits, the timing of decision-making, and budget restrictions. These constraints are created by the institutions and then sanctioned by politicians (see March/Olsen 1989: 164). Dependencies can thus be established, maintained and frozen over a long period through institutional power.

5.2.1   Institutional power that is exercised by institutions

The approaches above make it hard to see institutions as actors that could exercise power themselves. As Michael Barnett and Martha Finnemore point out, various schools neglect the political character that institutions may have and reduce them to technical instruments in the hands of states. Functionalism and utilitarianism regard institutions as mere facilitators of cooperation and of collective action of independent actors.[7] Scholars of neoliberal institutionalism and of principal agent theories presume that states delegate their power to institutions in certain cases. Institutional sociologists look at international organizations in terms of an accumulation of different

---

[7]   The functionalist way of describing international organizations has one of its roots in the development of the first international unions. These indeed had the aim to facilitate international trade, exchange and communications and were established with functionalist aims. Liberalism perceived them as motors of progress and development. It has regularly been pointed out, however, that even these technical institutions are a product of Western culture and have neither been apolitical nor norm-neutral.

cultures—but not as actors with their own autonomy (see Barnett/Finnemore 2005: 169). In all of these approaches, power is therefore regarded as a possession of states that can be passed to someone else and also be taken back. This neglects the reality that power also takes place in relationships. It also describes institutions in a rigid way as mere henchmen of states and therefore undervalues their performance as independent actors. As they present—but do not merely carry out—the policies of states, it would be mistaken not to acknowledge their influence. This is especially true of international organizations. Many of these have developed the ability to act independently in different fields; they form their own aims, influence state politics, and carry out actions. Especially in setting the international agenda, i.e. publishing reports, bringing up certain issues and holding others down, they wield a significant influence over world politics.

As soon as an institution becomes an actor that acts independently, it may not only exercise institutional power, but also compulsory, structural, and productive power. Institutions that exercise power therefore present an exceptional form of exerting influence. Even though they do exercise power, one has to note that this power is not necessarily institutional.

Barnett and Finnemore differentiate between four different kinds of authority that turns institutions into autonomous actors. First of all, they may stem from power that is *delegated* to them by states, and secondly from their *liberal* and *moral* values. As bureaucratic forms, institutions also dispose of *rational-legal* and *expert* power (see ibid.: 171 et seq.).

Delegated power is the most basic power that institutions may possess. Even if other sources of their power may erode, for example, if an organization's liberal values are perceived as dominantly Western or if their decisions are regarded as unfair, they remain authorities due to their delegated power. This power is drawn from the fact that their mission has been awarded to them by powerful states or by a community of states. As this power is delegated to them and can be taken back, they need to keep up the impression of neutrality and representation of the wills of all of their member states. Insofar as they present the will of the community, groups who may disagree with their policies will usually nevertheless feel obliged to them and act accordingly.

Moral power is connected to the liberal values accompanying the establishment of institutions. This power can be clearly seen in the field of worldwide norms. Due to the work of several international organizations, aims like the spread of democracy and human rights or the addressing of gender issues have achieved undeniable relevance in politics all around the globe (see ibid.: 161 et seq.). In many cases, international organizations are perceived as protectors of humanity and peace.

Today, some international organizations are even so recognized and regarded as a grant of international legitimacy that powerful states attempt to gain their approval in volatile international matters. Even though the United States could have conducted a military strike against Iraq in 2003 by their own means, they tried to get the support of the United Nations. The more powerful a state, the more likely it will be able to get the approval of the institution in support of its aims.

The acknowledgment of an institution's authority goes together with the term of "independence," in the sense defined by Kenneth W. Abbott and Duncan Snidal: due to their authority regarding norms, institutions do not only support inter-state actions but can also initiate these (see Abbott/Snidal 1998: 19 et seq.). Even more: international organizations can become active themselves and develop into major players in world politics, be it in UN peacekeeping missions or in financing development projects, as the World Bank does. Institutions, especially international organizations, therefore construct the reality of international relations to a considerable extent. Their power stems from the fact that they are viewed as embodiments of values and norms. They often even act as arbiters, be it in resolutions or in the deployment of peacekeeping troops. Most prominent examples are conflicts like the ones between Israel and the Palestinians, in Sudan, in the Balkans, in Rwanda or in Cambodia. Even if there are no means to enforce resolutions and decisions of the International Court of Justice, these are widely viewed as norms. The authority that institutions may have as moral instantiations also enables them to legitimizing military actions (see Barnett/Finnemore 2005: 161 et seq.).

Barnett and Finnemore also point to the form that institutions and especially organizations may have. Their form may be a proof that power is not only exercised through but also by institutions. As bureaucracies, they are organized in a *rational-legal* way. According to Max Weber, bureaucracies are hierarchies that carry out tasks in an impersonal and continuous way and in a highly expert manner (see Weber 1999: 109). They are more efficient than other forms of organization, as they are depoliticized and depersonalized and thus able to carry out decisions in a stable and decisive way (see Barnett/Finnemore 2005: 164). Because of their rationalized, technocratic form, Weber presumes that bureaucracies are powerful social forms. Barnett and Finnemore add that the modern form of international bureaucracies provides them with authority in that this form is regarded as modern and professional.

Furthermore, organizations contain specialized knowledge and have collected experience in special fields of international relevance. They have *expertise* in tackling topics like human rights, diseases, or nuclear proliferation (see ibid.: 170, 173). This assumption could be questioned in so far as bureaucracies do not always have the ideal reputation that their form suggests. In contrast, impersonality is often regarded as anonymity, and the working process of international organizations especially is often not efficient at all. Another problem occurs because the apolitical, impersonal and expert work of international organizations is in effect hardly neutral. To keep up their power, institutions like these are forced to present themselves as powerless players that act in order to fulfill the aims of the international community and to serve every group to the same extent.

5.2.2   Institutional power that works through institutions

This second facet of institutional power is especially relevant in the context of this study. Here, institutions present themselves as means through which actors, especially states, pursue their interests. Kenneth Abbot and Duncan Snidal have summarized the main functions of international organizations under the terms "independence" and "centralization" (see Abbott/Snidal 1998).

Organizations are "independent" insofar as they provide a neutral basis for talks between states (see ibid.: 19 et seq.). In conflicts, a neutral organization may be used as a mediator that is at least less biased than any other superpower or state will be. Without doubt, institutions generate trust and constitute a basis for talks. They also provide tools for conflict prevention, early warning, conflict resolution, and peace stabilization. The most famous example in this context is the United Nations Agenda for Peace (1992).

"Centralization" refers to the fact that collective action can be made feasible much more easily if there is a common body to shepherd it. Most scholars have studied this phenomenon by using rational-choice approaches and theories of functionalism. They claim that states use institutions in order to reduce the costs of cooperation. Actors are regarded as rational egoists that are looking out for their advantage. They use institutions only if they presume to gain a profit from it. Robert Keohane describes this fact as an "inverse link between effect and cause" that "is provided by the rationality assumption" (Keohane 1984: 80). As actors anticipate possible profits, they choose to cooperate by means of an institution. Institutions may enhance this profit in different ways. Most commonly, they reduce uncertainty about the behavior of other actors in a situation of imperfect knowledge (see Pollack 1997: 103). Actors therefore may choose to delegate authority to institutions, through which they may follow their interests and exercise power.

There are a number of cases in which actors typically use institutions to exert their policies: for instance, institutions can monitor whether and how member states comply with their international treaty obligations. In this context, institutions reduce the lack of information for each actor and enhance certainty in an unsure environment (see Barnett/Finnemore 2005: 161). Similarly, institutions may remedy problems of incomplete contracting. In most instances, contracts only go so far as to frame relationships, as not every single case can be predicted. In the case of a conflict, institutions can interpret the spirit of the contract and help to find agreements (see Pollack 1997: 103 et seq.). Moreover, most neo-liberal institutional scholars regard institutions as means of cooperation and peaceful conflict resolution. They enable collective action and deal with problems that one single state cannot solve, as they are either too complex or too wide-ranging. Problems like diseases or pollution, or even certain economical questions, require an appropriate body to deal with. Institutions, and especially international organizations, also offer stability. The way they work and carry out decisions has been tested and institutionalized through experience dealing with many issues over time, and therefore is less fragile than single inter-state actions. Organizations dispose of a bureaucracy that provides support in everyday actions as well as issues of conflict. They provide forums for the discussion of international issues in a wide range of topics. It has been pointed out as well that international organizations minimize risks for the single actor and reduce its transaction costs. In certain cases actors may profit from teamwork. Skills and resources may be complementary and help achieve success in a field in which a single actor would not have succeeded. A good example is the teamwork that NATO provides (see Abbott/Snidal 1998: 10 et seq.).

An important part of understanding international relations is discovering where power is located. This includes, of course, the analysis of dependency structures in formal and informal institutions. Some scholars dealing with institutionalism have examined these structures. They acknowledge that institutions may help to deal with everyday actions as well as with the resolution of international conflicts. Without any doubt, international organizations are an essential tool in international relations today and have to be regarded in a mainly positive way. They improve efficiency and enable collective actions, and present a fairly reliable instrument for states overall. In this optimistic view, however, many scholars do not adequately take power into account. They neglect that an organization is never as neutral as might be laid down in its constitution. Cooperation itself is a game of power and reflects structures of dependency. Actors who are favored in these structures—by the constitution of the institution or by their knowledge of how to use it—will likely direct the cooperation along the lines of their interests. Therefore, the conflict resolution may be peaceful, but the result is hardly as fair as many scholars of this approach like to claim. States use international institutions in order to get what they want, i.e. they exercise power in order to achieve their aims. Cooperation through institutions creates "losers" and "winners" (Barnett/Duvall 2005: 17). Looking at institutions in terms of dependencies and asymmetries does not make the examination of international politics any easier, and may even prove disappointing for those who prefer to look at institutions simply as peace-creating machines. These institutions, however, are also places of inequality and bear conflicts and power structures within themselves. They reflect the distribution of power outside the institution and, conversely, also contribute to it in various ways.

Stephen Krasner demonstrated the importance of power in institutions in the 80s by analyzing the fields of development policies. Analyzing dependencies and vulnerabilities, he points out that "most southern countries cannot hope to cope with their international vulnerability except by challenging principles, norms, and rules preferred by industrialized countries" (Krasner 1985: 3). Power and the means to determine one's own circumstances matter at least as much as wealth. Krasner even assumes that the degree of access to international organizations is the crucial factor in explaining why some developing countries succeed more and others less (see ibid.: 75). If a state cannot rely on its own capabilities, the access to agenda setting and decision making in international organizations will become even more relevant to its circumstances. Mostly, organizations (or regimes) reflect the hegemony of one or more actors. To provide the organization with legitimacy, certain concessions have to be made in favor of the weaker states. It is important to note, however, that these concessions will mostly not damage the stronger actors. For example, the distribution of votes in the General Assembly of the United States is equal, whereas the Security Council has just five permanent members with the right to veto. As grave decisions are taken in the Security Council and not in the General Assembly, the power of the stronger states is assured. The hegemonic actor A may also allow cases of minor issues that damage its direct interests but favor its broader goals (see ibid.: 76 et seq.). The United States and Europe may argue about economic interests. They will not let this break their political alliance, however. Therefore, it is possible that both sides will accept current disadvantages in certain economic questions in order to maintain their partnership in a long run.

5.3   Structural power

5.3.1   A third face of power

In the mid 1970s, the debate moved into a broader conception of power. In an attempt to combine the assumption of an agent exercising power and the understanding that power takes place not only through personal but also through social patterns, concepts of structural power were developed. This often-called third face of power has mainly been advanced by Steven Lukes. In a response to the argument of Bachrach and Baratz that power has a second face, he claimed that power can be found in even more places than Bachrach and Baratz maintain. Lukes points out that the scholars dealing with the first and the second face of power, mainly following Max Weber's definition, overemphasize the concept of free will. They mainly regard power as something that is carried out consciously and on a planned and considered basis. In what has become known as his *three-dimensional* view, Lukes leaves behind behavioralist assumptions and moves on to an idea of power that takes social structures, cultural patterns, and the practice of groups and institutions into account (see Lukes 1974: 21 et seq.). He asks rhetorically if it is not an exercise of power that shapes people's "perceptions, cognitions and preferences in such a way that they accept their role in the existing order of things, either because they can see or imagine no alternative to it, or because they see it as natural and unchangeable, or because they value it as divinely ordained and beneficial" (ibid.: 24). His definition expands the notion of power by taking desires, wishes and perception into account. Power does not only start where behavior and actions of the subordinate actor are concerned. Instead, it already determines B's freedom to decide what he wants. Researching perceptions turns out to be even more difficult than looking for nondecisions in the sense of Bachrach and Baratz. Finding out about power in Lukes' sense would require an objective and independent view of interests. Not surprisingly, Lukes has been criticized for the difficulties of operationalizing his theories and putting them into practice (see Bradshaw 1976). Nevertheless, today's power theories could not have been imagined without Luke's approach.

Like compulsory power, structural power is exercised directly. However, it works through social relations of constitution and not through interactions of specific actors. Thus, the definition goes beyond the examination of the relationship between the dominant A and the powerless B. It does not assume that power comes from individual or corporate agents or that it is "the production of intended effects" (Russell 1995: 25) as Bertrand Russell (1938) saw it. It even goes beyond perceptions that power can be exercised unintentionally, because also this case would require agency.

Structural power acts on the assumption that power may rest in non-agential constellations: agents only bear this power, as they are part of the structure. Nicos Poulantzas refers in particular to social classes to prove that power is exercised through structures rather than through agency. He claims that the power of a class can only be determined in relationship to other classes and that it depends in the first place on economic, political and ideological relations (see Poulantzas 2000: 147).[8] Hannah Arendt also conceptualizes power-giving structures in her definition of power that refers to Greek and Roman conceptions wherein the republic has its basis in the power of the people. This power is consensual, as it occurs whenever people act together. It "corresponds to the human ability not just to act but to act in concert. Power is never the property of an individual; it belongs to a group and remains in existence only so long as the group keeps together" (Arendt 1970: 44). Also Talcott Parsons emphasizes that power is a "generalized facility or resource" that rests on accepted norms of legitimacy. His aim is to show that social integration is based on common values. He therefore differentiates between power and types of coercion, manipulation and compulsion (see Parsons 1967: 331 et seq.). The analysis of structural power acts on the assumption, that structures are already defined. Therefore, the debate is still continuous and ties up to the discussions of Dahl, Bachrach and Baratz and their colleagues. It is maintained "that social power wears a 'face': that, within structured roles and relations sustained by agents peripheral to the dyad, powerful agents choose to use or to direct social power to constrain the free action of the powerless" (Hayward 2000: 22 et seq.).

---

[8]   Ralph Milliband critized this perception, claiming that political agents have a minimum of relative autonomy from class structures (see Miliband 1969; 1970).

Scholars of structural power have especially criticized the assumption that an advantaged actor that suppresses another actor possesses power. These dyadic concepts of power are right in highlighting relationships that clearly empower one actor and disadvantage another one. They neglect the fact, however, that a power relationship cannot be examined without regarding the social environment in which it takes place. Thomas E. Wartenberg has examined the role of the "social field" (Wartenberg 1992: 80) and the "social others" (ibid.) and developed a concept of power which he calls "situated social power" (ibid.). He claims that in most cases, the power dyad is only one element of two. The second is what he calls a social alignment. This means that the actors external to the power dyad will compose their behavior in accordance to the actions of the dominant part of the power dyad. They will also orient their behavior towards the weaker actor relative to his treatment by the dominant one. Moreover, and perhaps even more importantly, the coordinated actions of the external actors determine and constitute the power relationship itself.

This is the main disparity with regard to the assumptions of a dyadic power conception. These assumptions probably acknowledge that social actors external from the dyad are able to prevent A from exercising power over B and therefore may intervene in the power relationship, but do not take into account the presence of the whole social field within the power dyad. The social others make their presence felt by setting up alignments and determining which actor gets access to which rights and goods.

One example is the establishment of rules and criteria that an actor has to fulfill to be allowed into certain jobs. On an international level, European states interested in becoming member of the European Union must fulfill certain criteria before they will be allowed access. Alignments do not always have to be set up through rules or institutions. Many times they will be agreed upon verbally or even in an unstated agreement. This is especially true for structures inside societies, like sexism, racism or other forms of discrimination.

Alignments can be hold up over a long time, but can also be established for a special aim and for a limited timespan (see ibid.: 88 et seq.).

Scholars of institutional power consider identities and preferences of actors as granted. In their opinion, these actors deal with each other in a framework of procedures and rules that has been defined *ex ante*. In contrast, students of structural power "conceive structures as an internal relation—that is, a direct constitutive relation such that structural position A exists only by virtue of its relation to structural position B" (Barnett/Duvall 2005: 18). Structural power consequently takes place in relationships. It produces the social position of an actor, his identity and interests in relationship to another actor. Actors constitute each other mutually. Their positions and actions are determined by the structural setting in which they are engaged. Jeffrey Isaac, one of the most important scholars in the fields of structural power, explicitly rejects behavioral views that describe power in the sense of authority that A has *over* B (see Isaac 1987a: 6). In contrast, he defines structural power as "an enduring capacity to act" (ibid.: 72) that is "implicated in the enduring structural relations that characterize a society and is exercised by intentional human agents who participate in these relations" (ibid.: 9).

Therefore, even if A does not want to exercise power, he will nevertheless remain in the position of power assigned him by the social structure. Many scholars have cited judge-defendant or teacher-student relations to exemplify how structural power takes place. Usually, these kinds of relationships are regarded as typically dyadic: a stronger actor exercises power over a subordinate actor by shaping his behavior. The power a teacher has over his student is expressed in the fact that he can make the student work by threatening him with lowering his grades or even letting him fail the class. The student will behave well in class because the teacher has the power to punish him if he does not keep to the rules. This concept of power cannot explain, however, why a teacher and his student will also behave in the way they do in the case that a teacher does not take any measures to make his students work harder or to be silent.

This fact can only be explained when considering the social environment in which the dyadic relationship takes place. This means that the teacher's power also has a structural component. External agents influence the teacher-student relationship and therefore constitute it. Bad grades or the failing of classes may reduce the chance to receive scholarships, to be accepted at universities or to get good jobs. The student's parents may as well supply additional pressure. These external agents all have power over the student. All value similar outcomes, such as discipline and good grades. Moreover, these actors have expectations towards teachers and students that do not allow them to flee their roles. They are therefore present in the classroom and support or even establish the teacher's as well as the student's position (see Wartenberg 1992: 81 et seq.).

Thus, the social structures in which the teacher-student relationship is embedded give a certain role to the student as well as to the teacher. Within this structure, the teacher A may exercise his role in different kind of ways, depending on his character, convictions, and teaching concepts. Even if he abstains from instruments that would clearly show his dominance, like punishments, he will remain the dominant part of the teacher-student relationship due to the established structures. By contrast, the student, according to the prevailing structure, will always remain the weaker part in the relationship—even if he should have a broader knowledge than his teacher.

This conceptualization therefore dictates that the power of every actor A stems from the social alignment and the structure that provides him with it (see Hayward 2000: 24; Isaac 1987b). It is not a form of agreement between two actors, as the scholars of dyadic power models have sometimes claimed. Instead, power is a "socially structured capacity" (Isaac 1987a: 7). The ability to shape the behavior of another actor depends on the social relations that distribute different identities, statuses and positions to the actors (see Rupert 2005: 209). In case of a structurally asymmetrical, unequal distribution of these positions, elements of domination come in (see Isaac 1987a: 83 et seq.). It is possible to imagine that structures might also empower originally weaker actors or create equity. That is, structures will always exist in human societies but do not automatically produce better and worse positions for actors (see Rupert 2005: 209). This, however, seems to be a heavily theoretical argument that does not apply to reality in most cases. Even in the case that an actor A does not want to be the more powerful actor per structure, he will most probably not be able to avoid his role because external actors C, D and E will treat him according to his structural position. If the teacher does not exercise the power that he possesses due to his superior knowledge and the authority to grade his students, he will still be part of a power relationship. Even an anti-authoritarian teacher will always stay part of the social alignments in which his relationship to the students is embedded.

One could also imagine the case that a mother is tired of exercising the power that the mother-child structure provides her with. She will, however, hardly be able to flee her role as a mother because external agents like her husband, like teachers and neighbors will continue treating her in this role. The power dyad therefore might be perceptibly weakened, but will continue to work to a certain degree.

This pattern also holds in the opposite case: power may exist in its dyadic form without alignments, but it will then be weakened severely. Teachers, judges and parents gain their power in relation to students, defendants or children from their superior expertise or greater knowledge of life. A teacher may enforce this power through an authoritative teaching style in order to be regarded as an authority and gain power inside the dyadic relationship. If his power is based on his expertise only, however, he will not be able to exercise it in many cases. Situations of chaos in classrooms occur especially with disadvantaged students whose parents do not encourage them and who do not have any chances to climb up socially and to find good jobs. In such a case, the social field does not empower the teacher, and the power he has inside the relationship with the student declines (see Wartenberg 1992: 84 et seq.).

It is right to note that structures are formed over time and negotiated again and again throughout their history (see Isaac 1987a: 91 et seq.). Consequently, it is possible to change them. Structures are a constant matter of discussion and fight inside societies and on an international level. The question of ranks and classes in societies and international structures that favor some global players are prominent examples. As, in many cases, structural power goes along with wealth and the worldwide distribution of goods, these issues are especially volatile.

There are two main consequences of structural power: As noted above, structures do not tend to produce equality between actors, but rather favor the position of one. The less privileged actor rarely succeeds to reverse this situation of inequality, as these relational structures are often quite hard to overcome. It has also been pointed out that "structural constraints (or contradictions) make it impossible for any segment of the society to act to redress the *system* of inequality significantly without disrupting the basic capacity of the entire system to provide food, shelter, and security for its members" (Connolly 1993: 123). Consequently, "efforts by the beneficiaries or others to redress the inequalities significantly would work to the disadvantage of all segments of the population" (ibid.). [9]

---

[9]   Connolly speaks of „structural biases" that he does not summarize under the term power. In his opinon, power is only exercised if a powerful actor and a powerless actor can be determined. As he does not recognize a dominant actor or group in the case of structural inequalities, he does not speak of power. He acknowledges that structures cause a disproportional benefit for different groups, though (see Connolly 1993: 123).

5.3.2 Structural power in international relations

Even though, structural power has mainly been discussed by sociologists, it also plays a decisive role in the context of international relations. As much as processes of socialization take place in societies and structure them according to certain norms and roles, they are active in relations between states. The state system and the way states perceive each other and interact is based on created structures, i.e. on the fact that the participants in the international system are socialized into international norms and role as much as members of a society are (see Wendt 1992). Also in international relations, power can be exercised anonymously, and manipulations through processes or underlying structures form relationships. "Often, in fact, such structural power is the most pervasive form of power, and it clearly operates also in relation between states" (Ringmar 2007: 192).

In this context, especially the approach to explain the phenomenon of globally acting civil society groups has been structural,[10] dealing with the relationship between agents and structures (see Wendt 1987). Another approach of dealing with structural power in international relations distances itself from Wendt and provides a more Marxist understanding of agency. It claims that in international relations agents and structures cannot be considered separately, and that their interaction must be a matter of discussion. They are not only, as Wendt claims, parts of dynamic historical processes, but rather the result of structural inequalities that exist between state and market, public and private sphere (see Colás 2002: 17 et seq.). Even if this is

---

[10]   Ronnie D. Lipschutz offers different kinds of explanations regarding the emergence of global society organizations. He sums up that the emergence of these groups may not only be seen as due to structural reasons but could also be a consequence of agency: autonomous individuals form groups because it is their interest. The foundation of these groups takes place through the means of direct influence between the individuals and therefore can be regarded as compulsory power. The groups themselves use institutional power in order to promote their aims (see Lipschutz 2005: 230). Furthermore, international civil society groups could be regarded as a product of productive power. In this sense they are produced as actors fighting the world order (see ibid. et seq.).

assumed to be right, though, global civil society groups mostly do not and cannot exercise structural power themselves but rather use the means of institutional power (see Lipschutz 2005: 231 et seq.; ibid. 2007). James G. March and Johan P. Olsen, who deal with institutions and institutional power, point to a connection between institutional and structural power that is, in their case, exercised through political institutions. They write that actions "taken within and by political institutions change the distribution of political interests, resources, and rules by creating new actors and identities, by providing actors with criteria of success and failure, by constructing rules for appropriate behavior, and by endowing some individuals, rather than others, with authority and other types or resources. Institutions affect the ways in which individuals and groups become activated within and outside established institutions, the level of trust among citizens and leaders, the common aspirations of a political community, the shared language, understanding, and norms of the community, and the meaning of concepts like democracy, justice, liberty, and equality" (March/Olsen 1989: 164). This can also be applied to a broader framework like the EMP and the ENP and their processes and mechanisms. Power exercised through these channels has the potential to create new structures or even to change the identities of the actors in the international game.

Another example of structural power in the international arena is the creation of structures through labeling. Labeling takes place if states are arranged according to structured systems of political aims. A famous example is the Bush administration's casting aspersions on and pillorying so-called "rogue states." Also, the creation of groups of states, such as Bush's "axis of evil," or the distinction between an "old" versus a "new" Europe, are means to create structures. These structures do not only work de facto, but also have an effect on uninvolved states that are requested to behave accordingly, i.e. to take care not to become part of a stigmatized group of states, as well as to adjust their behavior towards these states in a way that the labeling (and thereby dominant actor A) demands.

Secondly, structures do not only produce the understanding the actors have of each other but also their perception of themselves. This fixes their positions and their relationship. The weaker actor will consider himself as weak and therefore will not dare to assert certain claims. And even worse: he will not even develop such claims because this is not part of his self-understanding (see Barnett/Duvall 2005: 18). This is where concepts of productive power originate.

5.4 Productive power

5.4.1 Producing the agents

Like structural power, productive power concerns social relations of constitution. Hence, they share some important characteristics. Both refer to the creation of actors' social positions, their perceptions of themselves and by others, and their respective interests. These positions are established and maintained by the practice of the actors—a fact that hints at the possibility that productive power occurs as actualized structural power. The conceptual basis of both types of power, i.e. of productive power as well as structural power, is the consideration of power as a relation that establishes the position of actors.

The difference between structural and productive power is that structural power takes place directly, whereas productive power is exerted in diffuse relationships. Structural power concerns structures per se, i.e. positions of dominance and subordination and their creation, maintenance, and reproduction. Productive power does not refer to the structures themselves but to structured systems of meaning. These systems are organized entities, but are not structures themselves. They consist of knowledge and discourse and can be described "as a network of boundaries that delimit, for all, the field of what is socially possible" (Hayward 2000: 3), and constitute social actors by granting them (or refusing to grant them) significance and relevance. Hence, productive power influences the structures that structural power deals with. "It does not simply act *upon* a (pre-political) agent, that is to say, constituting its preferences and delimiting how it might rationally act to realize them. It also produces this agent" (ibid.: 5). This gets very close to certain constructivist views, which hold that institutions as a set of routines, values and norms, shape identities either through authority or through socialization that leads to internalization (see Solingen/Saba Şenses 2006: 55).

A main divergence of productive power from concepts of compulsory, institutional or structural power lies in its perception of freedom. These latter concepts of power have looked at different facets, or faces, of power, as well as argued about the scope of power and how far it reaches. Different approaches have been taken to broaden and specify Dahl's definition. Scholars of structural power have pointed to roles that individuals attain through structure. Others have claimed that individuals are able to form autonomous decisions, desires and wishes and are consequently responsible for their actions (see Connolly 1993: 86 et seq.).[11] Nevertheless, all of these concepts— even that of structural power—base their argument upon Dahlian perceptions and compare two or more actors regarding their power. Their aim is to find out how B's freedom is limited by A. Be it for compulsory or structural reasons—the degree of freedom of which the weaker actor B disposes, depends on the power A exercises over him. Freedom had been defined in a behaviorist way as the sphere in which A does not shape B's actions. In the ongoing debate, the definition was broadened: B was regarded as free in cases in which A also did not interfere in his wishes and interests. If B acted only according to his own self-determined interests, he was claimed to be free in his

---

[11]   For Connolly's following considerations concerning responsibility not only regarding power see Connolly 1991.

actions. In any case, it was possible to distinguish between free, autonomous actions and those shaped by another actor.

Most students of power consider the limitation of B's freedom as fundamental in defining power. William Connolly calls this fact of constrained freedom a limit of choice for which the bidder is responsible. A has power over B when he has the potential to constrain B's actions. He may only possess this potential, use it actively, or profit from it insofar as B acts in anticipating the limits A could impose on him. According to Connolly, without this constellation, one cannot speak of power (see ibid.: 996 et seq., 102).

In contrast, the concept of productive power goes beyond comparing the influence of actors. It considers power to be *pre-structural.* Students of productive power do not agree with the perception that power is exercised by one actor over another. They do not judge whether A or B has more power and how the stronger one might limit the scope of action of the weaker one. Instead, the concept of productive power claims that power, seen as a network of social boundaries in the sense of Hayward, limits every social actor, be he A or B.

Consequently, productive power does not describe spheres of freedom. It claims that every individual is himself the product of power. His identity, his self-perception, interests, preferences, wishes, desires and even feelings are a product of his education, the culture he has been brought up in, and the expectations and demands of the society he lives in. The differentiation between free and constrained actions here becomes weakened, as the fields of action are determined already long before any action is taken or not taken. This leads Michel Foucault to the assumption that "the relations of power are interwoven with other kinds of relations (production, kinship, family, sexuality) for which they play at once a conditioning and a conditioned role" (Foucault 1980: 142). In her study "De-facing Power," Clarissa Hayward points out that in the context of productive power, freedom can only be seen as "freedom *to.*" This view contrasts with other concepts of power, which, when investigating a space without power, regard freedom as "freedom *from*": freedom from the interference or influence of the actor A. In the relationship between A and B, it is then possible to imagine that B's space of freedom could be enlarged. In rare cases he could even become the stronger actor and start shaping A's actions. Social boundaries, however, can never be overcome—at least not completely. Consequently, freedom from power does not exist, according to scholars of productive power. Instead, one should investigate "freedom to"—that is, freedom that enables the actor to participate in and shape his destiny despite and within social boundaries (see Hayward 2000: 30 et seq.).

For students of productive power, examining power means investigating a social network of limits rather than defining spaces of free or shaped action. These limits are not only visible in actions that B cannot take, but concern every single actor and his options of acting in a social context. Actions are not disturbed or enabled by A, but by mechanisms of power. These may be visible, like laws and regulations; or invisible, like social norms and standards, values or conventions, and traditions. They constrain or enable not only inter-subjective, but also intra-subjective action. Even if an actor is aware of these mechanisms and is determined to find out his pure self-interest and transform it into action, he will never be able to decide, act, or even think outside the limits set by the mechanisms of productive power. Power is therefore not an instrument that one strong actor possesses and applies according to his interests (see ibid.: 30).

Thanks especially to Foucault, productive power has become a major topic in the social sciences. In contrast to most major scholars dealing with power in the last centuries, Foucault does not investigate the constitution of power in the hand of a sovereign. Whereas Hobbes and his followers have been concerned with how to centralize power in a situation of chaos, Foucault is interested in "the myriad of bodies which are constituted as peripheral *subjects* as a result of the effects of power" (Foucault 1986: 233). Consequently, he does not deal with how a monarch or a group of people exert power, but investigates the multiple forms of domination inside a society. In this consideration, he regards the individual as "an effect of power, and at the same time, or precisely to the extent to which it is that effect, it is the element of its articulation. The individual which power has constituted is at the same time its vehicle" (ibid.: 234). Thus, Foucault examines the individual and its surroundings and does not look at society from a top-down approach. Ideologies may play a role in the exercise of power and may go hand in hand with it, but they will not be the reason for the particular organization of a society. This organization or constitution of a society and its individuals is instead caused by "the production of effective instruments for the formation and accumulation of knowledge—methods of observation, techniques of registration, procedures for investigation and research, apparatuses of control. All this means that power, when it is exercised through these subtle mechanisms, cannot but evolve, organize and put into circulation a knowledge, or rather apparatuses of knowledge, which are not ideological constructs" (ibid.: 237). As Foucault is mainly interested in these techniques of power and not on power exercised by states or by other apparatuses and their ideologies, his approach can be clearly divided from theories of compulsory power, and also of institutional power. Foucault claims that this non-sovereign form of power has its roots in the bourgeois society and was a decisive tool to built up industrial capitalism. It works through disciplinary instruments (see ibid.: 239), which derive from the erection and application of norms—so-called normalization. Judith Butler has followed up Foucault's writings on the production of identity through power in a specific feminist framework, and has further dealt with the construction of gender which "is produced precisely through the regulatory practices that generate coherent identities through the matrix of coherent gender norms" (Butler 1990: 17).

Foucault considers this normalization as a constraint. With regard to Habermas, Clarissa Hayward points out that this setup of boundaries is

136

not merely a limitation, but also may enable actors and lead to better understanding between them. Like Foucault, Hayward regards freedom as the social ability to act within a system of boundaries. She adds, however, that power also includes structures that enable action, not only those that limit it. Her aim is to find out which power mechanisms enable and which constrain in order to transform the constraining ones into those that allow freedom. She therefore recommends searching out the mechanisms and processes that define collective meaning (see Hayward 2000: 7 et seq.).

5.4.2 Productive power in international relations

Productive power is very hard to analyze in any conceptual context. This is also true in the framework of international politics. Nevertheless, one may regard certain examples of productive power in the international arena. Even though it is hard to examine systems of meaning themselves, it is possible to have a closer look at how meanings and identities are addressed on an international level. This gives the researcher the chance to maintain the approach of looking at power as a relationship and not as a network, but also to investigate characteristics in this relationship that create meanings and identities. Analyzing identities in regard to foreign policy and international relations goes far beyond realist or liberal approaches of looking at international relations (see Risse 2007: 49 et seq.). In this context, role theory, which usually refers to actors and tries to explain their individual behavior, has come up with enlightening insights. It suggests that roles also determine the behavior of actors on an international level. This postulates that every actor is subject to expectations that others address to him and thus to a collective normation (see Kirste/Maull 1996: 289). The basic assumption here, which has especially been developed by social constructivism, is that identities are subject to change. They grow and develop historically and are formed through the manifold social and political debates of societies and states (see Risse 2007: 50). This allows for the attempt to influence and to manipulate them. In this context, an expression of productive power is thus the motivation to establish meanings and identities, according to which the actors may adjust their behavior and future policies (see Williams 1996). The creation of identity and of identity differences, i.e. contrasting one's own identity against others (see Sen 2006: 105), is possible on different levels. It may refer to states as complete units as well as to societies, or to people in their identities as inhabitants of a region. Mostly, the addressing of identities has to reckon with understandings and perceptions resulting from historical and political processes, such as developments that went along with the creation of nations and the emergence of national pride or humiliation. These aspects normally form and reflect the self-consciousness and identity of a nation and thus also determine the relationship to political counterparts.

6　Setting up the case study

To this point, we have characterized a fourfold typology of power. Each type, i.e. compulsory, institutional, structural, and productive power, has been condensed into its civilian elements in international relations. The challenge to be dealt with in the following chapters is to find out how these four types of civilian power in international relations appear in order to arrive at a more precise notion. As the EU-Middle Eastern relationship presents a prime example of civilian power, it is subject of the case study to come.

As has been stated in the first chapter of this study, the basic questions that lead this cognitive process ask: (1) which of the four types of power characterizes the EU's respective civilian power relationships with Israel and Egypt in the given case; (2) which of the types appears in particular; (3) which of the types does not appear at all; (4) whether the appearance of the four types differs between the two examined cases; and (5) upon which factors does the appearance of the four types of power depend.

These basic questions need to be further specified to be operable for the case study. A further specification will allow for the collection and evaluation of data in as detailed a way as possible and for the possibility to break it down into assessable units. This specification finds its expression in a hypothesis that will be established and explored for each of the four types of power. It will contain the three main characteristics of each power type, which are set up in accordance to the prior description of the four types. As this study only deals with the first phase of establishing a differentiation of the four types of power, these characteristics are formulated as sub-hypotheses in order to allow for the necessary openness of the research.

This does not mean that the three chosen sub-hypotheses are conclusive; one might also find a number of other characterizations for each type. Nevertheless, these three sub-hypotheses have been established according to the literature reviewed above and represent a reliable and typical identification of the four types. That means that in the analyzed elements of the EU-Israel/Egypt relationship, at least one of the three sub-hypotheses should prove true if a certain type of civilian power was exercised.

In order to arrive at comparable results, it is necessary to ask the same questions and to set up the same hypothesis in each of the cases analyzed here. These should also be used in further studies to make results comparable and provide for the placing of other blocks in the same subject-framework. This allows for a similar approach as used in large-N statistical studies that ask the same questions of a large number of cases—a quantity the study at hand cannot come up with.

6.1   Hypotheses for compulsory power

What has been said before about the four types of power needs to be translated into assessable units. For the case of compulsory power, this means that the relationship should be dyadic and that there should be an element of force in it. The actors looked at are (1) the EU as a whole and (2) Israel and Egypt, respectively. As this study only examines civilian power, military bases of power are excluded. Bases in this case are therefore defined as sources that create dependencies. As these possible dependencies are rooted, fixed, and reflected in the EU's respective agreements with Israel and Egypt (i.e. Country Reports, Association Agreements, Action Plans and Progress Reports), these agreements are drawn on as a base of power in the relationship. They therefore represent one major channel of investigating whether the base of (compulsory) power has been used, as their policies and their relationship are thus determined. The typical element of compulsory power, namely the assumption that power is possessed in one way or another, is also included in this definition: The actor that possesses the bases upon which the other actor depends, is the one that may exercise compulsory power. Accordingly, the means of exercising compulsory power in this context are civilian.

The question of whether the EU's respective power towards Israel and Egypt is exercised intentionally will not be dealt with here. This is a rather theoretical question in the fields of power research and less relevant for the specific case. In general, one may assume that political actors do exercise power intentionally in order to pursue their policies and their aims. It has been taken into account whether compulsory power is actualized or remains potential. Both cases may take place in connection to threats with civilian means. Compulsory power that is civilian is mainly expressed through potential or actualized threats. Potential threats may be translated into conditionality, i.e. "the linking, by a state or international organization, of perceived benefits to another state (such as aid, trade concessions, cooperation agreement, political contacts, or international organization membership), to the fulfillment of conditions relating to the protection of human rights and the advancement of democratic principles" (Smith 1997a: 6). Whereas conditionality allows for different types of action but does not guarantee action (see Jepperson/Wendt/Katzenstein 1996: 56), actualized threats will be translated into action, and will thus mostly be expressed in sanctions. Moreover, compulsory power may be expressed through the positive counterpart to threats, i.e. incentives (see Smith 1997b: 15). Therefore, the three sub-hypotheses chosen in this study to characterize compulsory power as a type are *conditionality*, *sanctions*, and *incentives*. The hypothesis dealing with compulsory power therefore states that if compulsory power occurs, then conditionality, sanctions, and/or incentives must have been used.

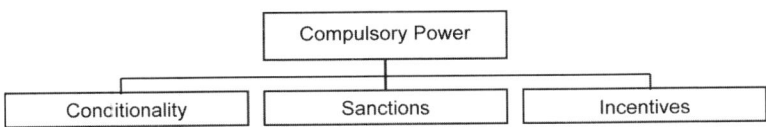

The first sub-hypothesis, *conditionality*, implies that if the EU threatened to take sanctions in the case of violation of essential elements of the agreements, civilian compulsory power was exercised by the EU. The opposite case may also prove true, namely that Israel or Egypt threatened to take sanctions in the case of violation of essential elements of the agreements: in this case civilian compulsory power was exercised by Israel or Egypt. Finally, one may think of the option that none of the actors threatened to take sanctions in the case of violation of essential elements of the agreements. Then, this form of civilian compulsory power would not have been exercised.

The question for *sanctions*, presenting the second sub-hypothesis, inquires whether the EU took so-called appropriate measures in the case of violations of essential elements of the agreements. In this case, civilian compulsory power would have been exercised by the EU. Again, the opposite case also has to be looked for: if Israel or Egypt took so-called appropriate measures in the case of violations of essential elements of the agreements, then civilian compulsory power was exercised by Israel or Egypt. Last, it is possible that none of the actors took so-called appropriate measures in the case of violations of essential elements of the agreements. Then, this form of civilian compulsory power would not have been exercised.

The third sub-hypothesis, *incentives*, states that if the EU promised further efforts in the case of good behavior, i.e. in the case of keeping to aims reflected in the agreements, then civilian compulsory power was exercised by the EU. If, on the other hand, Israel or Egypt promised further efforts, i.e. in the case of being satisfied with the EU's policy, then civilian compulsory power was exercised by Israel or Egypt. Finally, if none of the actors promised further efforts, then this form of civilian compulsory power was not exercised.

6.2   Hypotheses for institutional power

As has been discussed before, institutional power that works through an institution is based on the assumption that two actors are trying to influence each other in nonspecific and indirect ways through diffuse relations. In most cases, a spatial and temporal distance will characterize this relation. Institutional power is mainly expressed through biases in the institutional setting and through biases organized by the actors themselves. The latter refers to the various forms of agenda setting. These may be formal or informal. Formal agenda setting works through official bodies that allow for the setting of issues to be discussed. Informal agenda setting works through less official channels and relies on the ability to promote certain topics as important and to suppress other topics that are not in the interest of the actor. Thus, for institutional power, the three sub-hypotheses deal with a possible *bias in the institutional setting, agenda setting via the promotion or suppression of topics, and agenda setting via the reconceptualization of topics*. The main hypothesis dealing with institutional power therefore states that if institutional power occurs, then bias in the institutional setting, agenda setting via the promotion or suppression of topics, and/or agenda setting via the reconceptualization of topics must have been used.

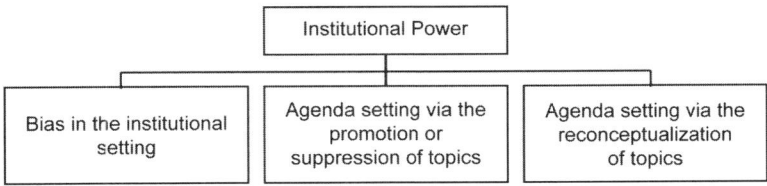

The first sub-hypothesis of institutional power refers to a possible *bias in the institutional setting*. It asks whether the EU was mainly at the established institutional controls of the cooperation or whether Israel or Egypt was mainly at the established institutional controls of the

143

cooperation. In the first case, civilian institutional power would have been exercised by the EU, whereas in the second case, civilian institutional power would have been exercised by Israel or Egypt. If none of the actors was at the established institutional controls of the cooperation, then this form of civilian institutional power was not exercised.

The second sub-hypothesis deals with *agenda setting via the promotion or suppression of topics*. It proposes that civilian institutional power was exercised by the EU if the EU set up topics and suppressed others. On the other hand, civilian institutional power was exercised by Israel or Egypt if Israel or Egypt set up topics and suppressed others. If topics of the same or very similar importance for the actors were chosen equally, conjointly and to the same degree between the EU and Israel/Egypt, then this form of civilian institutional power was not exercised.

Finally, *agenda setting via the reconceptualization of topics* has to be taken into account to meet the main characteristics of institutional power. This means that if the EU succeeded to grant topics a different meaning and/or a different urgency, then civilian institutional power was exercised by the EU. If Israel or Egypt succeeded to grant topics a different meaning and/or a different urgency, however, then civilian institutional power was exercised by Israel or Egypt. Finally, if none of the actors succeeded to grant topics a different meaning and/or a different urgency, then this form of civilian institutional power was not exercised.

6.3 Hypotheses for structural power

Structural power takes place directly. The relations in which it is active are diffuse, though. Its efficiency depends on a social environment rather than on specific actors. Social structures create perceptions and thus shape the social position and even the identity of an actor. A decisive element in the process of building up social positions is the establishment of the self against others and the differentiation between the actors. Inclusion and exclusion especially figure as means of deciding who belongs to which side, and are thus typical for systems of structural power. Inclusion and exclusion are established in various aspects. The relationship may be structured via the *political setup*, via *verbal classifications*, and via *values*. These three forms of structuring are all built on patterns of inclusion and exclusion as a principle of dividing among the actors involved. Even if structural power works as a network and not through the direct actions of actors, one can analyze the ways in which actors try to create these patterns of inclusion and exclusion, i.e. these networks of meaning. In this study, the three basic forms named above are taken as the most important features of structural power. One may note that these three basic forms of structural power can be considered a source of potential change of configurations in the longer term. As much as the structures themselves constitute a form of actualized power, they represent potential in reference to productive power. Productive power may be described as the actualized situation that structural power bears in it as a potential. The hypothesis dealing with structural power therefore states that if structural power occurs, then a structured relationship between the partners must have been established through the structuring of relations via the political set up, via verbal classifications, and/or via values.

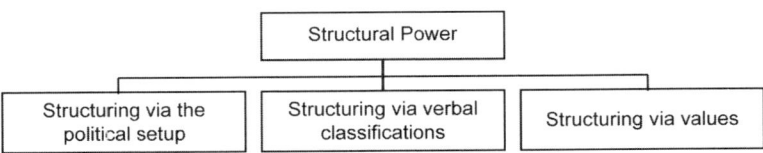

The first sub-hypothesis in the investigation of structural power asks whether *structuring via the political setup* has taken place. It asks whether it was the EU or Israel/Egypt that structured the relationship according to region and content. In the first case, civilian structural power would have been exercised by the EU, whereas in the second case, it would have been exercised by Israel or Egypt. If none of the actors structured the relationship according to region and content, then this form of civilian structural power was not exercised.

The second sub-hypothesis deals with the question of whether *structuring via verbal classifications* has taken place. It assumes that if the EU structured the relationship according to verbal classifications, it exercised civilian structural power. In the case that Israel or Egypt structured the relationship according to verbal classifications, civilian structural power was exercised by Israel or Egypt. If none of the actors structured the relationship according to verbal classifications, then this form of civilian structural power was not exercised.

Finally, structural power is concerned with a possible *structuring via values*. The third sub-hypothesis assumes that if the EU structured the relationship according to values, then civilian structural power was exercised by the EU. If Israel or Egypt structured the relationship according to values, then civilian structural power was exercised by Israel or Egypt. In the case that none of the actors structured the relationship according to values, this form of civilian structural power was not exercised.

6.4   Hypotheses for productive power

Productive power is similar to structural power in many aspects. It does not refer to structuring itself but to systems of perceptions that have been created through these structures. These systems produce the actor, which is a result of the systems of meanings in which it participates. In this respect, productive power may represent actualized structural power. Nevertheless, the actor itself is also a vehicle of these perceptions and meanings—so that productive power is not a strictly anonymous network but can be drawn back to actors. This makes it easier to get hold of, at least to a certain degree. Relationships between the actors are diffuse. Power in these networks or relationships of meaning, then, can be defined as the possibility of shaping one's own path. Productive power is best approached by looking at systems of collective meaning practiced by the various actors. Therefore, this study analyzes systems of perception, especially those that define what a state, a society and its members should look like and how they should build up their identities in a Euro-Mediterranean context. The study cannot come up with insights concerning a change of identities or a creation of new identities due to the exercise of power—it only examines how identities of actors are addressed in order to change them. This discourse has been broken down into three main parts:

The first basic form of productive power addresses an *actor's identity on a governing level*, i.e. how actors are subject to normative influence on the state level concerning Egypt and Israel, and on the governing level concerning the EU. The second form addresses the *identity of a society, or of a community* (which would apply to the EU more aptly than the term "society" would). The third form addresses *individuals in their regional identities*.

This means that productive power differs from structural power insofar as it goes further. It concerns addressing the actors' feeling of togetherness, i.e. their definition on a governing level, as well the actors' perceptions regarding their societies and themselves. At least one of these must appear in order to declare that productive power has occurred. Whereas structural power would only deal with classifications whose aim is structure, productive power concerns the addressing of inner classifications and the perceptions of the structured actors themselves. The hypothesis dealing with productive power therefore states that if productive power occurs, then the actors' identities on the governing level, as a society or a community, and/or

147

as individuals in the Euro-Mediterranean region must have been addressed.

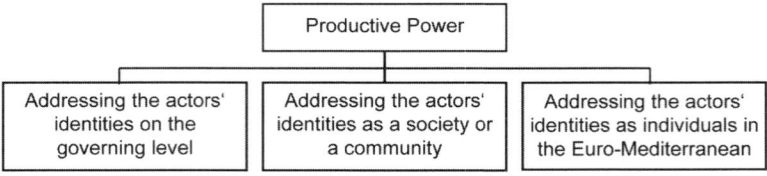

All three sub-hypotheses of productive power deal with the question of whether identities were addressed in an attempt to change them. The first sub-hypothesis asks whether *actors' identities were addressed on the governing level.* It assumes that if the EU mainly addressed Israel's or Egypt's respective identities as states, then civilian productive power was exercised by the EU. On the other hand, if Israel or Egypt mainly addressed the EU's identity on the governing level, then civilian productive power was exercised by Israel or Egypt. If none of the actors addressed the other actors' identities on the governing level, then this form of civilian productive power was not exercised.

In a second sub-hypothesis, the question of whether *the actors' identities as a society or a community* were addressed is taken into account. The basic assumption is that if the EU mainly addressed Israel's or Egypt's respective identities as societies, then civilian productive power was exercised by the EU. However, if Israel or Egypt mainly addressed the EU's identity as a community, then civilian productive power was exercised by Israel or Egypt. As always, none of these cases may occur: If none of the actors addressed the other actors' identities as a society or a community, then this form of civilian productive power was not exercised.

Last, it is asked whether *the actors' identities as individuals in the*

Euro-Mediterranean region were subject to the exercise of power. This means that if the EU mainly addressed the respective identities of Israeli or Egyptian individuals in the Euro-Mediterranean region, then civilian productive power was exercised by the EU. If Israel or Egypt mainly addressed the identities of European individuals in the Euro-Mediterranean region, then civilian productive power was exercised by Israel or Egypt. If neither of these cases holds, then this form of civilian productive power was not exercised.

The development of these four hypotheses and twelve sub-hypotheses, based on the academic research on power, presents the first main step of the study at hand. They are the main branches of a differentiation of civilian power. In order to specify its mode of functioning, the following case study was conducted.

7 Exploring civilian power: a case study

7.1 The development of Euro-Mediterranean relations

The relationship between the European Union and the Middle East has emerged out of a long and complex history. The bloody mission of the Crusaders has not yet been forgotten, and in more recent times, European colonialism and the Holocaust have marked the European-Middle Eastern relationship, and have often made dialogue and mutual understanding difficult. Nevertheless, both regions depend on each other economically, politically, geo-strategically, and with regard to migration and security issues.[1] In the beginning of the seventies, several cooperation agreements were made on a bilateral basis between European and southern Mediterranean countries. With the launching of the Global Mediterranean Policy in 1972 and the Euro-Arab Dialogue in 1973, the EC formulated its early policies in the region in order to become a player that would be able to pursue its interests. The major European interest was economic: its aim was to promote socio-economic development and to strengthen economic relationships. Until today, economic cooperation is the most developed field in the relationship. This is also due to the European assumption that economic prosperity in the MPCs would create spillover effects and reduce the dangers that may come out of poor and unstable societies (see Jünemann 2000: 66). With Spain, Portugal and Greece joining the European Union, there were hopes that this enlargement could deepen relations with the Non-European Mediterranean partners on a non-economical basis. This was not the case, however.

Only in the beginning of the 1990s did the cooperation receive new input, from the fall of Communism in Eastern Europe and its regional

---

[1]   For a comprehensive historical overview of European-Middle Eastern relations see Dosenrode/Stubkjær 2002.

150

and worldwide aftershocks. The European Union was keen to establish its part in the nascent new regional order and to promote its agenda of democracy as well as ensuring a maximum of trade benefits. The experience of the peaceful revolutions in Central and Eastern Europe is still a basis of the European policy of today. The EU pursues a policy of intensive civil society promotion—in the hope that the Eastern European miracle can be repeated elsewhere. Security issues were not as present in those days as they are now, even though some organizations, such as NATO, voiced the notion that the region's socio-economic problems could lead to an increasing violence of non-state actors (see Solana 1997). In October 1994, the European Commission (EC) developed new propositions concerning an enlargement and deepening of the cooperation. These propositions were designed to promote free trade and business relations, to ensure regional stability and security, to work together in specific fields, such as telecommunication and energy, and to lead a dialogue about social and cultural issues (see Webb 1996: 148).

7.2   The Euro-Mediterranean Partnership

Today, the relationship between the European Union and the Middle East takes mainly place within the framework of the Euro-Mediterranean Partnership and of the European Neighbourhood Policy. These policies are based on certain fundamental agreements, which provide for the EMP Association Agreements as well as for the ENP Country Reports, Action Plans, Country Strategy Papers, and Progress Reports. This study therefore examines these policies and their fundamental agreements in order to find out how civilian power is expressed thereby. Moreover, the 2005 Barcelona conference and two specific programs that are exemplary of the relationship are the basis of this study and will be dealt with in the following sections.

7.2.1   How the Euro-Mediterranean Partnership is set up

In 1995, the Barcelona Conference created a broader and more organized framework for several cooperative activities that were underway in the years before. Under the name European Mediterranean Partnership, it brought together all fifteen European Union member states with twelve Mediterranean states.[2] Today the Partnership consists of the twenty-seven EU states and the ten Mediterranean states of Algeria, Egypt, Israel, Jordan, Lebanon, Morocco, Palestinian Authority, Syria, Tunisia and Turkey. Besides the United Nations, it is the only forum that brings together Israelis, Palestinians and Syrians—a fact that is often highlighted as a typical European achievement. It comprises bilateral as well as multilateral cooperation. The bilateral part is mainly expressed in Association Agreements between the EU and single member states of the European Mediterranean Partnership with the aim of establishing a free trade zone that should in the long term comprise forty states and 600 to 800 million consumers. The bilateral part of the EMP makes up about 90% of the cooperation—a fact that shows clearly the level of emphasis put on economic interests (see Vasconcelos/Joffé 2000: 4).

The multilateral part of the EMP has been considered the more innovative part, however. Its establishment in 1995 was accompanied by the hope of creating a different reality of living together in the Middle East and a better understanding between European and Middle Eastern peoples. This part mainly consists of dialogue platforms, forums, programs and conferences about political, economic, and cultural issues. The Barcelona Declaration therefore created three major fields of partnership: A *political and security partnership,* an *economic and finance partnership,* and a *partnership in social, cultural and humanitarian fields*. The Middle East peace process was excluded from the agenda. The EMP is based on the experience of the European integration itself, where economic integration and shared

---

2   Libya did not take part, but has observer status since 1999.

values have led to a lasting peace and the development of mutual trust and friendship (see Menéndez/Youngs 2006).

The *political and security partnership's* aim is to create political stability. Dealing with conflicts in a peaceful way and creating means of conflict resolution are at the center of its efforts. Moreover, negotiations concerning security and stability are conducted in order to attain a more reliable and stable environment and fruitful cooperation. The political and security partnership has gained importance in recent years due to the escalating political situation in the Middle East. Europe feels increasingly threatened by the wars and conflicts in the Southern Mediterranean region and by growing Islamic fundamentalist movements. In connection with the European Common Security and Defense Policy (CSDP), a range of meetings between Senior Officials of the EMP, European Foreign Ministers, and Mediterranean partners have taken place in order to reinforce the security aspect of the EMP (see Ortega 2005).

Nevertheless, to this day the *economic partnership* remains the most developed part of the cooperation. The EU is the main partner of Mediterranean countries in trade of goods and services. With 36% of total foreign direct investment in the region, Europe is the largest direct investor; with an amount of almost three billion euros per year for loans and grants, the EU is also the largest provider of financial assistance and funding.

The economic aspect of the EMP comprises a number of fields of action: the establishment of a free trade zone including all European and Mediterranean countries by the year 2010; exemption from import duties for manufactured goods only; increasing liberalization of the agricultural sector. It is unclear, however, whether this formulated aim will be realized. A free trade agreement could only be arrived at with Israel in the absence of major harmonization problems. With Arabic countries a harmonization process must take place before even basic questions of economic cooperation can be solved. These questions and fields of harmonization also involve issues such as intellectual property, the formation of monopolies and cartels, and determinations concerning import and export of refined and composed manufactured products.

The European Union also promotes economic reforms in the partner countries. A new financial and tariff policy, modernization of industry, and reform of the public sector are especially being promoted. The primary aim is to support privatization, to afford technical support, to provide aid for problems typically created in transformation phases, to support social institutions such as hospitals and schools, and to promote regional cooperation, especially in the fields of tourism. The MEDA fund was established especially to finance this support. Its major resources go toward bilateral economic cooperation; a smaller amount is for regional and horizontal measures. The MEDA money mainly goes into privatization projects, support for the private sector, and support for social infrastructure. Moreover, it provides credits for the support of the productive sector. The distribution of financial means is checked and evaluated yearly, and changes for the coming year are made accordingly. If means are not used for the promotion of a free trade zone or foil efforts towards democracy building, they may be stopped (see Michalek 2005; Webb 1996: 150).

The *social and cultural partnership's* purpose is to enhance dialogue between cultures and to improve understanding of Western values in partner countries. In this context, the European Union especially promotes non-governmental organizations in the partner countries and encourages dialogue in academia between European and Arab or Israeli colleagues.

Ten years after the establishment of the Barcelona Process, disappointment is spreading. Political reforms or dynamics of democratization were not activated in most Arabic countries, the region does not prosper economically (see Blanc 2005; EC/EFA 2006; Luciani 2005; Radwan 2005), major deficits in education and gender equality persist, and demographic development remains startling (see Vasconcelos 2005: 67). Many southern partners are disappointed and even claim that the way the EMP deals with certain issues, such as security, borders on xenophobia and even racism (see Abouyoub 2005: 66; Guiza 2005). Others miss a greater emphasis on cultural cooperation (see Chenal 2005). On the European side, there are complaints concerning the lack of formulation of clear interests and the lack of a more promising strategy (see Marchetti 2005a: 6).

7.2.2 How the Euro-Mediterranean Partnership works

The EMP is built upon the Barcelona aquis[3], which consists of two parts, an institutional and a potential aquis. The institutional aquis is based on the decisions that have been taken from the beginning of the EMP in multi-level meetings. This includes the recognition of the legitimacy of EMP procedures and institutions. The Commission guards the EMP on behalf of the EU as well as of non-EU members. Moreover, it takes the function to coordinate multilateral and bilateral committees. The EU presidency chairs the Euro-Med committees. Things have gotten even more complicated with the extension of the cooperation onto a bilateral level and with the implementation of Association Agreements and Action Plans. The Barcelona Declaration serves as the original institutional aquis. Over the years, several other common institutions have been established which realize the partnership on the ground and animate it. The most important ones are "the Conference of Ministers of Foreign Affairs, the sectoral ministerial meetings, the Committee, the Senior Officials meetings on political and security issues and, more recently, the Parliamentary Assembly and the Anna Lindh Euro-Mediterranean Foundation for the

---

[3]   The term aquis comes from the European integration and its accession criteria. The Community aquis is the body of common rights and obligations that bind the 25 EU member states. For EU member states and candidate countries, the Barcelona aquis is part of the aquis communautaire (see EuroMeSCo 2005: 18).

Dialogue of Cultures" (EuroMeSCo 2005: 19 et seq.). It is crucial to note that the latter is exceptional: it is the first common institution of the EMP that is based in a Mediterranean Partner Country (Egypt) and co-financed by all members of the Partnership. In addition, the bilateral Association Council, Association Committees and Sub-Committees that are responsible for the implementation of the Association Agreements are part of the aquis.

The potential aquis refers to the principles and values of the Barcelona Declaration and provides the EMP with legitimacy (see ibid.: 18 et seq.). The targets, principles and values of which the Declaration speaks need not be fulfilled at present, but must be accepted as goals. As these goals have not yet been attained, the aquis is potential. It is important to note that the recognition of these values is a primary condition of membership of the EMP.

Since 1992, clauses defining respect for human rights and democracy have been included as basic elements in all Association Agreements. This is also true for the Israeli and Egyptian Association Agreements. As with all Association Agreements, those between the EU and Israel and between the EU and Egypt also focus on economic matters. It is obvious that the main concern for the undersigned parties is increasing their economic prosperity. The Association Agreement between the EU and Israel, about five times longer than the Agreement between the EU and Egypt, deals in detail with matters of industrial and agricultural production, trade, and capital movements. It sets standards for and addresses questions of intellectual property and of public procurement.

By contrast, the Agreement between the EU and Egypt is a lot less detailed. This may be explained by Egypt's less developed economy and the fact that it is not as much of an international economic player as Israel is. Both Association Agreements refer to political dialogue. Unlike the Agreement with Israel, there is an emphasis on migration matters with Egypt. In addition, cultural cooperation assumes a special place between the EU and Egypt. One can say that even though both Association Agreements put the most emphasis on matters of trade, its importance varies, as the Egyptian Agreement contains a relatively large part concentrating on political matters.

7.3   The European Neighbourhood Policy

In 2004, an additional instrument was established: the European Neighbourhood Policy. Proposed at the December 2002 Copenhagen European Council, the ENP states that while allowing new member states into the Union, the EU should also improve its relations with its neighboring countries. In contrast to the benchmarks, a EU candidate state has to fulfill in order to gain accession to the Union, the ENP states need not meet such standards.

The ENP is built on the EMP and uses its systems and structures, especially the Association Agreements. It was designed as a complementary program to enforce the EMP, strengthening ongoing politics, giving new impetus to existing cooperation, and providing a more differentiated framework for the relationship between the enlarged EU and the Mediterranean (as well as the Eastern) region (see COM (2004) 373 final). The Barcelona Declaration has been described as the political umbrella for European-Mediterranean relations, that takes multilateral and institutional aspects into account, whereas the ENP is the instrument used to bring about individual plans for the single countries (see Prat y Coll 2005: 64). The ENP also distinguishes itself from the Barcelona Process insofar as it affords the prospect of closer cooperation in fields such as regulatory structures, sustainable development, energy, and telecommunications, based on the harmonization of legislation. Moreover, it differentiates between countries, and can therefore take a country's specific situation better into account than the EMP can. Finally, since 2007 it has been financed by the European Neighbourhood and Partnership Instrument

(ENPI), which is more flexible than the MEDA financial assistance instrument. Nevertheless, there has been quite some confusion about the differences between the two programs, and the overlapping of approaches has largely been criticized.

The ENP does not only cover the Middle East as the EMP does, but applies to Algeria, Armenia, Azerbaijan, Belarus, Egypt, Georgia, Israel, Jordan, Lebanon, Libya, Moldova, Morocco, the Palestinian Authority, Syria, Tunisia and Ukraine. The EU claims the EMP is different from earlier policy instruments, as it is more focused and based on previous experiences of supporting reform and modernization in other regions. Moreover, it "covers a wider range of issues, with greater intensity, and throughout all fields of governance" (EC 2007: http://ec.europa.eu/world/enp/index_en.htm) and is "backed by increased and improved financial and technical assistance" (ibid.). More importantly, the EC claims that it "uses proven methodology (that has already helped us to support transition in central and southeastern Europe) and incentives to promote democratic and economic reforms, supporting the countries' own efforts" (ibid.). And it is designed to provide a framework for resolving issues that have arisen in bilateral relations.

Before its establishment, the ENP was outlined in several policy papers. Despite the fact that its policies overlap and are hard to distinguish, it is clear that the political focal point has shifted if one compares the political climate of the EMP's founding with that of the ENP policy programs. In 1995, political reform was not a high priority for the EU. Its efforts were mainly economic, and governance was not yet a major issue. In the aftermath of 9/11, policies changed clearly. A number of initiatives appeared that proposed a clear link between the lack of democratization and the security threat to the Western world. In May 2003, the Commission issued a Communication giving guidelines for reinvigorating action on human rights and democratization with Mediterranean partners (see COM (2003) 294 final), accompanied by Commission suggestions to provide additional

158

financial resources for MPCs that were willing to work on governance reform and to improve human right standards. These priorities were also outlined in the papers paving the way for the ENP, i.e. the European Security Strategy (see EC 2003b), in a Commission Communication on Wider Europe in March 2003 (see COM (2003) 104 final), a Communication on a New Neighbourhood Instrument in July 2003 (see COM (2003) 393 final), and a Strategy Paper on the ENP (see COM (2004) 373 final) in May 2004.

The Security Strategy named key threats more diverse and less predictable than large-scale aggression against EU member states. Among these are terrorism, the proliferation of weapons of mass destruction, organized crime, state failure and regional conflicts, "above all in the Middle East" (EC 2003b: 4). In order to tackle these threats, the paper highlights the necessity of building security in the European neighborhood and calls the resolution of the Middle Eastern conflicts and of the economic stagnation in the region a strategic priority for Europe (see ibid.: 7 et seq.).

The Communication on Wider Europe suggested the creation of a new policy in order to give "new impetus to the effort of drawing closer to the 385 million inhabitants of the countries who will find themselves on the external land and sea border" (EC COM (2003) 104 final: 3). Therefore, a new policy instrument, "which builds on the experience of promotion cross-border co-operation within the PHARE, TACIS and INTERREG programmes" (ibid.: 14) and ensures the development of "a zone of prosperity and a friendly neighbourhood—a 'ring of friends'—with whom the EU enjoys close, peaceful and co-operative relations" (ibid.: 4) was initiated.

In the Communication on a New Neighbourhood Instrument, the Commission examined in detail the possibilities of creating such a policy. One major aim was to develop the New Neighbourhood Instrument in a consistent way that would improve the coordination between the existing instruments, such as INTERREG and PHARE or

TACIS. It also deals with the problem of different legal and budgetary frameworks due to the separation between internal and external funding sources (see EC COM (2003) 393 final: 7).

The ENP took a more specific form in a Paper on general provisions establishing a European Neighbourhood and Partnership Instrument presented by the Commission in September 2004 (see EC 2004/0219 COD/628 final). The European Parliament and the Council of the European Union herein adopted the regulation of a new European Neighbourhood and Partnership Instrument "to provide assistance [...] for the development of an area of prosperity and good neighbourliness." The Regulation states that "the Union is founded on the values of respect for human dignity, liberty, democracy, equality, the rule of law and respect for human rights and seeks to promote commitment to these values in partner countries through dialogue and cooperation" (ibid.: 14). In order to promote these values, the Regulation suggests creating thematic programs such as human rights or migration management programs. Democratization and the spread of human rights and fundamental freedoms should be pursued through thematic programs that include "pertinent global, regional and country projects and programmes of local and EU non-governmental and civil society based organization" (ibid.: 44), and "cooperation with international organizations in the field of democratization and human rights" (ibid.).

Until December 31, 2006, funding for the ENP came from the appropriate geographical or thematic programs. The Middle Eastern fund was the MEDA or, for human rights promotion, the European Initiative for Democracy and Human rights (EIDHR). Since January 2007, funding has been reformed in order to make the ENP more coherent. Singular instruments have been replaced by the European Neighbourhood and Partnership Instrument that covers all the ENP activities, especially the programs of the Action Plans (see COM (2004) 373 final: 25 et seq.). For the budgetary period 2007 to 2013, approximately EUR 11.181 billion, 32% more is available in real terms than in the last budget period (see EC/IP/06/1676 (2006)). At least 95% of these funds are devoted to country and multi-country programs, and about 5% are allocated to cross-border cooperation programs (see Council 14087/06 (Presse 292) 2006). Funds for each country are allocated according to its specific needs.

7.3.1 Objectives of the ENP

It is the EU that sets up the criteria and objectives for cooperation in the ENP. According to the EC's notion, the ENP represents the common interest of the EU and its neighbors in encouraging and supporting "the rule of law, stable democracies and prosperity— prosperity, security and stability" (EC 2007: http://ec.europa.eu/world/enp/index_en.htm). These concerns, grounded in common values, form the basis for strengthening political dialogue and building up economic ties between the EU and its neighbors. Chief among specific concerns are economic reform and integration, democracy- and freedom-oriented political cooperation, and "development, environment, non-proliferation and counter-terrorism issues—in line with the European Security Strategy" (ibid).[4]

The Report of December 2006 on strengthening the ENP came to the conclusion that the ENP has already borne fruit but should be more concrete in its aims. It demands that the details of economic and trade integration should be made clear and go beyond free trade in goods and services. These should also cover non-tariff barriers and regulatory convergence. Moreover, mobility should be facilitated and visa procedures (especially for businesspeople, students, scholars, officials and journalists) managed better. This goes hand in hand with

---

[4]   It may be interesting to note that a recent survery conducted by the European Commission on the ENP reveals that EU citizens consider security issues, such as fighting organized crime and terrorism, most important for the relationship (see EC/Eurobarometer 2006).

161

dealing with migration matters. Moreover, supporting civil society and stimulating internal processes on a grassroots level are highlighted as a core element of the ENP. This should involve not only promoting contacts and organizing exchanges between European and Mediterranean societies but also supporting civilian societies in their countries. Highlighted are exchanges between regional and local authorities, educational, cultural, youth and research exchanges, business-to-business contacts, and training for the regulators of tomorrow. Civil society groups should deal more with democratization and conflict-settlement issues (see EC COM (2006) 726final).

7.3.2 Values, conditionality and incentives emphasized in the ENP

According to the EC, the ENP is "based on the concept of shared values and common interests" (EC 2007: http://ec.europa.eu/world/enp/index_en.htm). As shared values, the EC considers what ensures "prosperity, stability and security, i.e. democratic reforms (fundamental rights, rule of law), market economy and sustainable development (including reforms in sectors such as trade, competition, energy and transport, environment, people-to-people contacts etc)" (ibid.). The EC also assumes that it shares common challenges with its neighbor regions and that both sides are interested in finding a response to these challenges. Therefore, the reforms in these sectors are aimed to tackle such issues as migration, crime, the environment, public health, extremism, and terrorism. The ENP goes beyond existing relationship by offering deeper political relationships and economic integration. In consequence of the shift from economic cooperation to increasingly political interests, the ENP is based on the principles of conditionality and differentiation (see Menéndez/Youngs 2006).

Action Plans set out clear political targets and criteria that are meant to be as concise and as detailed as possible. In addition, political and economic benchmarks are used in order to allow evaluation in "key areas of reform and against agreed targets. Beyond the regulatory and administrative aspects directly linked to market integration, key benchmarks should include the ratification and implementation of international commitments which demonstrate respect for shared values, in particular the values codified in the UN Human Rights Declaration, the OSCE and the Council of Europe standards" (EC COM (2003) 104 final: 16). These benchmarks are intended to stimulate reform in the MPCs.

Secondly, the EU differentiates between the ENP countries and thus creates incentives to do better and to get more out of the partnership— compared to one's own possibilities, but also compared to the ones of the neighboring countries. The relationship with the partner country is linked to the fulfillment of the a priori established objectives and benchmarks: "The level of ambition of the relationship will depend on the extent to which these values are effectively shared [...]. Once monitoring shows significant progress and if the partner country is interested, it will be possible to consider deepening relations" (EC 2007: http://ec.europa.eu/world/enp/index_en.htm). Thus, the EU determines the objectives; the neighbor state receives technical help, political support, and aid money in exchange. In addition, the new ENP Instrument that has been proposed under the 2007-13 financial framework sharpens this approach of conditionality and incentives.

7.3.3   Country Reports and Action Plans

The ENP uses so-called Action Plans as its main policy instruments. These are worked out between a neighbor state and the EU. The aim is to agree on more specific and tailor-made cooperation programs than the ones of the broader Barcelona framework. The Action Plans are designed depending on the local political agenda and the will to undertake reforms according to the EU's understanding. Therefore, these may differ for each country according to its specific situation.

Plans were agreed on in early 2005 with Israel, Jordan, Moldova, Morocco, the Palestinian Authority, Tunisia and Ukraine, and in 2007 with Egypt. An Action Plan can be made only if an earlier Association Agreement of the EMP (or another bilateral agreement for non-EMP regions) is in force. Before a final Action Plan is worked out, the Commission prepares a Country Report for each country that assesses its political and economic situation and analyzes different aspects of its political and social life. This includes a discussion of the best strategies to deal with the country and its specific situation from a European viewpoint. The Country Reports are submitted to the Council, which decides if an Action Plan should be worked out or not. The European Commission sets the criteria for working on an Action Plan with the EU as follows: "Neighbours who want to carry out reforms to improve their standards of democracy and human rights, to increase their access to the Union's single market, to improve the environment or to step up their cooperation with the EU on issues like energy, transport or migration, have the chance to work on a joint Action Plan with the EU" (EC 2007: http://ec.europa.eu/world/enp/index_en.htm). Action Plans are based on a country's needs (i.e., the needs that have been highlighted in the Country Report). According to the EU, "they jointly define an agenda of political and economic reforms by means of short and medium-term (3-5 years) priorities. They cover political dialogue and reform, economic and social cooperation and development, trade-related issues and market and regulatory reform, cooperation in justice and home affairs, sectors (such as transport, energy, information society, environment, research and development) and a human dimension (people-to-people contacts, civil society, education, public health...). The incentives on offer, in return for progress on relevant reforms, are greater integration into European programmes and networks, increased assistance and enhanced market access" (ibid.).

164

There are Periodic Reports that monitor the implementation of the mutual commitments and the progress aimed at in the Action Plans. The Periodic Reports, prepared by the Commission, serve as a basis for adaptations in the Action Plan, such as setting new objectives or revising the EU's incentives. The first Periodic Report was issued in December 2006.[5]

The ENP has been criticized as a mere bilateral policy instrument that has given up the ambitions of the EMP and no longer considers the region as a whole (see Zorob 2007). Moreover, the renaming of the EMP's "partners" as the ENP's "neighbors" has caused criticism and frustration among the Mediterranean countries (see Schäfer 2007: 1). Nevertheless, others have welcomed the approach, saying that the Action Plans build on the positive elements of the EMP and give it a new dynamic by replacing the vague intentions of the EMP's Association Agreements with the relatively concrete policy programs of the Action Plans (see Emerson/Noutcheva 2005: 95).

The European Council adopted another instrument in June 2004. The EU's Strategic Partnership with the Middle East aims at promoting political, social and economic change in the region. Designed as a European concept for reform politics in the Middle East, the Strategic Partnership has been discontinued (see Schäfer 2007: 2), criticized for several inconsistencies, overlapping and lack of a clear strategy. Bilateral agreements have been judged as disregarding strategy for the region as whole. By contrast, the Barcelona Process has been questioned for its holistic approach, which is deemed inappropriate for such a diverse and complicated region (see Khader 2005). The tendency of recent years is to intensify bilateral or sub-regional cooperation, but not to put more emphasis on the region as a whole.

---

[5]   Concerning EU internal procedures, the Commission should submit reports to the European Parliament and the Council evaluating the implementation of the regulation dealing with the ENP (see EP/Council 2006: 13).

165

The Country Report and the Action Plan for Israel

Israel has signed an Action Plan in the framework of the European Neighbourhood Policy. In this framework it can be supported with about 14 million euros for the period 2007-2013. Moreover, it is eligible for the ENP regional and cross-border cooperation programs. The Action Plan for Israel is based on the Association Agreement of November 20, 1995, in which the EU and Israel agreed on a partnership that provides for mutually beneficial trade and investment relations as well as cooperation in economic, social, financial, civilian scientific, technological and cultural fields (see Council 16371/06 ADD 7; EC Commission Staff Working Document/SEC 1507 (2006)).

The Israel Action Plan is based on the Country Report for Israel from the year 2004. It refers to the Association Agreement and sets up two major chapters for the relationship: political issues and economic and social matters. The latter deals with macroeconomic questions, structural reforms, trade, market and regulatory reform as well as with related topics, such as energy, transport, information and innovation. The political chapter concerns democracy, the rule of law, human rights, regional stability, and justice and home affairs. The Report states simply that Israel is a democracy with all relevant elements and that it has a prospering civil society—it is a mere description of the status quo and neither offers criticism nor calls for change (see EC SEC (2004) 568/COM (2004) 373 final).

The Israel Action Plan was set up in the context of the 2004 enlargement round with the aim of intensifying the relations with EU neighbor countries in a way that is distinct from EU membership. For Israel this is a very interesting design, as it is a democracy with rule of law and as it has a highly developed, prospering market economy. A deeper cooperation with the EU is especially promising for economic, military, industrial and academic exchange and for a closer dialogue between the civilian societies (see Nathanson/Stetter 2006). Hence, it is not surprising that the EU-Israel Action Plan has a clear focus on topics such as economic cooperation and structural reforms, the promotion of trade relations, customs-related issues, facilitating the market assets of industrial products, improving administrative cooperation, tax issues, intellectual, industrial and commercial property rights, competition policies, and many more related issues (see COM (2004) 790 final; Musu 2007; Sade 2007).

The main aim of this cooperation is therefore to "develop an increasingly close relationship between the EU and Israel, going beyond previous levels of cooperation, including significant level of economic integration, and a deepening of political cooperation including in the area of foreign and security policy and in the resolution of the Middle East conflict and on human right issues, on the basis on the EU-Israel Action Plan" (COM (2004) 790 final).

Beyond the common interest in deeper economic relations, the Action Plan states that "the EU and Israel share the common values of democracy, respect for human rights and the rule of law and basic freedoms. Both parties are committed to the struggle against all form of anti-Semitism, racism and xenophobia. Historically and culturally, there exist great natural affinity and common heritage. Thus, we strive to build bridges and networks" (ibid.: 7).

Nevertheless, the Action Plan adds to this statement that "the level of ambition of the EU/Israel relationship will depend on the degree of commitment to common values as well as the mutual interest and the capacity of each party to implement jointly agreed priorities" (ibid.). It does not set any concrete objectives to be achieved. Instead, it speaks of working together, exploring and promoting these shared values— while not mentioning what that could mean in the context of Israeli society or the Israeli-Palestinian conflict (see ibid.: 10).

Concerning people-to-people contacts, the EU-Israel Action Plan calls for increased academic cooperation, for example, exchange programs for students and academic staff, talks on education and a closer cultural cooperation. Moreover, civil society cooperation should be enhanced through programs bringing together civil society organizations, intellectuals, politicians, journalists, experts and others (see ibid.: 28).

One of the ENP's aims is to promote peace between Israel and its Arab neighbors. Even though the ENP is based on bilateral relations, peace-related issues can be addressed as well. The EU aims in its bilateral relationships to work for a pragmatic and facilitative atmosphere in the region that will allow better relations among the different countries. It reinforces regional and sub-regional cooperation by recommending cross-border cooperation, especially concerning trade and infrastructure, involving local and regional authorities as well as civil society actors. The Action Plans for Israel and the Palestinian Authority also have some common elements aimed at promoting dialogue. The Action Plans for Israel, the Palestinian Authority and Jordan include commitments on regional cooperation, for example, in the fields of trade. Jordan and Israel have already signed an agreement to export joint products to EU markets under tariff-free arrangements. The EU has also initiated and sponsored joint offices between Israel and the Palestinian Authority concerning energy and transport, as well as established a trilateral group between Israel, Jordan and the Palestinian Authority on trade issues. These initiatives were suspended in 2006 after the Hamas came to power, but may be resumed in the future.

In its Assessment of the ENP in 2006, the EC claims that the implementation of the Israel Action Plan was successful and has opened the door for a closer cooperation between the EU and Israel in fields such as political dialogue, trade, science and technology, as well as justice and security. In addition, a number of workshops and smaller projects preventing terrorist financing, fighting racism and anti-Semitism, and promoting judicial and police cooperation were conducted on the basis of the Action Plan (see EC Commission Staff Working Document/SEC 1504/2 (2006): 4; EC Commission Staff Working Document/SEC 1512/2 (2006)).

168

The Country Report and the Action Plan for Egypt

The EU-Egypt Association Council adopted the EU-Egypt Action Plan for Egypt on March 6, 2007 in order to deepen their relations economically, politically and socially. The EU acts on the assumption that Egypt is a key geographical and historical player with great influence on stability and peace in the region (see EC COM (2006) 282 final: 7). The Action Plan sets the cooperation agenda for the next three to five years. It is meant to fulfill the objectives of the Association Agreement, which is the legal framework for the bilateral relations between the EU and Egypt, and of Egypt's national development aims.

The Action Plan for Egypt deals with several fields of action, such as political, security, trade, technological and cultural relations as well as regional and sub-regional cooperation. Above all, it sets up a list of objectives in the framework of enhanced political dialogue and reform. The Recommendations for the Action Plan already call for "specific actions which reinforce adherence to shared values in areas including respect for international obligations, democracy and the rule of law, including the holding of democratic elections, administration of justice and human rights and to certain objectives in the area of foreign and security policy" (see EC COM (2005) 72 final: 6 et seq.) as key priorities. The Action Plan itself calls for democracy and the rule of law, human rights and fundamental freedoms, a better cooperation on foreign and security policy, combating of terrorism and the non-proliferation of weapons of mass destruction and their means of delivery.

In its Country Report on Egypt, the EU states that Egypt has ratified most of the major UN human rights conventions, though with reservations. The main obstacle for improving the human rights situation and the acceptance of fundamental freedoms is the Emergency Law that has been continuously applied since 1981. It allows for arbitrary arrests and detentions without trial, also severely restricting freedoms of opinion and expression and of assembly and association. The Press Law and the Publications Law allow for censorship, and the Islamic Centre al-Azhar has the permission to seize material that is not in accordance with the Sharia. The government owns all ground-broadcast television stations and controls the printed press. Moreover, there are no real efforts to achieve better human rights standards, despite the creation in 2004 of the National Council for Human Rights, mandated to work out a national plan on human rights (see EC SEC (2005) 287/3/COM (2005) 72 final).

According to the Action Plan, democracy and the rule of law are to be reached through measures such as strengthening participation in political life, exchanging election experiences and raising public awareness and participations in elections, fostering the role of civil society and enhancing its capability to get more active, demanding a reform of decentralization and a strengthening of local administrations, and supporting modernization of public services by building on accountability and transparence for the citizens. Moreover, the goal of an independent judiciary, including capacity-building of bodies entrusted with the implementation of law as well as the improvement of prison conditions, is pursued (see EC COM (2006) 282 final: 11). The Action Plan also calls for the protection of human rights and fundamental freedoms in line with international conventions to which Egypt is party, and for the further alignment of her laws and practices in accordance with UN standards. Moreover, Egypt should consider signing optional protocols of the international human rights conventions to which it is already party. Awareness and respect for human rights should be strengthened in Egyptian institutions as well as in society as a whole. Especially important is a dialogue about how to put signed conventions into practice should be launched. This includes talks concerning the death penalty and the circumstances of pre-trial and administrative detention systems as well as detention conditions and the access of detainees to legal counsel and families (see ibid.: 11 et seq.)

Furthermore, the Action Plan calls for the promotion of rights of women and children, i.e. the promotion of gender equality in political, economic and social life, the fight against gender-based violence, and the eradication of female genital mutilation (see ibid.: 12). The freedom of association and expression and the pluralism of the media is another core aim of the Action Plan. The International Covenant on Civilian and Political Rights should be implemented, and an independent media should be allowed. Moreover, it calls for a fight against discrimination, intolerance, racism and xenophobia, and for fundamental social rights and core labor standards (see ibid.: 13).

On the foreign and security policy level, especially a dialogue in the CFSP and ESDP frameworks is thought of. Also disarmament and regional issues are to be discussed. Notably, also in this chapter, the Plan calls for the respect of international humanitarian law. Human rights issues are also mentioned in the chapter about combating terrorism. It points to the fact that all measures of fighting terrorism should be in accordance with the international humanitarian law. Moreover, it calls for a closer exchange of information, means and methods used to counter terrorism (see ibid.: 14).

As in other Action Plans, here also the "level of ambition of the EU-Egypt relationship, leading to continuing trade liberalization including in agriculture and services, a stake in the EU's internal market, increased financial support and enhanced political cooperation, will depend on the degree of commitment to common values as well as the implementation of jointly agreed priorities to mutual benefits. The pace of progress to the relationship will acknowledge fully the efforts and concrete achievements in meeting those commitments" (ibid.: 6). In addition, future cooperation depend on the implementation of the Action Plan: "In light of the fulfillment of the objectives of this Action Plan and of the overall evolution of EU-Egypt relations, consideration will be given to the possibility of a new contractual relationship" (ibid.: 8).

7.3.4 Country Strategy Papers and Progress Reports

A Country Strategy Paper is published for each country that receives EU aid, serving as a basis for designing and implementing the programs. The formulation of a Country Strategy Paper is in the hands of the European Union; however, it is based on "discussions with the partner country. The process of CSP preparation should promote clear 'local' ownership of the strategy so as to facilitate successful implementation" (EC 2004c: 26). A Country Strategy Paper has to contain a description of the EU's objectives as well as of the partner country's policy objectives. Moreover, it has to make statements concerning the political, social and economic situation of the country. It should take into account lessons learned from previous EU, government or other donor programs. As a result, some limited and specified fields must be chosen. These should complement other, already existing donor programs in order to avoid multiple and wasteful transactions.

The Country Strategy Paper is drafted under the National Indicative Programme (NIP), which serves as a management tool for a framework of between three and five years. It describes measures and instruments to be taken in order to tackle the problems and reach the objectives set up in the Country Strategy Paper. It must also specify the objectives described in the Country Strategy Paper, selecting certain fields out of broader issues and describing them in detail so that they may be tackled by special programs. In a second step, financial means must be indicated for every field in which the EC plans to become active. In addition, indicators are to be established for the chosen fields of action. These serve as instruments to formulate programs and to measure their results in the medium term. Moreover, the Indicative Programme should include crosscutting issues, i.e. questions of gender and environment. Finally, it may formulate ideas for projects, which should specify the fields of activities, the partners and the timeframe. Thereby they should take into account the key stakeholders in the field of activity, their needs, the concrete problems on the ground and how they can be dealt with, and the instruments of project management that can be used in order to assure success and sustainability for the concrete project.

The Country Strategy Paper, the National Indicative Programme and the Progress Report for Israel

The current Country Strategy Paper for Israel is set up for the period 2007 to 2013, and the according Indicative Programme from 2007 to 2010. Funding is provided under the ENPI. This amounts to about about 14 million euros in the timeframe of 2007 to 2013 (see EC/Israel (without date)).

The Country Strategy Paper for Israel does not come up with decidedly new policies but is closely linked to the existing agreements, such as the Association Agreement and the ENP policies. It puts emphasis on Israel's status, which is exceptional in the EMP and the ENP. Unlike most other MPCs, Israel is a democracy with a highly developed high-tech sector and therefore faces the specific challenges that most EU countries also face. More important, the EU is Israel's largest trading partner, with 35% of its total trade (excluding diamonds). The Country Strategy Paper reflects the fact that both sides have significant economic interests in the relationship (see ibid.).

Consequently, Israel does not receive bilateral assistance from the EU, and EU/EC cooperation with Israel is therefore limited. It is active, though, in the fields of civil society promotion, mostly under the umbrella of the EU Partnership for Peace Programme and the European Initiative for Democracy and Human Rights, and also concerning regional MEDA programs.

The Strategy Paper becomes explicit when it comes to the conflict with the Palestinians. The paper criticizes the building of the separation barrier by the Israeli government and points to the fact that this fence is partly built on occupied Palestinian land. It also expresses concerns regarding human rights violations in the context of the Israeli-Palestinian conflict (see ibid.).

The ENP Progress Report for Israel was published in 2006. In accordance with the previous policy strategies, it has a strong focus on economic aspects. It states that Israel and EU exports to each other were increased by 10.5% and 4.9%, and it lists concrete measures that were initiated to strengthen the partnership, such as the establishment of an Israel-EU Chamber of Commerce (see EC Commission Staff Working Document/SEC 1507 (2006)).

In political fields, the Progress Report also lists concrete projects that have jointly been conducted, such as a seminar on how to fight terrorism. The EU stresses that international law and especially human rights issues must be fully respected in the fight against terrorism, but also claims that it is ready to learn from Israel's experience in these fields (see ibid.).

The Country Strategy Paper and the National Indicative Programme for Egypt

The first relations between the EU and Egypt were established in 1966. Ten years later, a first Cooperation Agreement was signed, but only with the inauguration of the EMP was a deeper and more ambitious policy established. In 2001, the Association Agreement with Egypt provided a more specific bilateral framework for the relationship. It entered into force in 2004, providing the relationship with a broader spectrum of cooperation fields and a number of political and economic aims to be worked for. It is the legal basis for Egypt's relations with the EU.

The Country Strategy Paper provides a strategic framework for the cooperation. It sets objectives under the ENP, dealing with political reform and good governance, competitiveness and productivity of the economy, and socio-economic sustainability of the development process. The current Country Strategy Paper is made for the period 2007-2013. Against its background, the National Indicative Programme presents details on measures to be taken, results to be expected and financial assistance to be provided by the EU.

The Country Strategy Paper is prepared in consideration of Egypt's policy agenda, set out in its National Plan for the period 1997-2017 and the Five Years Plans, which describe the details. They deal especially with the improvement of the living standard and with questions of economic growth and investment. In its policy, the EU focuses on issues selected according to its own strategic interest, consistency with the Egyptian National Development Plan, relevance to the conclusions of the subcommittees on the implementation of the Action Plan, and a strategic approach to donor coordination (see EC/Egypt 2007: 19). Therefore, the EU names three key objectives for its strategy in Egypt in 2007-2013. These are: 1) enhancing reforms in the fields of democracy, human rights, good governance and justice, 2) supporting the development of the Egyptian economy, and 3) ensuring sustainability regarding social, economic and environmental policies (see ibid.: 20). The EU claims that all these objectives are in accord with Egypt's own development aims and that it especially finances Egypt's own policy priorities. The first objective is to be pursued through financial assistance, "in particular enhancement of the effectiveness of institutions entrusted with strengthening democracy and the rule of law, including legislative institutions. Assistance will be made available for reviewing and supporting the electoral system, for capacity building in civil society and for supporting the process of decentralization and reform of the local administration, including local elections. Civil society will play an enabling and awareness-raising role in these areas. Modernisation and development of public services delivery, including improvement of good governance and measures to combat corruption and encourage transparency, especially of public finance, are major priorities for

Egypt" (ibid.: 21). Regarding human rights, the Strategy Paper aims at strengthening the "culture of respect for human rights and fundamental freedoms, and the capacity and effectiveness of all competent institutions, including the security apparatus and the police, and at supporting formulation of a national human rights strategy by the authorities. Cooperation will be provided to support protection of women's and children's rights and to enhance the freedom of expression and independence of the media. Special attention will be paid to enforcement of protocols and international conventions related to human rights to which Egypt is party (on political and civilian rights, economic, social and cultural rights, women's rights, children's rights, torture, racial discrimination, the death penalty and the status of refugees)" (ibid.: 22).

In order to reach these strategic objectives, the EU comes up with a range of different programs and operations and the according financial means. The EU is one of the major donors to Egypt. Between 1995 and 2006, the European Community assisted the country with over one billion euros in various programs, especially in the regional and bilateral MEDA framework.

The MEDA program is the main financial instrument of the EU to implement the EMP. It is thus based on the Barcelona principles and has financed not only economic and social programs but also programs on human rights and democracy that are part of the National Indicative Program with Egypt (and other Mediterranean partners). In the MEDA framework, the promotion of human rights is established as one principle of European policy in the Nice Charter on Fundamental Rights of December 2000 (see EC 2000/C 364/1). The Commission's Communication one year later on the "European Union's Role in Promoting Human Rights and Democratisation in Third Countries" (COM (2001) 252 final), specifies these objectives. Article 2 MEDA regulations stipulates that measures include the strengthening of democracy, respect for and defense of human rights, and the promotion of good governance through supporting key institutions and key protagonists in civil society (see Council 1488/96, amended by EC 780/98: Art. 3). If there is a violation of respect for democratic principles, the rule of law, human rights or fundamental freedoms, appropriate measures may be decided upon by the Council (see ibid.: Art. 16). MEDA includes some regional programs, such as the Regional Indicative Programme (RIP) to promote human rights on a regional level. Moreover, the European Initiative for Democracy and Human Rights (EIDHR) was established in 1994 in order to promote human rights in third countries by funding activities of NGOs and of international organizations. Providing 100 million euros for worldwide activities, the EIDHR was designed as complementary to MEDA programs. While MEDA mainly works through government channels and often takes place in a bilateral framework, the EIDHR worked directly with civil society organizations (see COM (2003) 294 final: 10). The special MEDA line for democracy promotion was fused with the EIDHR.

As a reaction to the attacks of September 11, 2001, the Valencia Euro-Mediterranean minister meeting one year later insisted on a greater emphasis on good governance and democracy, deciding to launch the "Anna Lindh Euro-Mediterranean Foundation for the Dialogue of Cultures" in order to promote these aims through creating better understanding and dialogue between the peoples of the Mediterranean.

On January 1, 2007, the European Instrument For Democracy and Human Rights was established, replacing the European Initiative for Democracy and Human rights (EIDHR) that expired on December 31, 2006. It was designed to simplify the regulatory architecture of external assistance and to be more strategic and flexible than the EIDHR was. As it acts on the assumption that democracy and human rights are inextricably linked and need to be pursued together, it takes an according form as a thematic program. Its key objectives are "to enhance respect for human rights and fundamental freedoms where they are most at risk and provide support and solidarity to victims of repression or abuse" and "to strengthen the role of civil society in promoting human rights and democratic reform, in supporting conflict prevention and in developing political participation and representation" (EC COM (2006) 23 final). Democratization is seen as a process that may take time, whereas human rights are regarded as values that have immediate relevance on an international level (see EC COM (2006) 354 final/2006/0116 (COD): 9). As they are issues of global concern, they should be pursued in a thematic program that is not geographically limited (see ibid.: 26). That means that the ENP and the human rights programs in Egypt are embedded in a broader approach that is one of the core policies of the EU.

Financing is provided by the EIB to Egypt, mainly for energy, transport, small and medium enterprises and environmental projects (see EC/Egypt 2007: 15). Most of the financial assistance in the period 2007-2013 falls under the National Indicative Programme, which is designed above all to enhance reforms in the Egyptian political system. Through the European Neighbourhood and Partnership Instrument, the EU supports the implementation of the Strategy Paper and the Action Plan with 558 million euros. As it is expected that this will also help attract lending for investment of an estimated 250 to 300 million euros, the total value of the Commission support is about 800 million euros for 2007 to 2010.

Measures for the support of political development, decentralization and good governance are financed by 13 million euros. These are spent in order to increase the number of registered voters and participation in elections, to achieve greater participation of citizens in local decision-making, to improve the provision of services at a local level, to reduce the social and economic gaps between the governorates and to improve administrative processes in general (see EC/Egypt 2007: 28). The total budget planned for the promotion and protection of human rights is 17 million euros. It should help to consolidate a strategy for the protection of human rights, to increase the capacity of civil society organization to contribute to the political, social, economic and environmental debate, and to help women get into the labor market and make their voices be heard in society and politics (see ibid.: 30).

Another 10 million euros are allocated to the modernization of the administration of justice and the enhancement of security. This includes the training of the justice administration personnel and of capacity building in this field, increasing the access of citizens to justice, decreasing of court backlogs, and a dialogue with Egyptian administration and government on migration-related issues (see ibid.: 31).

In summation, that the emphasis on promoting civil society has become much stronger on account of the above initiatives. The recent Action Plans for Egypt also clearly reflect development issues.

7.4   The examined project in Israel: the EU Partnership for Peace Programme

One of biggest civil society programs of the European Union in Israel is the so-called EU Partnership for Peace Programme. It is not an integral part of the ENP but a special, focused measure to promote peace in the area. Nevertheless, it is based on the Barcelona aims and is in line with the ENP and serves as an instrument to fulfill the goals of the Action Plan (see EC/Euromed 2006: 19).

Before 1998, the European Commission supported a number of People to People Programs under different programs and budget lines, such as the MEDA Micro Actions or MEDA Democracy. The starting point for all of these programs was a development aid approach. Each EU Delegation could propose certain projects to Brussels, and the headquarters there would decide about their promotion. With the 1998 Luxembourg Declaration and the reform of the Commission, the different approaches were unified in the People to People Program. In the EU framework, this meant a de-concentration and a shift of

179

responsibilities from Brussels to the Delegations. The People to People Program was designed as a civil society program: during the time of the peace process, Israeli and Palestinian government officials would be in touch with each other and promote common interests, such as tourism. This dialogue stopped even before the second Intifada, however. Thus, the EU approach was then to create a program that would involve Jewish and Arab civilian societies. A dialogue on the grassroots level should be kept on going, even in times of silence between the political counterparts.

The first project of the People to People Program was carried out in 1999. It was connected to the MEDA-framework only with regard to its financial resources. All Barcelona countries could apply to it. The specific People to People Program was therefore created in order to bring these activities under a common roof and focus on peace projects (see EC 2000: 2). According to the EC, it could become a vital instrument to transform the aims of the Barcelona Declaration in particular, and the goal of peace in the Middle East in general, into projects on the ground (see ibid.). Therefore, it was based on the Barcelona Declaration, which aims at "turning the Mediterranean basin into an area of dialogue, exchange and co-operation guaranteeing peace, stability and prosperity" (EC 2008: http://ec.europa.eu/external_relations/euromed/bd.htm). These aims should be reached through "strengthening of democracy and respect for human rights, sustainable and balanced economic and social development, measures to combat poverty and promotion of greater understanding between cultures, which are all essential aspects of partnership" (ibid.).

The People to People Program was heavily criticized, however, its assumption that entire societies could be brought closer to each other seemed illusionary. Therefore, it was decided to concentrate on more specific issues. The People to People Program was transformed into the Partnership for Peace Program in 2002 (see EC/Euromed 2006: 20). It was designed exclusively for the Israeli-Palestinian conflict

180

with the inclusion of neighboring Jordan. Therefore, it supports peace-related initiatives only.

7.4.1 The objective of the Partnership for Peace Programme

According to the European Union the "overall objective of the EU Partnership for Peace Programme is for the EU to work jointly with civil society organizations to build conflict transformation capacities within societies in order to help re-create the conditions for re-launching the peace process and provide a solid foundation for a just and lasting peace in the Middle East. The creation of a sustainable process to reach a just peace relies both on strengthening and increasing direct civil society relationships and co-operation based on equality and reciprocity between Arabs and Israeli societies, including the Arab-Palestinian minority in Israel. (…). The program aims to support initiatives assisting in areas which are likely to have an impact on people's everyday life by including less-politicized, more practical actions, which will aim to rebuild mutual trust through reconciliation, build capacity for conflict resistance, empower marginalized parties and launch joint development policies and strategies. These initiatives should broaden the basic support for the Middle East peace process through promoting communication, and understanding by demonstrating the advantages of working for mutual benefits and tangible results" (EC 2005a: 3).

In this framework, the EU has set up six major priorities. These are:

1) Embedding a range of alternative mechanisms for handling disputes

2) Educating communities about concepts and skills for dealing with conflict and promotion of peace

3) Supporting marginalized groups in achieving a positive voice in society

4) Opening the political space for political discussions among conflicting groups

5) Clarifying issues that will need to be settled in permanent status negotiations

6) Complementary development actions (see ibid. et seq.).

The first priority aims to promote initiatives that spread capacities for handling disputes and especially teach them to community leaders, supporting programs that increase these capacities and even are innovative enough to find new mechanisms for conflict resolution. According to the EU, conflict resolution means avoiding conflicts as well as handling them in a peaceful and just way. As examples for such programs, the EU mentions "training sessions; courses; media presentations; common activities; people to people exchanges; outside experts; on-line materials; simulations; development of materials; case studies; internships" (ibid.: 3).

The second priority supports initiatives that promote dialogue at a grassroots level. These attempt to overcome conflicts through introducing people to each other on a personal level and through initiating dialogue and even friendship. The key elements of this work are spreading shared ideas or common interests within key groups or exposing them to cross-boundary experiences on the basis of shared humanity. Typical programs could be workshops and training sessions, especially with blocker or veto communities to expose them to new concepts and the development of grassroots plans for community change (see ibid.: 3).

Thirdly, according to the EU program, groups are to be supported that are either marginalized or especially resistant to transformation in their societies. These groups are mostly found in regions that suffer due to the political situation, i.e. the Gaza Strip and the West Bank, especially Jenin, Hebron, Tulkarem and Nablus. Promoted programs should aim to empower weak populations, give them a voice in political processes, and fight against discrimination. Measures could be advocacy training, the promotion of social and economic development, teaching participation and media projects that help to give people a voice (see ibid.: 4).

The fourth priority tries to create space for alternative concepts in academic discourse and public discussion. The discussion of new ideas and non-mainstream approaches to deal with the situation of conflict needs a local, national and international arena in which it can develop and prosper. Instruments may be networking, simulations and games as well as reports and data gathering (see ibid.).

Moreover, initiatives are supported that help to clarify the issues on which the ongoing conflict is based. These are mainly the recognition of Israel, the nature of a Palestinian state and its borders, the question of refugees, the status of Jerusalem and access to natural resources. Initiatives may be active in data gathering, report production, conducting surveys and researches, simulation games, networking, conference organization and participation, and cooperation between experts in these fields (see ibid.).

Finally, a bottom-up approach is promoted in order to improve daily life. In these programs, hope should be created, and improvements should made be tangible in the everyday reality of individuals. The main tools could be joint initiatives between regional partners that try to tackle common problems together. The jointly developed concepts for a better everyday reality would promote mutual understanding for the situation of the counterparts and could create a dynamic of change and hope. Instruments could be "local need assessment teams, strengthening of stakeholders' analysis and negotiation skills, ad hoc action groups, city-to-city long term networks, business association cooperations, local projects for change, specialized surveys and analysis, the organization of thematic workshops with the participation of governmental and private sector representatives" (ibid.).

7.4.2   Types of promoted civil society groups

There are eleven types of civil society groups that are promoted in the framework of the EU Partnership for Peace Programme. All of these share the purpose of transforming conflicts and "provid[ing] a solid foundation at civil society and intergovernmental level for a just and lasting peace in the Middle East by strengthening and increasing direct civil society relationships and interagency/intergovernmental co-operation based on equality and reciprocity between Arabs/Palestinians and Israelis, including the Arab Palestinian minority in Israel" (EC/Euromed 2006: 19). The specific goals of each type and the techniques they use are different, though.

According to the information gained during the interview with Mrs. Meir of the European Delegation to Israel, there are eleven types of promoted projects:

1. Mutual Understanding Work

2. Peace Education Work

3. Conflict Resolution Capacity Building

4. Political Options Work

5. Cultural Identity Work

6. Embedding Justice and Peace Concepts

7. Empowering Marginalized Communities

8. Shifting the Environment of Threat and Intimidation

9. Crafting an Open and Positive Political Space

10. Functional Projects for Development

11. Projects to Empower and Build Capacity for the Programme for Peace Work

Projects in the *Mutual Understanding Work* framework aim to create cross-boundary understandings of shared humanity, shared interest, willingness for reconsideration and reconciliation, possibilities of dialogue and the desire for peace. The approach is to transform conflicts by enabling the combatants to get to know each other and understand the opposite side better and on an everyday level. The techniques that may be used for projects in this framework are dialogue groups, art and theater, common activities, and exchange programs.

Peace Education Work aims at spreading concepts and skills for dealing with conflict and for a promotion of peace within local communities. Leaders with influence in different local groups, such as youth groups, local associations, certain authorities or the media are chosen in order to embed notions of a peaceful social life in local communities. Instruments to be used are workshops, training sessions, programs designed for children or students, Internet presentations, curriculum development and diplomas.

The goals of *Conflict Resolution Capacity Building* are to diversify the range of mechanisms for handling conflicts. Again, influential leaders and decision-makers should become familiar with such new (as well as traditional) mechanisms in order to use them and to spread them within societies. It is important that grassroots organizations as well as leading figures in the communities increase their capacities and abilities in dealing with internal disputes, and in the long term also with conflicts with different groups. Techniques to be used are workshops, internships, courses and training programs, simulation models and case studies.

Political Options Work attempts to inspire decision-makers. Its aim is to prompt leading figures to consider alternative ideas that they have not thought of before. This is how circles of conflict should be broken and turned into processes that free the way for innovative solutions. Therefore, a database on which one can argue for alternatives is being built, and knowledge and ideas developed in dealing with other conflicts or in academic studies must be provided. Moreover, a network between the EU in Brussels, the Delegations and the conflict parties on the ground has to be established to make information, new ideas and innovative solutions flow. If a process of dialogue and conflict resolution has been launched, it is critical to be aware of changes that may threaten the ongoing process. The techniques that may be applied are data gathering, workshops, conferences, networking, scenario development, simulations, media campaigns, off-the-record meetings, protest groups and model games.

The fifth type of supported programs is *Cultural Identity Work*, which assumes that groups need to be empowered internally. The assumption is that the more assured people feel and the more confident they are regarding their identity, the more they will be able to speak to others on an eye-to-eye basis. They will be able to express their interests and also to understand the interests of the other side only if they do not feel threatened in their existence and their cultural, religious and social ways of life. Institutional capacity building, activities for retention of heritage and cultural forms, media representations of identity and self perception as well as avenues for expression of one's interest may be the instruments used to reach these goals.

Projects that are designed to *embed Justice and Peace Concepts* have the purpose of spreading basic values and concepts such as justice, pluralism, multiculturalism, reciprocity, the rule of law, civitas, tolerance, and win-win constellations. It is assumed that institutions and societies that believe in and practice these concepts are more likely to engage in peace building. Possible techniques for embedding Justice and Peace Concepts may be to work especially with blocker or veto actors and to make them familiar with these concepts. Furthermore, civil society and grassroots institutions should be empowered to work on these topics. They should be helped to develop action plans and campaigns in these fields. Moreover, workshops, simulations, and civic training are instruments that can be applied. They should focus on the legal system and help establish an alternative dispute process.

The seventh type is designed to *empower Marginalized Communities*. It is based on the assumption that a greater voice and participation in social decision-making strengthens minority and marginalized groups in resisting violent conflict and participation in early warning and mitigation. Conflict transformation is about empowerment, removing discrimination, shifting the structures of conflict that maintain asymmetrical power relations, speaking truth to power, building resistance. The techniques that may be used for achieving this aim are teaching of fundraising and organizing, advocacy training, workshops to teach participation and non-violent resistance, the support of economic and social development and the empowerment of vehicles to express one's voice.

The type *Shifting the Environment of Threat and Intimidation* aims at creating space for win-win situations and dialogue, with the aim that threat and intimidation in situations of conflict be reduced and replaced by positive engagements. It is important not only to reduce feelings of humiliation and destructiveness, but also to replace them with different and constructive strategies of conflict resolution. Techniques include training to learn alternative instruments of dealing with conflict, to identify the actors of hatred and to address them directly in order to break the circle of destructiveness, and to show that alternative approaches reach results and that the initiation of compromise is not a sign of weakness.

The ninth type, *Crafting an Open and Positive Political Space*, attempts to broaden and deepen the political space, so that discussions and ideas that have been suppressed may find room. Discussing and creating alternative ideas on a local, national and international level can make the actors understand each other and change their internalized behaviors of conflict. Such an enlargement of the political space can only take place on the basis of trust and regularity. If alternative ideas are not taken seriously and are not regarded as realistic, the old schemes of conflict will persist. Techniques to be applied can be the establishment of agreed principles, procedures that create transparency and lead to trust, fair and regular elections, and pressure from external actors.

Supporting *Functional Projects for Development* is meant to transform the daily life of people and make them feel hope and an atmosphere of change and improvement. People should feel that their own engagement as well as the engagement of their counterparts makes a difference and improves their lives. To achieve this aim, people need to identify with the projects they engage in and enjoy changing their lives and those of like-minded others. Techniques to be used are local needs assessment teams that work with support from technical experts. To every project there should be a counterpart: a good example is city-to-city-networks, twinning, association connections, and supportive friends-groups.

Finally, *Projects to Empower and Build Capacity for the Programme for Peace Work* are supported. The goals are to make projects and institutions supported by the EU-Programme for Peace effective and sustainable. Techniques may be training, consultations and giving advice, capacity building, and the creation of networks between projects and people who have experience in similar projects.

7.4.3 Promoted projects

At the moment there are about thirty ongoing projects. Each project runs between one and three years. Per call for proposals the EC provides five to ten million euros. Each year about fifteen to twenty projects are chosen. The call for proposals is issued by the European Commission Technical Assistance office for the West Bank and Gaza Strip in Jerusalem. The proposals are sent either to Jerusalem or to the European Commission's Delegation to Israel in Tel Aviv. The decision about the approximately 200 proposals that reach the EU per call is made in Jerusalem. In 2006, there was no call for proposals because the EC was working on a new instrument for choosing the projects. About one third of the proposals to the EU Delegation are dismissed because of administrative reasons. These lack required documents or do not meet the basic criteria for being promoted. For reasons of fairness, only minor changes are allowed to be made in the proposals after a proposal has been handed in. Every proposal is analyzed by two evaluators according to a standard form. These evaluators come from external evaluation firms from Brussels; in Tel Aviv they get a briefing and write their evaluations. If the two evaluations concerning a proposed project differ extremely, a re-evaluation is possible. In the end, a EU committee decides about the proposed projects. There may be non-EU advisors taking part in the discussion, but the final decision is in the hands of the EU. After the call, groups have about two to three months until the deadline to hand in their proposals. The evaluation takes another two months. All in all, the process takes almost one year; mostly from September until June.

Before 2005, only projects were promoted that involved at least two different ethnic or religious groups. The aim was to get people together and to create understanding for each other's situation and opinion. In 2005, one-group projects were supported for the first time. In Palestinian society, projects were carried out to decrease internal violence and to create the ability to deal with conflicts peacefully. In Israel, projects with so-called blocker communities were especially promoted. Mainly, this was educational work in religious and Russian communities and in poorer development areas. Moreover, Jewish-Arab cooperation among Israelis was promoted. In addition, tolerance projects as well as minority projects found support. All in all, a certain balance has been considered: Projects should not concern only one country, ethnicity or religious group. In projects with more than one group involved, only one group signs the contract with the EU, and the other stakeholders involved are considered partners. The signing actor should be Israeli or Palestinian. If a European organization wants to lead a project, it needs to prove its suitability.

In the last seven years, most projects that were supported belong to the types of mutual understanding and of peace education. They mainly targeted students, youth, religious leaders and journalists. Moreover, there were a great number of projects dealing with specific political options to find alternative solutions for the ongoing conflict between Israelis and Palestinians. They involved mid-level political figures, academics and certain NGO leaders. In contrast to the mutual understanding and peace education projects, they cannot be called real grassroots projects.

Other types of promoted projects were hardly represented at all. These were especially the following types: Cultural Identity Work, Crafting an Open and Positive Political Space, Shifting the Environment of Threat and Intimidation as well as Empowering and Building Capacity for the Program for Peace Work.

The actors involved in the projects were local Palestinian (or occasionally Jordanian) as well as Israeli partners and the EU. In Jordan, the Palestinian Authority and Israel, over seventy projects were funded that reached thousands of participants and beneficiaries.

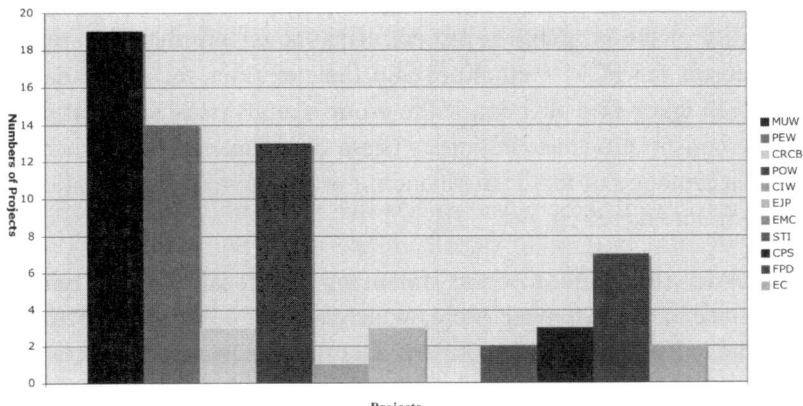

Chart of Distribution of Types of Projects

MUW   Mutual Understanding Work
PEW   Peace Education Work
CRCB   Conflict Resolution Capacity Building
POW   Political Options Work
CIW   Cultural Identity Work
EJP   Embedding Justice and Peace Concepts
EMC   Empowering Marginalized Communities
STI   Shifting the Environment of Threat and Intimidation
CPS   Crafting an Open and Positive Political Space
FPD   Functional Projects for Development
EC   Empowering and Building Capacity for PfP Work

(see Stanley 2005:12)

7.4.4 Financing

In the framework of MEDA the decisions to finance the different policy programs are made at the end of the so-called identification phase. Financing decisions are taken as follows: First, a quality assessment of the draft financing proposal is conducted, and then changes are made. This proposal is appraised by the quality support group, which may either be led by the Directorate Quality Support

Group on the level of the operational unit or by the Office Quality Support Group. The appraisal needs to assess the relevance and feasibility of the program or project. It has to ensure that the program is based on the PCM Guidelines and that previous recommendations have been taken into account. If the group's analysis is accepted, inter-service consultations are initiated. These consultations will either lead to the acceptance of the draft-financing proposal, to a modification, or to a complete rejection.

EuropeAid then submits the financing proposal to the relevant committee of the Member State, which is chaired by DEV/RELEX. One and a half months before the Committee meets to discuss the proposals, they have to be ready and are translated in that time.

If the committee approves the proposal for the program (or for single projects), EuropeAid leads the financing procedure and sets up the financing agreement in accordance with the approved proposal. The financing agreement should be flexible enough to allow itself to be adjusted to new situations while the project is implemented on the ground. Furthermore, it may be completed by a complementary contractual procedure in case that timeframe does not allow the inclusion of certain arrangements in the agreement itself. The final financing agreement is negotiated and signed between the European Commission and its partners. Governments as well as non-state actors may be partners (see EC 2004c: 24 et seq.)

The overall amount for one call for proposals in the context of the EU Partnership for Peace Programme is about 7.5 million euros. Not all of it must be spent if there are not enough appropriate proposals. A grant for a chosen program has to be at least 50,000 euros and not more than 500,000 euros per program (see EC 2004b: 4; EC 2005a: 4). This is in contrast to the earlier programs: in the year 2000, the minimum amount was 150,000 and the maximum 500,000 euros (see EC 2000: 4). In 2002 and in 2003, the minimum amount was 100,000 and the maximum 500,000 euros (see EC 2002: 6; EC 2003a: 4). A grant needs to be at least 50% of the total eligible costs of the action (see EC 2005a: 4). Moreover, "no grant may exceed 80% of the total eligible costs of the action. The balance must be financed from the applicant's or partner's own resources, or from sources other than the European Community budget" (EC 2004c: 4). However, the grant may cover the entire cost of the action if this is essential to carry it out. If that is the case, the applicant has to justify it in detail in the grant application form. "Nevertheless, if an applicant proposes activities that involve annual funding of more than twice its annual expenditures, it will be assumed that this is beyond the management capacity of the applicant" (ibid.). Applicants who do not keep to these financing rules may be rejected.

The overall amount for the Partnership for Peace Programme from 2007 to 2010 will be 20 million euros, from which 10 million is allocated in the first two years and the other 10 million is committed in 2010 (see EC/Euromed 2006: 53).

7.4.5 Evaluation of the People to People Programme

The most up-to-date evaluation of the ongoing program is conducted by a consultant for the European Commission (see for the following Stanley 2005), who states that the aim of the People to People Program is to achieve methods of conflict resolution—rather than repressing conflicts. Stopping suicide bombings or house destructions would not be enough, as it is a stopgap and not a transformation. As conflicts will come up again and again, it is important to know how to deal with them in a peaceful way. This means that behavior and attitudes must be addressed. Specific conflicts may also be solved through addressing their causes and conditions. For the EU, this means that their work has to be "collective, complex and holistic" (Stanley 2005: 3).

According to the evaluating consultant, this program's approach is correct, but the term People to People is fuzzy. There are various (also non-EU) programs that call their civil society programs People to People Programs, but some of them have very different aims. Moreover, the People to People approach is only one instrument in dealing with conflicts and building peace. Thus, the evaluation is built on the questions of whether the EU People to People Program is doing enough for its high aims, whether it fits with complementary measures that are being carried out, and whether it has created the critical mass to change things—in short: has the program been effective, and is it sustainable?

The evaluation report summarizes the success of the program in eight points (see Stanley 2005: 3 et seq.). These are:

1. Decrease in ignorance of the "other":

The evaluation comes to the conclusion that the attitudes and perspectives of many participants changed due to the projects. Participants in various projects got to know their counterparts. Not only did they learn about the other's views and attitudes, but they also learned how to get along in joint programs. Moreover, the concepts of pluralism and accepting different views were promoted in special programs via media and education in shared projects. This success is limited, though, as not all beneficiaries said that they had been touched by the projects. In addition, it is questionable whether this change will remain for a longer period and will also be applied in other situations than the project-framework.

2. Opening up of communication where blockage or gaps existed:

The evaluation comes to the conclusion that new connections of communications were created on a bilateral and multilateral level. New groups were created and started discussion ideas and opinions. In addition, old networks were restored. Only a small part of participants continued networking beyond and after the end of the projects, but this networks proved to be robust.

3. Good focus on veto (or blocker) groups:

Projects concerning groups that are not open to peace building are of the most difficult projects to undertake. Mostly, groups that are a priori open for dialogue and peace-projects are chosen for promotion, but veto groups are not considered. This is due to the fact that they are often regarded as "hardliners" that are too hard to convince and to win over for productive peace work. Nevertheless, some projects were carried out in the Israeli Jewish sector. The evaluation comes to the result that these were relevant and produced limited, but good results. It states that one would not have expected better results than these in such a complicated environment. Therefore, the projects are called successful.

4. A multiplier effect beyond the direct beneficiaries, which helped to decrease the ignorance of the "other" in a broader frame:

The evaluation record was not able to measure this multiplier effect and warns against overestimating it. Nevertheless, it states that it "appears that what was being transferred was a willingness to listen, to not automatically classify the other as evil or malevolent, a decline in suspicion, and a willingness to consider that the other was not a homogenous group" (ibid.: 4). The spillover effect mainly took place in families or among friends. A broader impact on a whole community could not be seen, though. The broader public has remained suspicious of its counterparts and the atmosphere of threat prevails. Most of the spillover effects were reached through mutual understanding projects and interfaith workshops.

5. Support for local heroes who take leading roles in peace building in a broader community:

So-called local heroes are exemplary figures for a whole community.

If these people manage to act in an alternative way that is different from the mainstream perception, they may cause a change. These actors cross boundaries and set examples in their brave otherness. Nevertheless, they need support in times of severe crisis and regarding divides that seem to be too deep to be crossed. The example of diversity and of fearless commitment to unpopular ways may impress communities. At least, it may show publicly that there are alternatives to the current way of thinking and acting.

According to the evaluation report, the projects of supporting such individuals found respect and appreciation among key actors in government and civil society. It also encountered resentments from many sides because of the polarizing effect, the opinion and way of life these local heroes represent.

6. Promotion of the concept of dialogue:

These projects act on the assumption that dialogue has to continue despite the prevailing tension or even war situation. Dialogue ensures that the partners will not lose each other completely during wartime and provide the way for a future peace. The key principles that the EU promotes in such dialogues are: mutual understanding and listening, belief in the possibility of cooperation and peace, rejection of violence, and a process to build trust.

The projects succeeded insofar as participants recognized the necessity of dialogue and contributed to it. Even though, concrete questions about how to create a peaceful Middle East remained open, but the main aim, to continue debating solutions, was fulfilled. The evaluation puts forth the criticism that dialogue should be embedded in a broader political frame with clearer objectives. Speaking with each other for its own sake is not enough. If dialogue projects take place in a political vacuum, the door is open for criticism concerning their usefulness and impact.

7. Spreading awareness, knowledge and skills for conflict management:

These projects are regarded as successful by the evaluation team. They state that notions and skills for dealing with conflicts were spread among key actors as well as in a broader community. Actors taking part in specific programs were business, sports and religious groups. There were also certain spillover effects from the people trained in conflict resolution on their social environment.

8. Strengthening the peace building sector by promoting diverse projects:

Peace building projects were one major focus of the program. Due to their intensive promotion, a number of diverse projects took place. In addition, partners' expansions and the deepening of already ongoing activities were promoted. Projects that had been established before and individuals that were already committed to the peace movement, but were suffering from a lack of financial resources and from harsh criticism because of the tenseness of the current situation, were supported in their work. Due to EU support, these projects and individuals could maintain and widen their influence and made their voices heard more loudly in society. In addition to already existing projects, the EU supported new ideas and approaches in order to make innovative and counter-mainstream notions heard. Most of these projects can be called successful (see ibid.: 3 et seq.).

The report finds nine points that need to be improved in order to ensure the success of the promoted projects. It claims that "the successes were significant, but neither sufficient nor all that they could have been" (ibid.: 6 et seq.). The nine points are:

1. Too many one-off activities were supported:

The evaluation report criticizes that too many projects were not able to create a long-term impact. Their design only allowed one-off activities that did not lead to a broader effect and did not have a multiplied impact on participants and institutions. This is mainly because of the fact that already while choosing certain projects, the program managers did not put enough emphasis on these questions and did not select projects accordingly. During this phase, they should already have attempted to include elements that would ensure long-term impacts. Also during the Implementation Phase, they should have stressed this matter and helped to establish mechanisms for sustainability. In particular, mutual understanding and peace education projects lost a major part of their potential effectiveness. Thus, existing opportunities were missed in a great number of cases.

2.   The program did not support long-term capacity building:

The above is also true for capacity building. Even though long-term success is a major aim of EU policies, the projects were not chosen accordingly and actors were not asked to include these components in their project proposals. Moreover, long-term capacity building was hindered by the fact that approaches or projects of weaker and not yet established actors were hardly considered in the promotion. They therefore remained marginalized, and the way for a broader change that would have included these groups and institutions was not established.

3.   The program did not establish mechanisms to regularly bring staff together for consultation, sharing, discussion and joint evaluation:

The program also lacked effectiveness because it did not establish mechanisms that would have brought the involved actors together on a regular basis. Such meetings are crucial for the success of the programs and also for the internalization of ways to work together between the different actors in the future.

4.   There was no mechanism to support risk management by partners or to evaluate the potential of unforeseen events on

projects:

Especially in the context of a tense region, unforeseen events do not only occur in exceptional cases, but are rather an everyday reality that one has to deal with. To create effective projects, the element of unforeseen events should have been included in the normal project framework. Dealing with such events and managing risks is a crucial part of ensuring effectiveness. The projects did not include these aspects on a regular basis, though. Contingency plans and up-front considerations should have been included in the projects in order to make sure that they would come up with the planned results.

5. There was no leading code of conduct:

For reasons of fairness, transparency and clearness, the EU, as the actor that intervenes in the fields of conflict and promotes certain initiatives, should have formulated a so-called code of conduct. In this code it should have stated its principles and concepts in dealing with the ongoing Israeli-Palestinian conflict area. It was not enough to formulate the aims vaguely or implicitly; rather, the EU should have formulated a specific code of conduct and made its aims and tasks in the projects visible a priori. This would have made it possible to better know and understand the EU's strategy concerning the projects and to take into account. its aims in the application process as well during the Implementation Phase. Without such a code, the EU remained the dominant actor with non-transparent strategies and aims. The lack of transparency did not allow the Israeli and Palestinian actors to establish their initiatives according to the EU's purposes and therefore is doubtful from a moral, cooperative and legitimacy perspective. If such aims and strategies are kept hidden, there is no equality and no shared commitment between the actors, but rather a structure of dominance and dependence.

6. The impact on the peace process on a macro level was too small:

The program succeeded only on a limited micro level. Certain individuals were touched and changed their attitudes and behaviors, but it was hard to perceive a change in the notions and programs of organizations. The peace process did not profit from the program, and it was impossible to find an indication of the program broader than appeared on a personal level. This may be a typical problem of such programs like these—however, it may have been aggravated by the fact that the program's design had not taken this perhaps most crucial aspect into account.

7. There was no strategy to develop spillover effects or sustaining impacts:

The program did not come up with a strategic approach to build, enhance and sustain its impacts. Even though there are evaluations and grid requirements, and the EU states its interest in sustainability, there was no aspect of the program that was concerned with broadening impacts and enhancing sustainability strategically.

Though there was a certain sensitivity among project stakeholders about the enlargement of the projects' impacts, this sensitivity was not channeled in a focused way and did not have the instruments necessary for a systematic approach. While the project staff may have ensured the effectiveness of the project they are concerned with, they did not consider a broader impact. This impact would have been created only by chance or the good luck of the project constellations— but it is more probable that it would not in fact have been created, as the constellations and surrounding influences of a project would not have been in favor of such an impact. Most likely, these influences would even have worked against a broader impact, acting instead to keep the changes created within the framework of the limited project. Especially in civil society projects, a broader influence could have been achieved if the project had taken the necessary measures into account. Instead, projects were designed on the assumption that the civil society would pass on the ideas of the project without further efforts of the project staff.

It was especially problematic that financing and planning capacities were not passed on to the local partners. These functions remained in the hands of the program staff during the projects, so that the partners did not gain the know-how in these fields necessary for further projects and broader initiatives. In addition, the single projects were not embedded in local institutional structures. Therefore their impact remained limited.

8. There was a lack of local stakeholder involvement:

Sustainability also was threatened due to a lack of stakeholder involvement. Local staff was only involved through regular interactions. The program itself was designed by the EC only, and local stakeholders were not consulted as a group. Also, while the program was carried out, local stakeholders were not organized in a way that would have allowed them to give their opinions and input into the projects. Single persons were consulted, but institutions, organizations and groups with formalized structures were not taken into sufficient account as stakeholders. There was no regularized method or even strategy of consulting stakeholders about the program and the projects. Consequently, stakeholders neither felt the necessary ownership of the projects nor acquired the skills and abilities to run the projects in the future on their own. More than that, the program did not create deeper and broader connections among the stakeholders. By ignoring and not consulting them as a group, the program missed the chance to establish a broader peace-minded community and reach out beyond the single individuals who already support peace building approaches. The dynamics of the projects were not used to create a broader ownership and did not contribute to sustainability. A better approach could have been to link the single stakeholders strategically in networks for regional conflict transformation and disrupt the limits of the small peace building community that already exists. Therefore multiplier effects were lost.

9. There was a bias towards the promotion of particular types of peace building projects:

In addition, sustainability was not attained because of the focus on certain types of projects. Over 50% of the projects and 45% of the money was attributed to either mutual understanding or peace education work. Together with political options work, the three mainly supported projects type made up as much as 70% of the projects and 60% of the money. This means that most of the support went to previously existing networks and concepts, and consequently that untried and less popular notions were not well supported or disseminated. Thus, the program did not manage to widen the range of its topics and lost the chance to develop mechanisms for sustainability (see ibid.: 3 et seq.).

The evaluation report comes to the conclusion that the program suffered from four major problems: Effectiveness was not assured, as the program dealt only with limited topics and was not conceived with a longer-term strategy. Rather, it concentrated on ad hoc projects without planning their future and working for sustainability. Moreover, the involvement of local stakeholders was very limited. Key tasks remained in the hands of the EC. Again, this threatened effectiveness and sustainability. Impacts were also lost because multiplier effects were not taken into account. Instead, projects were designed with an "atomistic nature" (ibid.: 10). Finally, projects dealt with conflict management rather than with conflict transformation. A long-term perspective was not reached.

7.4.6 Recommendations to improve the People to People Programme

According to the evaluation and the problems it highlighted, the Evaluation Report recommends seven main points to be improved (see Stanley 2005: 10 et seq.).

202

First of all, the program should be set up more strategically and consciously. There should be more time invested in planning projects appropriately and deliberately. A regular strategic evaluation would help to fulfill this goal.

Secondly, the immediate as well as long-term impact of the program could be enlarged by increasing the focus on capacity building. This should take place within communities, whether or not they lie across state boundaries.

In addition, it is crucial to keep in mind that peace building is a process. It cannot be achieved in single short-term projects that end after a limited time. Rather, the projects themselves are part of the process of conflict transformation. In order to anchor the objectives of the projects in a longer-lasting process, there should be mechanisms to include feedback and discussions of best practice between the different stakeholders in the projects.

Furthermore, sustainability is a major issue that needs to be integrated into the projects more carefully. Instead of concentrating on specific short-term aims, projects should provide the local stakeholders with basic skills and empower them. The evaluation report suggests distinguishing between concrete aims that are on the agenda and longer-term objectives. Concrete decisions should be taken with decision-makers according to the immediate political agenda. Transforming the environment of hatred and building a peaceful future is a different thing, and should not be linked to specific short-term decisions.

The work of the so-called local heroes should be supported more. It is crucial to highlight the achievements of these individuals and make them visible to a broader public. This could be done by certain awards, or publications in the relevant media or the Internet. One must consider, though, that supporting local heroes could endanger them and their work if it gives the impression of supporting bias. Therefore, local stakeholders should be consulted and integrated in possible award granting.

The EU should take care to support a broader range of projects. Mutual understanding projects are important and should be continued in the future, but other peace building approaches should not be neglected, and the proportions between different focuses should be more equal. Moreover, short-term political aims and long-term conflict transformation objectives should be unlinked and tackled separately.

Finally, local stakeholders should be better integrated into the program. There are several instruments that would help to ensure their participation. Progress could be made especially by the establishment of a formal advisory committee with an institutional set-up that would be consulted regularly. It should be involved in the program design, the project selection and the evaluation. Local experts should also be used for training and outreach toward a larger local community.

Above all, these kinds of projects require patience. Their results are hard to measure and will only become apparent in the long run. It is crucial, though, to set up projects carefully and continue checking their outcomes. Best practices should be identified and plans modified if necessary. The program's highest aim should be not to produce specific minor outcomes, but rather to make a broader difference that means to produce change.

7.5 The examined project in Egypt: democratization, human rights and civil society under the EC-Egypt Cooperation Programme

One of the most urgent priorities emphasized by the EU in almost all of its declarations and statements dealing with the Euro-Mediterranean relationship is the promotion of democracy and human rights. This policy gained momentum after 9/11 and is now a central issue in

Western-Arab relations. Despite the impression prevailing in the West that Arab states might be averse to more democratic governance, the discussion on reform is not new in the Arab world. One may or may not agree with those who cite the liberalist constitutional period under Ottoman rule (1870s-1910s), the period of parliamentarism under colonial dominance (1920s-1950s), and movements of political liberalization in the 1980s as examples of a certain history of debates on democracy (see Kubba 2003: 29; Menéndez/Youngs 2006), but without doubt the current policies are based on the assumption that the current lack of democracy in the Middle East is not culturally intrinsic. This argument of the "Arab exception" has been made by some who see a basic incompatibility between Islam and democracy (see Lewis 1990). In contrast, others blame current socio-economic conditions, colonialism and the years of Western-supported autocratic governance for the lack of democracy and point to certain democratic elements in Arab culture and institutions (see Piscatori 1991). The discussion continues (see Brynen/Korany/Noble 1995; Chartouni-Dubarry 2000: 55; Khader 1997; Salamé 1994), but Western politics are based on the assumption that change is possible and desirable. The EU acts on the assumption that "political reform in Egypt is not only crucial for development of the domestic process of democratization but also will have significant repercussions in the region" (EC/Egypt 2007: 20).

In 2002, the UN Arab Human Development Report made the lack of good governance and democracy the main topic and called for reform with uncommon clarity (see UNDP 2002). Also the reform of the Egyptian constitution prior to the parliamentary elections in 2005, the introduction of human rights reforms in Morocco, the Lebanese movement for an open Lebanon as well as the Palestinian elections stimulated the debate further. At the same time however, Arab regimes made headlines by undermining reform. Syria, Tunisia and Libya have not been willing even to pretend a will to reform. And Egypt has become a police state more than before, not only heavily cracking down on minorities but also fighting intellectuals, thinkers who are in favor of democracy as well as opposition leaders, such as Ayman Nur.

Egypt's estimated 16,000 non-governmental organizations are mainly active in the fields of social services. They have mostly very limited capacities and are subject to the restrictive Egyptian NGO-Law. All in all, one may say that democracy has not found its way into the region, but that structures remain more or less the same (see Feliu 2005: 368). The EC's Democratisation, Human Rights and Civil Society Programme takes place in this complex context. In the following, it will be characterized in detail. In contrast to the Israeli program, there will be no chapter evaluating the program. Due to the relative newness of the EC program in Egypt there has not yet been an evaluation one could draw on. The following information is based on the interview conducted in Cairo.

7.5.1 The objective of the Democratisation, Human Rights and Civil Society Programme

The program for Democratisation, Human Rights and Civil Society was established on May 7, 2006, with the signature of its Financing Agreement. The program started in November 2006 and will be finished in December 2009. It is a EU project implemented through the UNDP, the National Council for Women and the National Council for Human Rights. The project comes under the authority of the Ministry of International Cooperation. Efforts concern citizens' rights, strengthening of civil society groups and support of human rights. According to the EC, the main objectives of the program are "to support the Egyptian efforts to further consolidate governance in the broad sense; to support the development and implementation of institutions, policies and strategies that are in line with the relevant international human rights instruments and standards; and to increase the capacities of the Egyptian NGOs and of their umbrella organisation" (EC's Delegation to Egypt 2008: http://www.delegy.ec.europa.eu/en/eu_funded_programmes/program mes3.htm).

206

7.5.2 Types of promoted projects and groups

The EU uses a combination of a top-down and a bottom-up approach to set topics, such as human rights, on the agenda. The top-down approach attempts to enhance good governance through a direct dialogue with the Mediterranean Partner Countries in the various forums provided by the EMP and the ENP. These range from the lower levels up to the regular conferences of the Ministers of Foreign Affairs, which is the highest body of the EMP. In 2004, the Euro-Mediterranean Parliamentary Assembly (EMPA) was inaugurated in Cairo in order to link the top-down with the bottom-up approach. As many Arabic parliaments are non-authoritative bodies, they may constitute a link to civil society (see Marchetti 2005b: 48 et seq.). In this context, the EC Egypt Cooperation Programme promotes public institutions and business as well as the civil society and populations according to specific needs. Topics are political, economic and social reform as well as good governance. The projects are carried out in a classical approach of technical assistance used in development aid. In order to achieve political reform, activities such as the support of the General Federation of NGOs—a partly UNDP supported initiative—are carried out.

First, the EU helped to establish a Complaints/Ombudsman Office at the National Council for Human Rights with a 900,000 euros budget in order to deal with the great number of complaints about human rights violations it receives. The Ombudsman`s task is to monitor and assess the human rights situation in Egypt. He must also respond to the violation of fundamental freedoms and human rights granted in international agreements and declarations. Moreover, he must mediate between the Egyptian authorities and the citizens who are or who feel violated in their fundamental rights (see EC`s Delegation to Egypt 2008:http://www.delegy.ec.europa.eu/en/eu_funded_programmes/prog rammes3.htm).

Secondly, the EU supported the Ombudsman's Office at the National

Council for Women with 700,000 euros. This office had been set up in 2001 with EU funds. Between 2001 and 2006 more than 20,000 women turned to the office with complaints about discrimination and human rights violations. The Ombudsman's Office supports these women in their complaints and helps process them through to government authorities (see ibid.).

Moreover, other human rights programs in cooperation with the UNDP and in discussion with the Ministry of Interior and the Ministry of Justice were supported, especially the UNDP's activities in human rights capacity building. Capacity building aims at raising awareness among Egyptians about human rights and spreading information about their rights according to international human rights standards and the treaties Egypt has signed. People with key positions in Egyptian society, such as legislators, teachers, and NGO leaders, are targeted especially.

Finally, the EU supported the UNDP with a grant to help transform the General Federation of NGOs and Foundations into an organization that would be more open and participatory and more innovative and stronger in its actions when representing Egyptian NGOs in policy making. To make things more efficient and to increase the publicity of the organization, a volunteer unit, a coordination office and a complaint officer have also been provided for.

The European Initiative for Democracy and Human Rights (EIDHR) deserves a special focus when bottom-up measures are conducted. It currently runs 24 projects and has a total volume of 4.7 million euros. Implementation is delegated to NGOs over public bodies at a ratio of twenty-five to one in order to create a prospering civil society, which is considered to be a basic prerequisite for any democratic development (see Marchetti 2005b: 48 et seq.).

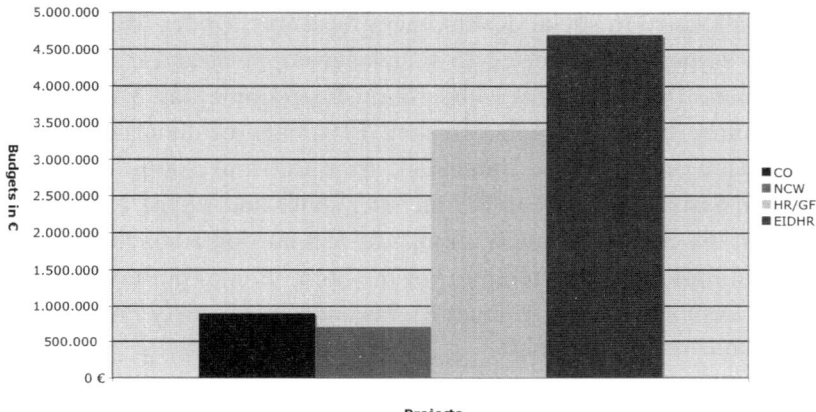

Chart of Budget Distribution to Projects

CO	Establishment of a Complaint/Ombudsman Office
NCW	National Council for Women
HR/GF	Human Rights/General Federation of NGOS
EIDHR	European Initiative for Democracy and Human rights

7.5.3 Financing

Due to its key political position, Egypt has traditionally received most of the EU's financial aid among the Mediterranean Partner Countries. There are two main periods of financial cooperation. Between 1977 and 1995, there were a number of four-year bilateral protocols amounted to 661 million euros, as well as loans of 806 million euros provided by the European Investment Bank (EIB). With the inauguration of the Barcelona Process in 1995, the system was changed in order to meet the Barcelona criteria and the Association Agreement more precisely. Instead of financing single projects as had been done before, large-scale programs in selected sectors are financed according to what has been determined in the Association Agreement. This policy continues up to the present. Funding was provided under the MEDA I regulations from 1995 to 1999 (686 million euros, which is 20% of total MEDA I funds) and under MEDA II from 2000 to 2006 (351 million euros). 115 million euros of MEDA I were allocated to social development measures. Under MEDA II 29 million euros were allocated to social development and civil society promotion. The EC Egypt Cooperation Programme has a volume of 812 million euros in grants. To that, EIB loans of about 2.3 billion euros were added in the framework from 2002 to 2006, as well as bilateral assistance between EU member states and Egypt. From 2007 to 2010, the cooperation will provide of 558 million euros through the National Indicative Programme. For the promotion of political reform, i.e. the Democratisation, Human Rights and Civil Society Programme, 5 million euros are provided.

8 Analysis of Europe's respective relationships with Israel and Egypt through the focus of compulsory power

The last chapter demonstrated how the EU's respective relationships with Israel and Egypt are laid down in basic agreements as parts of the bigger framework of the EMP and the ENP. Only elements of cooperation in political, security and civil society questions were included in the foregoing description—economic and technical elements were not considered. Moreover, it depicted the details of the civil society programs the EU promotes in Israel and in Egypt.

In this and the coming chapters, these elements are analyzed under the focus of civilian power. Where and how does which type of civilian power, i.e. compulsory, institutional, structural, and productive power, appear?

The first hypothesis of this paper stated the following: If compulsory power occurs, then conditionality, sanctions, and/or incentives must have been used. That means that in the analyzed elements of the EU-Israel/Egypt relationship, at least one of the three characteristics should appear if compulsory power was used.

8.1 Evaluation of the analyzed policies regarding compulsory power

8.1.1 Conditionality

Conditionality is mainly used as a management instrument to advance political reform. It is based on the assumption that it makes a party undertake actions it would usually not undertake or makes it refrain from certain actions it would usually undertake, and is thus both a means to limit as well as to encourage the behavior of actor B (see Feliu 2003: 96). It was introduced into the Euro-Mediterranean relationship as a strategy after it became clear that mere financial support would not automatically lead to spillover effects that would enhance democracy. Therefore, conditionally is a trade-off that takes place between the economic area and democracy, including good governance and human right issues. This concept is especially highlighted in the Commission's Communication on Wider Europe, where it is stated that engagement should "be introduced progressively, and be conditional on meeting agreed targets for reform" (EC COM (2003) 104 final: 16). This is visible in the case of human rights and civil society promotion, a field in which the interest of the EU and its partners do not necessarily go hand in hand—or are even opposed to each other.

After controversies between the European Parliament and the Commission, with the latter rejecting the EP's request for a legal mandate for the European Community on human rights, in 1989 the Lomé IV agreement was the first EU accord including a clear human rights clause within its body. With the Single European Act, human rights conditionality gained momentum. The EP used its new powers and refused to give assent to financial protocols with Turkey and Israel demanding reforms, even though no conditions had yet been included in the relevant protocols with these countries. The post-Cold War atmosphere, however, was generally in favor of human rights issues and even of their legal codification (see Fierro 2003: 65 et seq.).

Since 1995, all new Association Agreements, Action Plans, and agreements on bilateral trade and cooperation have contained special chapters or clauses concerned with human rights and democracy promotion. Originally, these human rights clauses were created to provide a legal basis for sanctions against countries that violate human rights standards. In addition, the Barcelona Declaration highlights human rights issues in its political and security dimension. Even though the Declaration is a legally non-binding document, it may be of legal significance because it may be used to interpret the human rights clauses and the sanctions connected to them in Association Agreements and in Action Plans. Thus, it does commit the signatories to keep to the Declaration's words via their Association Agreements and Action Plans (see Bartels 2004: 372 et seq.).

Even though the human rights clauses are not the same in every Association Agreement and in every Action Plan between the EU and the MPCs, one can say that three provisions are basic and appear in almost all of the Euro-Mediterranean agreements. These are first of all *essential elements*, secondly *non-execution clauses,* and third *appropriate measures* which the non-execution clauses provide for.

Essential elements

The essential elements clause states that principles of human rights and of democracy are considered essential elements and therefore must be respected. For Israel and Egypt, this is laid down in the Association Agreements. The clause for Israel says that, "Relations between the Parties, as well as all the provisions of the Agreement itself, shall be based on respect for human rights and democratic principles, which guides their internal and international policy and constitutes an essential element of this Agreement" (EU/Israel AA 2000: Article 2). Almost identically, but with a special emphasis on human rights, the EU/Egypt Association Agreement states, "Relations between the Parties, as well as the provisions of the Agreement itself, shall be based on respect of democratic principles and fundamental human rights as set out in the Declaration on Human rights, which guides their internal and international policy and constitutes an essential element of this Agreement" (EU/Egypt AA 2004: Article 2). This most important mechanism of conditionality in the EMP (see Schmid 2004: 404) means that the principles listed in the Universal Declaration on Human rights (UNDR) must be kept.

Lorand Bartels points to the fact that this form of creating essential elements goes beyond the UNDR, as it includes the principle of democracy. This has not yet attained the status of customary international law, and therefore constitutes a more ambitious obligation in the Euro-Med framework (see Bartels 2004: 374). Thus, the Israeli and the Egyptian Association Agreements with the EU include the full spectrum of civilian, political, social, economic and cultural rights of the UNDR, and they go even further with the reference to democratic principles.[1] These elements are emphasized and strengthened through reiteration in various speeches and in different other communications. Moreover, they are pursued through political dialogue. In its Regional Strategy Paper for 2007 to 2013, the EC claims that its policy "has helped to maintain and step up the domestic political reform momentum, not through external pressures but through political dialogue and strengthening of underlying domestic political institutions (…) Partner countries will be assessed on their progress in these reforms for the purpose of the ENP progress reports and for the ENPI Governance Facility (…) There are no specific EC bilateral or regional programmes that are aimed directly at domestic political reforms. However, a number of programmes aim to enhance the enabling environment for the development of civil society, the rule of law, justice and security, both at bilateral and at regional level—including some that are part of the present regional programme" (EC/Euromed 2006: 12).

Article 4 of the Israeli Association Agreement calls for a political dialogue that "shall cover all subjects of common interest, and shall aim to open the way to new forms of cooperation with a view to common goals, in particular peace, security and democracy" (EU/Israel AA 2000: Article 4). Similarly, the EU-Egypt Association Agreement states that "the political dialogue shall cover all subjects of common interest and, in particular, peace, security, democracy and

---

[1]   This is also true for the other Euro-Mediterranean Association Agreements, with the exception of Tunisia.

regional development" (EU/Egypt AA 2004: Article 4). Hence, the essential elements are defined as a common interest. In reference to that, they may be implemented through the establishment of a subcommittee. In addition, the Action Plans refer to these essential elements by setting objectives "based on joint ownership, common interests, reciprocal commitments, differentiation, shared values" (EC COM (2006) 282 final: 1). The significance of human rights and fundamental freedoms is emphasized several times in the EU/Egypt Action Plan (see ibid.: 2; 4; 6; 7; 9). The Action Plan also calls for a formal and regular dialogue about human rights and democracy in the framework of the subcommittee provided for by the Association Agreement (see ibid.: 6). For Israel, the Action Plan claims that "the EU and Israel share the common values of democracy, respect for human rights and the rule of law and basic freedoms" (COM (2004) 790 final: 1). The text mentions common efforts in pursuing these values several times, but does not call for a dialogue or even a subcommittee in this field.

Non-execution clauses and appropriate measures

Secondly, a non-execution clause that provides for appropriate measures is included in the Association Agreements with Israel and Egypt. For Egypt, this clause states that under the Agreement "the Contracting Parties shall take any general or specific measures required to fulfill their obligations under this Agreement. They shall see to it that the objectives set out in this Agreement are attained" (EU/Egypt AA 2004: Article 86/1). In case that one party considers that the other party has failed to fulfill these obligations, "it may take appropriate measures" (ibid.: Article 86/2). Concerning these appropriate measures, the Association Agreement states that "priority must be given to those which least disturb the functioning of this Agreement. The Parties also agree that these measures shall be taken in accordance with international law and shall be proportional to the violation" (ibid.: Article 86/3). Except for the reference to international law, the formulation is identical in the EU/Israel Association Agreement (see EU/Israel AA 2000: Article 79).

This non-execution clause dates back to the EU's trade agreements of the 1970s. It does not refer explicitly to the essential elements clause because it also applies to all other obligations of the Association Agreements. There has been an argument about whether the essential elements establish an obligation at all, or if they may rather be seen as a condition on which the agreement is based. In his legal analysis dealing with this question, Bartels does not come to a final result, but conducts his study on the assumption that non-execution clauses do apply to violations of essential clauses (see Bartels 2004: 378 et seq.).

As all parties, in this case the EU with Israel and Egypt, respectively, have signed the Association Agreements and the Action Plans, all of them make use of conditionality and are subject to it at the same time. One can conclude that all of them have used the instrument of conditionality. Compulsory power has therefore been exercised through one of its characteristics.

8.1.2 Sanctions

To impose sanctions would mean to actualize the potential provided by conditionality. Compulsory power would then reach a more severe level than by using only conditionality, which is a quasi-threat.

As stated above, appropriate measures may be taken in the case of a violation of the essential elements. These measures include sanctions. Cases of material breach or special urgency are excluded (see EU/Egypt AA 2004: Article 86/2; EU/Israel AA 2000: Article 79). The agreements do not go into further detail about the types of sanctions, but according to the historical origin of the human rights clause, it is obvious that "appropriate measure" could mean the suspension of any of the benefits provided for in the agreement. In its 1995 Communication on the Inclusion of Respect for Democratic Principles and Human Rights in Agreements between the Community and Third Countries, the EC names the following measures that may be taken in case of violations or severe interruptions of democratic rules: "alteration of the contents of cooperation programmes or the channels used, reduction of cultural, scientific and technical cooperation programmes, postponement of a Joint Committee meeting, suspension of high-level bilateral contacts, postponement of new projects, refusal to follow up partner's initiatives, trade embargoes, suspension of arms sales, suspension of military cooperation, suspension of cooperation" (COM (1995) 216 final: 17). What Israel and Egypt mean when speaking about appropriate measures remains unsaid, but one may suppose that at least some of the measures named by the EU are common diplomatic instruments used in cases of violations of agreements. The suspension of the Association Agreement and the Action Plan are the sanctions that suggest themselves most saliently in this framework.

The exceptional cases that are not allowed to be sanctioned are further determined in the agreements, and it is made sure that the appropriate measures are taken in accordance with international law. Except in the agreements with Israel (and Tunisia), this formula is explicitly integrated in all Euro-Med agreements. If a party wants to take appropriate measures because of the other's party failure to keep to their obligations, it must turn to the Association Council. This body, in which both parties have an equal number of voices, will deal with the failure. This process does not apply to human-rights violations, however. A party may act unilaterally then, without turning to the Association Council. In this case again, the formulation for Israel is weaker than the ones with the other Mediterranean States, including Egypt. For Egypt, unilateral measures may be taken in situations of material breach. For all the other Arab MPCs (except Tunisia), unilateral measures may be taken in case of any violation of human rights or of democratic principles. For Israel, this only applies to situations of "special urgency"—a term that remains undefined, however (see Bartels 2004: 384).

Whatever appropriate measures may mean, exactly, and whatever sanctions one may imagine, in reality none of the actors has made used of them in the context of the cooperation. Israel and Egypt have never taken any sanctions in this context against the EU. Neither has the EU made use of appropriate measures. It has never applied sanctions, nor cancelled or suspended Association Agreements or funding. Even during the second Intifada, when criticism of Israel increased in volume in the European Institutions and the European Parliament even called for a suspension of the Association Agreement with Israel, no sanctions were taken and the Association Agreement was never suspended. The same is true for Egypt: When the Egyptian government jailed the well-know Egyptian human rights activist Saad Eddin Ibrahim for his MENA-sponsored project on human rights, the EU did not take any sanctions and continued with its bilateral funding instead. None of the parties have used the appropriate measures provided for in the agreements. No sanctions have been taken. One can therefore conclude that none of them has used the instrument of sanctions. This form of compulsory power has therefore not been used.

8.1.3 Incentives

Instead of insisting on the negative mechanisms of sanctions, the EU rather pursues a more positive approach in its de facto relations. In its Communication on Actions on Human Rights and Democratization with Mediterranean Partners, it states that enforcing human rights as an essential element does not always require a negative or punitive approach. Instead, dialogue and cooperation may be used as instruments to encourage the partner to keep to human rights and implement them (see COM (2003) 294 final: 11). Thus, the EU increasingly puts emphasis on human rights and democracy issues in its communications, describes them in more clarity and detail and proposes conferences or forums dealing with them especially. The agreements do not reflect this policy shift, though. They continue to include human rights clauses as a basis for sanctions in the form of suspension of a part or the whole of the agreement.

More than that, the EU dangles incentives as rewards for good behavior: when MPCs meet specific targets, the EU promises deeper or further relationships (see Herman 2006: 373). And what may be even more interesting for certain states is the EU's open announcement of increased financial aid for partners that commit themselves to political reforms (see Calleya 2005: 15 et seq.). In the interview conducted with Christian Berger in Brussels, it became clear that it is part of the EU's strategy not to link economic cooperation and financial aid to political reform and civil society promotion, but rather to embed the latter in economic frameworks. Hinting at the saying that the EU speaks softly and carries a big carrot, it was also emphasized in the interview that this informal link is well clear to all involved parties.

The EU incorporates incentives in the pursuit of its aims and interests into the framework of the agreements. Israel and Egypt have not done the same, however. Hence, it is possible to conclude that this form of positive compulsory power has been used, but it is located only on one side of the actors and therefore is distributed unequally.

8.2 Tracing the exercise of compulsory power back to the political context

8.2.1 Conditionality

The former EC Director for the Middle East and South Mediterranean (DG External Relations), Christian Leffler, claims that "it is certainly not Europe's role or intention to impose the necessary reforms; home grown change is the most acceptable and durable" (Leffler 2005: 63). In contrast to this European statement, if one looks at the compulsory elements of the relationship, it becomes clear that there is certainly an element of force involved.

As not only the EU, but also Israel and Egypt have signed the agreements, conditionality and the right to take appropriate measure in the case of a violation of the agreement applies to all three. One has to take into account, however, that the agreements and the politics they promote are mainly European-made. This is more relevant for the relationship with Egypt than it is for Israel because a major part of the agreements deals with democracy and good governance—issues that are more problematic in non-democratic Egypt than they are in Israel (or Europe). However, neither Egypt nor Israel necessarily agrees with European perceptions concerning human rights. De facto, these are more threatening for Egypt than they are for Israel, and least threatening for the EU. Even though the EU has not used sanctions in its demand for democratic reforms and for good governance, some authors have emphasized that Egypt, or the MPCs, feel a certain threat that "behind the co-operative rhetoric is hidden nothing less than a European will to impose EU concepts on the partners and that good governance might as well be translated into the less co-operative concept of regime change" (Marchetti 2005b: 53). This perception seems exaggerated. It likely stems from the impression of general events in the region and has more to do with US policies than with the

ENP. Nevertheless, this perception reflects the compulsory element of the relationship, even if it is not actualized.

On the other hand, the compulsory power the EU uses is not intangible. Conditionality does not function if it is not conducted coherently and suffers from ambiguities. This is also true for the EMP/ENP context and becomes obvious in different aspects. First of all, there are internal inconsistencies from the EU's side and arguments about how to deal with MPCs when it comes to sanctions. After the opposition of some EU countries, the European Parliament was excluded from the decision to take sanctions. Only the Council decides with a qualified majority about sanctions after a suggestion of the Commission. The exclusion of the EP was intentional and due to the fact that the EP is known for its stricter stance on human rights issues (see Gillespie 1997: 35). Thus one political institution that might have insisted on taking sanctions was excluded.

Also, most benchmarks given in the EMP/ENP agreements, and especially in the Association Agreements and the Action Plans, are not exact enough to serve as clear criteria for measuring performance. The absence of clear objectives and precisely formulated aims is a clear weakening of compulsory power on the side of the EU—if one assumes that the agreements reflect the EU's agenda, as will be argued for in the chapter dealing with institutional power. All EMP member states are forced to sign and accept the potential aquis, for example,. They give their word that they believe in these European-set values and principles and promise to pursue them. As no benchmark system exists to check if and in how far the potential is realized over the years, the potential aquis is not "a guiding force of the Process" (EuroMeSCo Report 2005: 20), but rather a "rhetorical flourish" (ibid.). This matter was discussed prior to the Barcelona summit in 2005, but EU officials argued that more precise benchmarks were too difficult and also inappropriate to set.

More than that, it is not by chance that there are no concrete benchmarks in the agreements. Most MPCs did not like the fact that in the mid-1990s the focus on good governance and civil society promotion gained momentum. As they depended on the EU economically, they were not able to fight this increasingly important dimension of the Euro-Med relationship. Instead, they tried to limit or to neutralize these European efforts and were successful in avoiding the inclusion of too detailed objectives in the agreements whose violation could be seen as a reason for sanctions. A good example is the negotiation process of the EMP. Southern Mediterranean governments that opposed change insisted on not adopting the Barcelona Declaration if it was to be more than a politically non-binding document. Moreover, the MPCs managed to get a major condition agreed on and included in the Barcelona Declaration: the clarification that civil society activities must be launched within the framework of national law.

Also for Israel, it is true that most commitments, especially the ones in human rights standards, cannot be benchmarked efficiently. Terms used in the Action Plan are weak and do not ask for more than promotion, working together and exploring. Therefore, there is no demand for a concrete change in ongoing politics and no means to measure any outcome whatsoever (see EMHRN 2005: 9).

Furthermore, MPCs have managed to use a de facto veto about which civil society organizations may financially be supported by the EU. Theoretically, money goes directly to the NGOs by using MEDA (in this case the MEDA Democracy line) or the EIDHR. De facto, the EU is highly sensitive in taking its partner countries' perceptions into account. As the case of Egypt shows (for details, see chapter productive power), consultations are first of all made with the government. Money is provided to certain organizations only if the MPC government gives its say-so. This procedure has already become standard with Arab countries. It is not only a gesture of showing a will to cooperate and to discuss matters: the EU will not finance projects that its Arab MPCs do not agree with. This means that declared opposition groups do not profit from EU money. Neither are Islamic oriented or ethnic minority groups, such as Kurds in Turkey or Syria, or Saharawis in Algeria, supported. This Arab exercise of power reached a climax in 2003, when the Commission withdrew funding of opposition groups in Egypt that had previously been approved, because Egypt claimed that some of these groups were close to terrorist activities.

Furthermore, despite its agreements with the EU, Egypt has increasingly repressed civil society activities since the beginning of the 1990s, so that it has been hard for the EU to even find groups or projects that could be supported. As a result, for example, in the EIDHR promotion of 2002-2004, large sums of EU money remained unused at the end of the financing period. Egypt therefore de facto prevented the EU's policy of civil society promotion and violated the common agreements (see Johansson-Nogués 2006: 8 et seq.). Therefore, it is not only the EU that sets up conditions: the MPCs also manage to resist conditions—and thereby to set up conditions themselves.

8.2.2   Sanctions and Incentives

It is obvious that even if benchmarks are set clearly enough, and MPCs do not reach them, there will be no serious political impact. Neither side has made use of sanctions. In the case of incentives, it is only the EU that exercises compulsory power. This reflects Europe's perception that it may have more to offer to Egypt or Israel than the latter have to offer to the EU. It promises deeper relations that may go hand in hand with more financial means. In addition, financial incentives have been given on the basis of a separate evaluation of a country's performance. As benchmarks are not set clearly and financial support does not only depend on governance reform but also on a series of other factors, such as a country's strategic regional importance, incentives are not very credible for many countries. These countries also may ponder the benefits they will receive in return for the reforms they have to make—and may decide that it's not worth it. Rather, they may try to gain financial support by cooperating in other fields. That means that if the EU presses its agenda too hard, the MPCs may no longer be willing to cooperate—no matter what financial support the EU promises. The EU therefore depends on a certain supportive framework of within the MPCs. It cannot afford the impression that it interferes in the internal affairs of the MPCs and thereby disregards their autonomy (see Marchetti 2005b: 54).

Besides that, the EU's reluctance to use rewards and sanctions causes a credibility gap concerning the question of how serious the EU is in its demands. MPCs may (and do) suspect that the EU is not sure about its own policies and does not mean what it is saying: out of fear of weakening more or less West-friendly regimes like Egypt, the EU does not insist on reforms and human rights issues. More paradoxically, the EU has increased financial aid to certain countries that fare increasingly poorly in good-governance and human rights issues (see Youngs 2006; ibid. 2008: 3). Elisabeth Johansson-Nogués highlights the case of Morocco and Egypt: the better Morocco was doing in terms of good governance and allowing civil society organizations to work quite freely, the less money and technical support was allocated to these organizations. By contrast, Egypt, being increasingly illiberal and cracking down on oppositional groups (see Brownlee 2003), received more attention, technical and financial aid (see Johansson 2006: 9). Moreover, the fear of terrorism has caused the EU to cooperate with regimes that crack down on minority groups (among these Islamist fundamentalists) rather than to press them to keep to human rights standards.

The MPCs are very aware of this logic and of the lack of consistency in European policymaking. Moreover, the incentives the EU offers are badly defined and not strong enough for authoritarian regimes to be worth giving up on undemocratic practices (see Del Sarto/Schumacher

2005: 19; Tovias 2006: 206), especially as the EU is not consistent in granting any of the promised rewards (see Youngs 2008: 10). Therefore, there is not only a lack of power on the EU side, but rather an advantage in power on the MPC side. They "have been skillful in deflecting reform pressure playing the counter-terrorism card" (Menéndez/Youngs2006:http://www.ipri.pt/artigos/artigo.php?ida=10 9). The EuroMeSCo Report even states that "under the pretext of fighting terrorism, and based on a very wide interpretation of the term, most countries adopted measures and legislation that were used to repress internal political opposition, limit freedom of religion and expression, discriminate minorities, and to legitimate torture and deny the right to an equitable and fair trial, among other problems. Progress in cooperation in the fight against terrorism within the EMP can therefore only be observed at a declaratory level although even this has its value" (EuroMeSCo 2005: 60 et seq.). Bartels comes to the conclusion that "it might be observed that while the human rights clauses in the Euro-Mediterranean Association Agreements (EMAA) could have a genuine application, it seems that it is only with a significant change of heart on the part of the EU's political leadership that their potential can be realized" (Bartels 2004: 387).

Lastly, one may point to the fact that the short-term success of compulsory power may turn into a lack of power on the EU's side in the medium or long run. Conditionality, sanctions and incentives may work in the short term, but could have reversed effects later on because their approach is doubtful in strategy and content. The policy of conditionality and the system of rewards and sanctions creates the impression that democracy, good governance and human rights are burdens which must be borne in order to earn rewards and avoid punishment. Instead of making it clear that democracy and human right standards are values in themselves, the EU's policy of incentives makes them look like something MPCs must accept as a necessary evil in order to receive financial aid. This negative perception may be especially true for autocratic governments, such as the Mubarak regime in Egypt. Consequently, the incentives are a means of power for the EU. However, it is doubtful whether these means are chosen rightly and whether they will help the EU reach its aims. From a European perspective, it is unclear whether communicating democracy in a negative way makes sense in the medium term. Therefore, in this field, compulsory power may work in the near future but have an opposite effect in the middle-term.

8.3   Conclusion about the exercise of compulsory power

One can conclude that the EU exercises compulsory power, but that this power is limited due to a lack of coherent strategies and a number of design and operational inconsistencies. Neither Egypt nor Israel exercises compulsory power comparable to the EU's. For Israel this is less relevant, as its own motivations go hand in hand with the EU's aims in many cases, but Egypt feels to a stronger degree the agreements' conditionality and the EU's pressure for different policies. Even if Egypt does not succeed in exercising compulsory power itself by establishing a system of rewards and punishments as the EU does, it succeeds in resisting the EU's power and continues determining which reforms are undertaken and which NGOs are supported—and, even more importantly, which European efforts in these fields are shot down.

Regarding the whole picture, the EU exercises slightly more power towards Israel than the other way round. Both actors dispose of potential power due to the common agreements which both have signed. When it comes to actualized power, both exercise conditionality and neither exercises sanctions. Differences arise concerning incentives. Both actors have the potential to set up incentives due to their economic strength, but are thus also relatively independent when it comes to incentives set up by other actors. The EU is obviously the economically stronger actor. Thus, it succeeds in catching Israel's interest by coming up with economic incentives to a greater extent than Israel does regarding the EU. These results can be visualized in the following charts, which demonstrate who realizes civilian power in the two specific cases. It must be noted, however, that the charts simplify the results to a certain extent.[2]

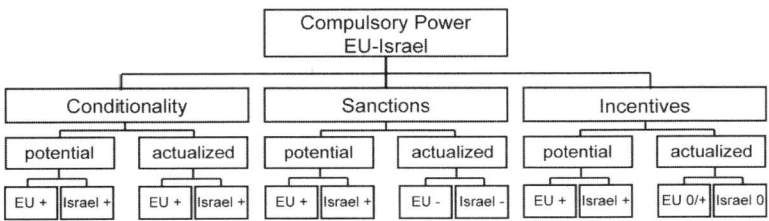

In the relationship between the EU and Egypt as well, both actors dispose of all kinds of potential power as well as actualized conditionality. None of them imposes sanctions. Egypt is less interesting economically for the EU than the other way round. This is expressed in the fact that Egypt exercises less potential and no actualized compulsory power when it comes to incentives. The EU's power in this field is limited, however, due to a number of strategic

---

[2]   A minus (-) indicates that no power was exercised by the respective actor towards the second actor. A zero (0) means that power was exercised but with severe limitations. A plus (+) shows that power was exercised by the respective actor towards the second actor. Moreover, a differentiation has been made between potential and actualized power. "Potential" means that an actor exercised potential power but does not indicate whether potential power exists absolutely. "Actualized" means that an actor exercised actualized power. This is also possible in a case where potential power does not exist, as it is not a gradation of potential power, but a different type. For example, one might hypothetically imagine that compulsory power is not included in the agreements, i.e. no potential power is exercised, but that the EU does exercise actualized power if it uses compulsory measures.

Finally, it must be noted that for certain types of power, not actors but networks (for example, of knowledge or significance) are decisive. Therefore— according to the type of power— actors may be referred to here only as parts of networks and not as actors in a dyadic relationship.

inconsistencies. Neither Egypt nor Israel exercises compulsory power comparable to the EU's. In the interviews conducted, from the EU's side it was even said that the lack of military means may increase the civilian power the EU possesses, as it is seen as less threatening and more cooperative and friendly—a fact that makes a subtle exercise of power easier.

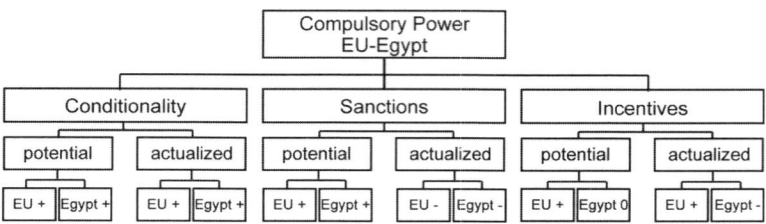

In the analyzed case, compulsory power depends on interests and values, the consistency of strategies, and the will to pursue announced measures and make them credible. Because the EU and Israel's interests and values concerning democracy overlap and only the EU's pressure for human rights is cause for friction, compulsory power is less visible in this case. With Egypt, an autocracy that lacks human right standards to a greater extent than Israel, compulsory power is more relevant. Egypt partly resists this power, though, by using inconsistencies and European fear of pursuing its policies with hard measures.

9 Analysis of Europe's respective relationships with Israel and Egypt through the focus of institutional power

The second hypothesis of this paper stated the following: If institutional power occurs, then bias in the institutional setting and/or agenda setting via the promotion or suppression of topics and/or agenda setting via the reconceptualization of topics must have been used. That means that in the analyzed elements of the EU-Israel/Egypt relationship, at least one of the three characteristics should appear if institutional power was used.

9.1 Evaluation of the analyzed policies regarding institutional power

9.1.1 Bias in the institutional setting

The EMP and the ENP are based on a complicated institutional system that reflects the particularities of European decision-making and is clearly determined by European actors. First of all, the EMP does not have its own secretariat. Instead, the European Commission fulfils this function de facto. An independent EMP Secretariat would include both sides of the Euro-Mediterranean Partnership, but in this setting only the European side is at the controls of the cooperation.

It is also the European Commission and the Council that prepare and follow up the work of the two institutional EMP Committees, the Senior Official's Committee and the Euro-Med Committee. The Senior Official's Committee is chaired by the EU, i.e. by its revolving Presidency. It works with the support of Senior Officials who are almost always European. European Commission teams in Brussels are responsible for the follow-up of the Barcelona Process, crucially determining the face of the EMP. A true partnership would have been based on a revolving presidency among all the EMP states, but here non-EU states are excluded. In the last years, a slight change has taken place: Senior Officials that prepare common declarations are encouraged to get in touch with the southern partners and take their views into account. This is not a must, however, and it is only a minor development, even more as it is only an item of advice and not officially linked to institutional procedures. More important, this development was not pushed for because of criticism or encouragement from the MPCs, but came from the European side, namely the then Dutch Presidency. Therefore, even changes that have the objective of lessening the asymmetry between the sides are European-made. Practically all EMP and EMP-related meetings take place in European countries. However, this is also due to the fact that most Arab states refuse to hold meetings that include Israel in their countries (see EuroMeSCo 2005: 47).

Given these facts, it is not surprising that the institutional setting of the EMP is said to be Euro-centric (see Aliboni 1998). Dealing with the institutional asymmetry, or rather one-sidedness of the program, the EuroMeSCo Report even suggests creating a co-presidential system (with a rotating co-presidency from the South), a troika system (with the chair of the Ministerial Conference jointly held by the EU Presidency, a coordinator for the Arab countries and either Israel or Turkey on a rotating basis) (see EuroMeSco 2005: 11, 50). Not surprisingly, suggestions like this have not borne fruit.

Moreover, the institutional setting has been criticized for its lack of transparency and inefficiency. Some reforms have helped to improve things. For example, the MEDA management system now functions better in disbursing aid, and the creation of EuropeAid managerial units as well as the decentralization process from the Commission's delegations have improved processes (see ibid.: 47).

Nevertheless, the EMP structure can only be called asymmetrical. The only existing institution with an equal north-south representation is the EMPA, a forum that was created in 2004 to bring the EMP closer to the people. It may also become active as an adviser and monitor for the EMP. Until today, the EMPA has not been able to influence the EMP or to provide expertise that would change the agenda. It is not able to monitor the EMP in any important matter and also has not helped to improve the EMP's visibility. It remains a powerless forum.

Thus, one can conclude that MPCs do not contribute significantly to the EMP through institutional procedures, due to the European-made setup of the EMP. It is mainly the EU that exercises this form of institutional power through the setting of the EMP.

9.1.2 Agenda setting via the promotion or suppression of topics

The fact that the EU dominates the institutional setting of the EMP goes together with forms of agenda setting. The EU regularly may determine the subjects to be discussed and those to be excluded from the agenda. Not only is it inherent in the institutional setting of the EMP, but the EU also tries to spread its ideas prior to signing agreements with its partners and thus exercises pressure on them.

A good example of this is the organization of a seminar on "European Neighbourhood Policy: Human rights in EU-Egypt" in Cairo on January 26-27, 2006. It was organized by the Euro-Mediterranean Human rights Network (EMHRN) in cooperation with the Cairo Institute for Human Rights Studies (CIHRS) prior to the setting up the Action Plan. The EMHRN is a network of about eighty human rights organizations and individuals of thirty countries in the Euro-Mediterranean region. Due to its self-description, it "aims at developing and strengthening partnerships between NGOs in the Euro-Mediterranean region and facilitating development of mechanisms for protecting and promoting human rights, for democratic reform, and for disseminating the values of human rights as well as generating capacity in this regard" (EMHRN 2006: 8). The CIHRS is an Egyptian NGO that was established in 1994 and works for the promotion of human rights in Egypt. It has a consultative status for the UN Economic and Social Council and the African Commission on Human and People's Rights.

Tellingly, the seminar was inaugurated by the Austrian Ambassador to Egypt, with Austria then being the EU Presidency. Representatives of the European Commission, as well as of European Countries (UK, Austria, France, Netherlands, Sweden), attended the seminar—but representatives of the Egyptian government refrained from attending even though they had been invited. About seventy people attended the seminar, not only EU or European officials and Egyptian NGOs but also civil society representatives from Jordan, Tunisia, Morocco, Lebanon, Palestine, Ukraine and France. The aim of the seminar was to ask civil society organizations for their opinion on the Action Plan in order to make their voices heard in the then ongoing political consultations about the Action Plan. The four main topics discussed were EU-Egyptian relations in the EMP regarding democratization and human rights issues, the experience gained in establishing Action Plans in Central and Eastern European countries, and how to make human rights and democratization issues heard during the negotiations of the Action Plan. Finally, NGOs gave recommendations on how to draft and implement the Action Plan. Of special interest was the criticism during the seminar that the reference to "common values," which appears again and again in EMP and ENP documents, should be avoided—or rather, that these values should be named and made concrete. Only if both sides agreed about what is meant by "common values" would it be possible to refer to and insist on them (see ibid.: 8 et seq.). Also meaningful was the fact that no government officials attended the seminar. They refused to take part in the conversation on human rights issues and made it clear that these issues were not in their interest and that there was nothing to talk about.

A second example of attempts to influence and resist the agenda is the Barcelona Conference of November 27-28, 2005, which has gained fame. Despite the MPCs' internal division and their failure to find a way to concentrate their interests and work together in a more promising way, they displayed a remarkable sign of interest during Barcelona. This conference was set up as a summit in order to mark the ten-year anniversary of the EMP. It was jointly planned by the then EU Presidency Great Britain with Spain as the host country. Even the preparations were accompanied by plenty of attention from the media and the public. Expectations were high, and there was a certain hope that the summit could bring about a rapprochement between Ariel Sharon and Mahmoud Abbas. Therefore, the beginning of the conference was already an éclat: All the EU countries were represented at the highest level (barring Luxembourg). In contrast, however, not one single Arab country sent its most senior representative. Despite some excuses for the absences, it was obvious that the absence was not only a lack of interest or the decision to deal with other matters, but rather a clear political statement.

Except for President Bouteflika of Algeria, who was in hospital in Paris, none of the MPC heads of state had an excuse that could have held up to diplomatic scrutiny. King Abdullah of Jordan and President Hosni Mubarak of Egypt preferred to stay at home and to deal with internal affairs, and as did Israel's prime minister, Ariel Sharon. President Bashar Al-Assad of Syria and President Emile Lahoud of Lebanon preferred not to show up because of criticism for their lack of cooperation in the Hariri investigations. Morocco, Tunisia and Libya (as an observer) did not find the summit important enough and did not expect any outcome that would have justified their personal attendance. Some sent their apologies only at the last minute, while others, such as King Mohamed VI of Morocco (who had gone to visit Japan), already had other plans in advance. One can conclude that the MPCs' rulers were not willing to attend a summit whose outcomes were unclear and not necessarily favorable for their countries and their politics, and which would make human rights violations and Middle

Eastern conflicts a topic. Therefore, the word of the Arab boycott made the rounds and marred the history of the EMP and the already fragile relationship (see Gillespie 2005: 272).

The absence of the senior Arabic and Israeli rulers was even more blatant as, especially as the European side was present on the highest political level, with the heads of state of Germany, France, Italy and Britain in attendance. Due to the high expectations and the media coverage that had already accompanied the summit in advance, the atmosphere was one of disappointment and tension.

The éclat of this summit suggests that the EMP is a project dominated by European interests so much that Arab leaders simply step back from it. This is, of course, not an official withdrawal from the agreements. Rather, one can assume that it is an inner withdrawal that comes to light through a lack of interest and a lack of active contribution. More than that, the summit showed that the Arab reaction is not only inner withdrawal, but even open opposition to the European-made principles and topics of the EMP. In this case, during the organization of the summit, security issues were already at the top of the agenda. These are typical topics of European interest that regularly place the MPCs at a disadvantage.

The President of the Palestinian Authority, Mahmoud Abbas, and the Turkish PM, Recep Tayyip Erdogan, were the only non-EU heads of state who attended the summit. This was clearly due to their own interests. Abbas wanted to show his qualities as a Palestinian leader who is willing to play a constructive role in an international context, and Erdogan's attendance was a must in the light of Turkey's efforts to gain accession to the Union (see ibid: 273 et seq.).

9.1.3   Agenda setting via the reconceptualization of topics

A form of institutional power that is subtler and already touches spheres of structural power is the attempt to change the focus on issues. These issues may thus become more or less important, and may be dealt with in different forums and with different urgency. In the analyzed framework of the EMP/ENP this can be seen mainly in the fields of security. The EC makes this emphasis clear by stating that through "the ENP, the parties will strengthen their political dialogue and make it more effective. This encompasses foreign and security policy issues including regional and international issues, conflict prevention and crisis management and common security threats (e.g. terrorism and its root causes, proliferation of weapons of mass destruction and illegal arms exports). Areas of enhanced dialogue with each country will be identified in Action Plans. The EU and partner countries should also work together on effective multilateralism, so as to reinforce global governance, strengthen co-ordination in combating security threats and address related development issues. Improved co-ordination within the established political dialogue formats should be explored, as well as the possible involvement of partner countries in aspects of CFSP and ESDP, conflict prevention, crisis management, the exchange of information, joint training and exercises and possible participation in EU-led crisis management operations. Another important priority will be the further development of shared responsibility between the EU and partners for security and stability in the neighbourhood region" (COM (2004) 373 final: 13).

In recent years, several researchers have dealt with the question how and why redefinition in the field of security takes place. They have come up with the term of *securitization,* pointing to the fact that issues that were not previously connected to questions of security are securitized. The concept of securitization was developed mainly by the Copenhagen School. It began to be discussed after the end of the cold war (see Buzan 1991) and gained importance when agendas were reshaped in the aftermath of September 11 (see Gillespie 2003). Even though it is connected to social constructivist approaches by its basic assumption that security is socially constructed, it is nevertheless distinct from traditional discussions of security and has developed its own dynamics and ideas. Instead of treating security as an objective, it is regarded as the outcome of a process (see Williams 2003: 513). It may already be seen as a first basis for structural and even productive features of power, but differs from them insofar as it deals with setting agendas and changing informal institutions.

Securitization means to characterize topics as so threatening that they are to be put on the top of the agenda, as they require immediate actions. Thus, topics are reconceptualized in different frameworks and perceived differently, that is more favorably in terms of the actor's agenda. Not only does it allow him to determine the order on the agenda, but it also gives him the right to deal with matters more quickly and to determine the action to be taken in the case at hand. As Buzan, Wæver and de Wilde have put it in their trailblazing book on securitization, the priority of security issues is communicated in a way that makes us believe that "if we do not tackle this problem, everything else will be irrelevant (because we will not be here or be free to deal with it in our own way)" (Buzan/Wæver/de Wilde 1998: 24). On the other hand, a region that is not generally regarded in terms of security may fall off the map of world security interaction as a whole (see Buzan/Wæver 2003: 57). The Middle East is far away from such a dynamic, though. On the contrary: in the framework of the EMP and the ENP, matters such as migration are put in a framework of threat and emergency. Thus, an atmosphere of fear is created and it appears that a fight has to be conducted against the phenomena of migration. The topic then loses its human dimension. It is also not dealt with in an appropriate and thoughtful way because the atmosphere of alert makes it impossible to consider options more reasonably. Therefore, it has been argued that securitization lifts subjects out of the normal rules and procedures of politics and thus leads to their de-normalization. This limits the space for discussion.

Despite the EU's attempt to securitize issues in the Euro-Mediterranean framework, it is obvious that the EU has not been able to establish a wide-ranging and stable security dialogue or even to find

236

a consistent security strategy or focus on what its concrete objectives are. The EuroMeSCo Report lists three main stages that show how the attempt to make more headway in security matters failed: The first stage focused on developing a Plan of Action in the spirit of security cooperation and arms limitation. Confidence-building measures did not bear fruit in this typical field of hard security and were not continued after the assassination of Yitzhak Rabin in 1995. Except for an Italian-Egyptian cooperation in this field, most initiatives were stopped and no new ones have been launched in recent years.

Reflecting the failure in hard-security matters, in a second phase in 1997, confidence-building measures were renamed "partnership building." During the talks concerning the establishment of a Euro-Med Charter for Peace and Stability, it became particularly clear that confidence building did not work. The idea of the Charter was dropped in 2000 when tensions in the region were so high that more attempts in reaching security through confidence building seemed in vain.

In a third phase, a more pragmatic approach was adopted than that of the Charter. In 2002, the Spanish Presidency addressed specific fields of security cooperation instead of looking for a broad common ground. Topics were especially anti-terrorism cooperation, civilian protection, and non-proliferation. The Valencia Action Plan contributed to this approach in an attempt to reduce southern suspicions towards European security and defense issues (see EuroMeSCo 2005: 54 et seq.). One may conclude that the EU's civilian, institutional power remains limited in hard-security issues.

9.2 Tracing the exercise of institutional power back to the political context

9.2.1 Bias in the institutional setting

The EU represents a big weight. Economically, (as a whole) it outclasses the MPCs. Due to its structures, it is able to use established and practiced mechanisms of cooperation and internal decision-making. It uses the weight of its 27 member states and, at the same time, is able to channel its interests and to speak with one voice in the EMP-framework. It uses know-how regarding contents and functions that the southern regional unions do not possess to the same degree. The most important and even the oldest of these unions, the Arab League, is not even able to agree about its own regional matters. It is mostly unable to formulate common positions regarding regional and worldwide issues and often interrupts its meetings because of severe arguments and even insults among the leaders. The Southern Mediterranean is characterized by cultural, political and religious fragmentation. Despite several attempts to create a Mediterranean togetherness and to strengthen the region's influence, the region remains deeply divided, and there is no a single political or economic framework that functions (see Calleya 2006: 121). All the calls for Pan-Arabism, the attempts to find a way out of the economic crisis together, and the spiritual hegemony of Islam cannot conceal the fact that the region is highly heterogeneous. Not only has the project of Pan-Arabism failed, but also up until today the region's leaders have not even been able to create effective and functioning organizations. This does not even take into account the tensions between the Arab states and Israel, but is already true for the Arab states in the region only (see Chourou 2003).

If one does not look at the EMP with its regional framework but at the ENP, then institutional asymmetry is even more blatant: Several single

238

states deal with one big actor consisting of a number of weighty national states. More than that, the EU does not only profit from the relative powerlessness of the southern partners due to their lack of organization and ability to agree; it uses this situation according to its own interests. The tailor-made Action Plans for each country show the gaps among the countries and create a certain frustration about who gets what from the EU's (financial) attention (see Marchetti 2005b: 53). The EU may use this jealousy as a stimulus to enhance its own goals.

It is obvious that this form of institutional power is weighted clearly toward the side of the EU. This is not only because of the EU's attempts to determine processes, but also due to the lack of cooperation and know-how on the southern side.

9.2.2 Agenda setting via the promotion or suppression of topics

The examples of the seminar on human rights in Cairo and of the Barcelona Conference in 2005 have shown that agenda setting is pursued by influencing the actors a priori as well as by setting up topics on the agenda itself. Some of the major topics dealt with in the EMP and ENP framework are democracy, good governance and human rights. The pursuit and promotion of these topics is one of the EU's top priorities in enhancing its relations with the Mediterranean Partners: "Above all, the disinclination of the EU to form a Euro-Mediterranean region has been demonstrated in its handling of the questions of democracy and human rights. The EU has included clauses concerning these principles in every EMAA in order to affirm its 'civilian nature'" (Tzifakis 2007: 55). The Arab Mediterranean Partners regard this mainly as a European interest that works to satisfy its security wishes. They do not share the European notion that the promotion of democracy and human rights serves them, too. Instead, in their eyes, this is merely a European standpoint that is forced on them and on their populations. Reflecting the EU's wish to gain more security through the EMP, it prioritizes the first EMP basket. In contrast, most MPCs favor the second basket and perceive the first and the third basket only as a necessary evil (see Jünemann 2003b: 8). Therefore, the EU's commitments in these fields have "frequently been regarded as external involvement in domestic affairs" (Marchetti 2005b: 51). The MPCs were not able to put their topics on the Euro-Mediterranean agenda and the EU has not managed to convince them of the profit for themselves.

But not only does the EU decide which topics are parts of the agenda. It also determines which topics are not to be discussed. On a political level, the Middle East peace process was excluded from the EMP agenda, which preferred the promotion of peace on a grassroots level only. This led to the fact that the Israeli occupation of Palestinian territory was removed from the agenda, and Arab countries did not find the agenda fair and did not cooperate in confidence and security-building measures (CSBM) that would have reflected the regional security problem as a whole (see Jünemann 2000: 74; Tzifakis 2007: 51). Israel also did not find itself and its interests on the agenda, its main political considerations being its conflicts with different Arab states and not social development and democratization. Israel considered the regional approach inappropriate and thus of minor interest. With security as a key interest, it was rather interested in military balances in the region than in cooperation. The separation of the peace process from the EMP made the EMP almost look ridiculous in the eyes of many Israeli politicians; neither did the Israeli public attribute significant importance to it. This kind of agenda setting made the EU, an actor that due to historical reasons and to its policies is often perceived as too pro-Arabic, even less credible in Israeli eyes (see Peters 2006: 230). Moreover, the progress of the EMP had greatly depended on the peace process. Therefore, it was an illusion to just remove the topic from the agenda and hope that it could be ignored.

In addition, other topics are not part of the agenda, even though they are of great significance for the MPCs. The most interesting example is probably religion. Religion is one of the most basic factors that determine the life, culture and identity of most Arabs and of many Israelis. Europeans, however, are widely disconnected from religious issues and regard them as not worth talking about or even embarrassing. Due to the separation of state and religion, they especially do not see why religion should be talked about in political forums. This leads to a complete exclusion of religious issues from the Euro-Mediterranean agenda (see Kühnhardt 2005: 91 et seq.). Instead, the EU promotes (human rights) values that stem from a typical European context, such as the freedom of the individual, gender equality, or non-discrimination against homosexuals.[1] Allowing religion and its meaning into the discourse on values instead of limiting the dialogue on to a European framework, would have led to a more fruitful outcome.

Regarding actions and topics, agenda setting is a tool located on the European side. Not surprisingly, this is regarded as an expression of power from the MPC side. In the case at hand the European Delegation felt this very clearly, as was expressed in the conducted interview. The Egyptian partners were not willing to accept every topic and only allowed issues in after long negotiations involving the conversion of the topic into more acceptable labeling and a more inoffensive format for the projects on the ground.

This one-sidedness of institutional power is not only a result of the EU's will to set its priorities and to determine the relationship, but also comes from a lack of involvement from the MPC side. The Arab side has been notably passive in giving input to the documents and papers that the EU (as well as national governments and NGOs) usually

---

[1]   As Cilja Harders has argued, the EU does forget about gender issues, however. According to Harders, gender is not only an issue in human rights questions, but is also decisive in dealing with security, as there are blatant differences among the exposure of men and women to violence (see Harders 2003).

241

produces during the political processes, for example, before and after conferences. More than that, the MPC side has produced no decisive papers or statements regarding the very basics of the EMP/ENP. Even at the end of the Barcelona Conference in 2005, MPCs were not involved in the final press conference. Instead, it was a European event only—as much as the final paper was merely a British conclusion to the conference (see Gillespie 2005: 271, 277).

However, the events at the Barcelona Conference in 2005 also show that overly unilateral agenda setting and a too obvious attempt of the EU to use the relationship for the pursuit of its own interests, is counterproductive. The EU's failure to at least suggest that the relationship was on an eye-to-eye basis or to create ownership of the agenda on the Arab side makes it lack power and gives the MPC side only one effective option of determining the agenda—simply not to attend. It is worth noting that the MPC's simple absence is a means of power, but a weak one. It blocks the European attempt to set the agenda according to its own interests and to criticize the MPCs for their policies. It does not allow the MPCs to set their own agenda or pursue their own interests, though. The MPCs are obviously so weak as a group of states that they do not even try to get their aims discussed in the framework of the EMP. One can conclude that "the EMP has come to be seen as a process in which the European partners develop initiatives and the southern partners either accept or reject them" (EuroMesSCo 2005: 47). This means that this form of institutional power is mainly located on the European side.

9.2.3   Agenda setting via the reconceptualization of topics

The EU clearly pursues a policy of securitization. In a typical approach of reaching one's aims by extending the agenda with the claim that a more secure environment is a number one priority that needs to be tackled urgently (see Wæver 1995: 51), it puts other topics in a context of security. Frédéric Volpi explains this with the fact that "the type of economic and normative regional development fostered within and by an (expanding) European Union can provide the impetus for a more secure regional community around the Mediterranean. This economic-normative process of reappraisal of the regional behaviour of states dilutes specific security aspects into a wider pool of policy initiatives designed to address what are perceived to be the root causes of regional insecurity—economic underdevelopment, poor governance, and so forth" (Volpi 2006: 123). Thus, security becomes an act of speech. It puts issues verbally into the place of necessity and thus allows the EU to take the measures it considers right in different fields (see Wæver 1995: 55).

The reconceptualization of topics by means of securitization affects the southern partners especially, mainly in terms of the restriction of migration, the granting of visas, and the sealing off the north. Not by chance, a complete section of the Work Programme of the Barcelona Conference in 2005 dealt with "Justice, security and freedom, including migration and social integration" (EC Communication/SEC 1521/2005: 12). The EU tries to extend its inner experience in dealing with justice and home affairs on a European level into the EMP. The EuroMeSCo Report criticizes these policies, saying that migration "cannot be addressed from a security perspective, but rather in a way that makes migrants and their descendants central actors in the process of regional political and economic integration" (EuroMeSco 2005: 10).

It is noteworthy that securitization also determines the inherent conflict between democracy promotion and the suppression of civil society groups that are regarded as fundamentalist or religiously extremist (see Volpi 2004: 157). The promotion of democratization and good governance is "less a goal in itself than a means of attaining prioritized security goals" (Jünemann 2003b: 7). Therefore, security considerations will always determine EMP politics—and democratization measures will be pursued only if they are regarded as

243

helpful in this context. Even if the EU is not very successful in hard-security issues, it clearly succeeds in putting matters under the label it desires. Therefore, it wields institutional power by reconceptualizing topics.

At the same time, MPCs are also trying to gain more influence in security fields. After the events at the frontiers between Spain and Morocco at Ceuta and Melilla, Spain and France tried to increase dialogue and cooperation regarding migration. For the first time, an MPC succeeded in being a real partner in this cooperation as it made the point of being a "victim" of irregular migration itself. The migrants who perished by trying to gain access to Europe via Morocco were of African origin. Therefore, Morocco was recognized as a country of transit and not only of origin of migration. It became a European partner in a discussion with Algeria about where migrants came from. The lack of south-south cooperation and the interest in Morocco as a partner in the eyes of the EU made Morocco a wooed actor that could demand better cooperation, such as improved mechanisms for the transfer of remittances, in exchange (see Gillespie 2005: 276). That means that Morocco did not manage to break the securitizing attempts of the EU. Instead, it even took part in them— but changed the sides and thus attained the power to securitize itself.

Nevertheless, labeling matters as security-relevant remains a good example of European institutional power. Security is a topic of primarily European interest. It is the EU that sets it on the agenda and that tries to pursue its security interests, especially concerning migration. These interests overlap only seldom with MPC interests, such as the case of Morocco cited above. Securitization is mostly carried out on account of the MPCs. It is therefore uncertain whether the dialogue has led both sides "to converge on a common understanding of security or if, by contrast, it has sharpens the gap. Whether it is possible to speak today, ten years after Barcelona, of a "common security culture" is questionable, but given the values and principles of Barcelona, it is certainly possible to speak of a particular

244

security culture that the Partnership, as a dynamic project, aims to promote" (EuroMeSCo 2005: 53).

9.3 Conclusion about the exercise of institutional power

The power that stems from the institutional setting is clearly located on the EU's side. The EU gives the guidelines of how the EMP and the ENP are set up, and both Egypt and Israel (as well as all the other partner countries) must keep to this setting. When it comes to agenda setting, it is also the EU that suggests topics, prepares them and puts them onto the agenda. The follow-up process is also EU-determined. The reconceptualization of topics is another means of power located on the EU's side. It securitizes issues systematically and thus provides them with the urgency and the places on the agenda that fit European interests.

Nevertheless, the MPCs are not completely powerless in this process. Even though they do not manage to put their own interests on the agenda, they do succeed in rejecting the EU's attempts to promote issues that are against their own interests. The EU therefore has the power to promote and to suppress topics, whereas the MPCs dispose only of the latter. Even though Israel does not manage to reconceptualize the agenda in favor of its own topics, it is less affected by the EU's securitizing measures than the Arab MPCs are. Migration between Israel and Europe is not a political issue, and turning non-security issues into security issues is rather an Israeli interest itself. Israel might also have a certain chance to try to bring its topics in if it left the established institutional paths. Consequently, when it comes to actualized power, the EU is powerful in all three aspects of institutional power, whereas Israel is institutionally powerless and only succeeds to a limited degree to reject the EU's topics or to promote its own interests.

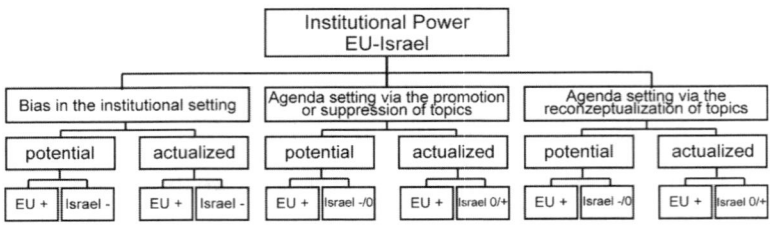

Similarly, the relationship between the EU and Egypt is characterized by the European exercise of institutional power. Institutionally, Egypt does not have great options to influence the agenda, and it also does not succeed in pushing for its own topics. In certain cases, however, it did succeed in rejecting the EU's agenda. If the Arab MPCs succeed in making their point, it is mainly because they adopt this European agenda.

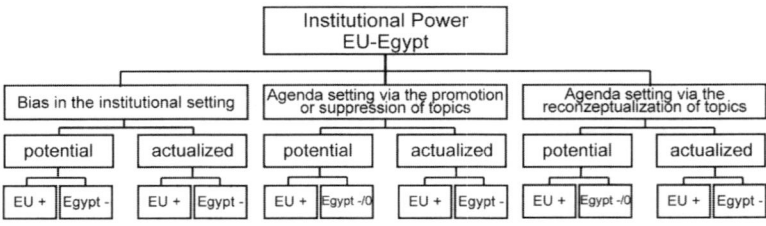

The EU's institutional power is mainly due to the setting of the EMP and the ENP, which favors the EU's position, and because a chain reaction in different aspects dealt with by institutional power does not allow for the possibility that actors outside the EU might be equally or more powerful than the EU. One can conclude that only a change of the fundamental setting of the relationship would make a change in this case.

10 Analysis of Europe's respective relationships with Israel and Egypt through the focus of structural power

The third hypothesis of this paper stated the following: If structural power occurs, then a structured relationship between the partners must have been coined through structuring the relations via the political setup, through structuring via verbal classifications and through structuring via values. That means that in the analyzed elements of the EU-Israel/Egypt relationship, at least one of the three characteristics should appear if structural power was used.

10.1 Evaluation of the analyzed policies regarding structural power

10.1.1 Structuring via the political setup

Looking at the way, structures are built up politically, one can depict two main dimensions. These are regional and content structuring.

Regional structuring

Even though the differentiation between Orient and Occident may suggest a clear border, the Mediterranean is both oriental and occidental. Over the centuries, it has been a bridge rather than a frontier between regions and cultures. That does not mean, however, that it was not subject to ongoing conflicts about its political, cultural and identity-related "ownership." It has been claimed to be the *mare nostrum* not only by the Romans. The seizure of Gibraltar by the British Royal Navy and Napoleon Bonaparte's invasion in Egypt in

247

1798 are only two major events in the centuries-old power game in the Mediterranean (see Demmelhuber 2006). Also the EU's policy towards the Middle East is an approach that draws and consolidates boundaries (see Bicchi 2006b). Boundaries may concern regions on the ground[1] as well as rather abstract concepts of inside and outside. In any case, they separate between "us" and "others." As a consequence, identities may be formed anew. Differentiation between inside and outside creates gaps—but also has the potential to bridge them. According to Nikolaos Tzifakis, "the EU policies and instruments towards its southern and eastern adjacent countries can be viewed as institutional endeavors to construct spaces and regions in order to deal with them" (Tzifakis 2007: 48).

Based on Karl Deutsch's research of the 1950s (see Deutsch et al. 1957), most political analysts dealing with regions and region-building claim that a high degree of cultural and institutional similarity is crucial to improve political cooperation and to eventually create common norms that solve existing conflicts and avoid the emergence of new ones (see Adler/Barnett 1998a). This assumption is based on the condition that groups remain culturally stable and do not undergo major social changes while they are in the process of regional community forming. In more current research, this approach has been confronted with the fact that regional communities are formed despite great heterogeneity and due to common problems regions may share. In this view, regions gain importance as communities because they are exposed to global trends and dangers and therefore have interests in cooperating with one another (see Attinà 2006: 240). This has especially been analyzed in the fields of security because security interests are vital to different actors and have gained supra-regional importance during recent years. Emanuel Adler and Michael Barnett

---

[1] The author believes that even widely-known and recognized regions, or so-called natural boundaries such as rivers, mountains or sea narrows, are not objective historical or geographical facts, but rather conceptual constructions that can be changed.

suggest in their article about security communities[2] that shared norms, shared practices, a shared definition of a problem and—most important—a feeling of belonging together regarding the security situation, are the basis for the creation of a security community on an international or regional level (see Adler/Barnett 1998a: 3 et seq.).[3]

Because the Northern and the Southern Mediterranean region differ greatly in various social, cultural and political aspects, the EMP and the ENP come up with tools that try to overcome common (security) challenges with regional approaches. The very basis of the EMP and the ENP has a structural impact: both programs structure the Mediterranean region through the inclusion and exclusion of states from the program and ascribing them a certain place. The policy programs create a binary relationship between "Europe" and "the Mediterranean," neglecting the fact that various EU member states such as Spain, Italy, France and Greece, are located in the Mediterranean themselves. More than that, the approach does not consider the fact that Libya and the Balkans are also part of the Mediterranean. Instead, it includes Jordan, a country that is not situated on the Mediterranean Sea. Establishing a single policy framework for a certain group of countries is a legitimate and common strategy. However, the fact that this framework is not based on mere geographic matters but rather on assumptions of a European versus a Mediterranean unity shows the constructive and structural approach that is behind this policy. It is a deliberate measure to differentiate oneself from the Mediterranean, a region that is regarded as problematic and unstable. More than that, this differentiation between Europe on the one hand and the Mediterranean on the other, the de-Mediterraneanization of Europe's south, aims to create a Europe-wide

---

[2]   For theoretical approaches to security communities see Adler/Barnett 1998b; Russett 1998; Tilly 1998. For detailed analyses and case studies concerning security communities see, for example, Gonzalez/Haggard 1998; Higgott/Nossal 1998; Hurrell 1998; Shore 1998; Wæver 1998.
[3]   This assumption is closely linked to constructivist approaches in international relations (see, for example, Katzenstein 1996; Kratochwil 1989; Ruggie 1998; Searle 1995; Wendt 1994).

sensitivity and understanding for the national issues with which the European Mediterranean states are faced in dealing with the Southern Mediterranean. Besides that, it creates a specific Europeanness in dealing with these issues. Or, as Nikolaos Tzifakis has put it, "the location of the Mediterranean EU countries on the European side of the dyadic relationship coupled with the negative presentation of the Mediterranean as a problematic place intends to render the latter as something external to Europe, something alien towards which the EU positions itself. The representation of the Mediterranean as the 'Other' in relation to which Europe defines itself presupposes the subjectification of this 'Other'" (Tzifakis 2007: 49).

At the same time, the EU does not only define and determine the Southwestern Mediterranean as the non-European "other" but also fixes this construction in establishing the relationship of close neighbors who should be dealt with according to these regional "we-and-you" assumptions. Therefore, the EMP with its declared aim of creating a common Euro-Mediterranean region of peace, security and prosperity, has rather had a further dividing effect on the ground. Borders have not been eliminated or weakened, and the often cited bridge-function of the Mediterranean sphere has not been built upon, but rather borders have been drawn and deepened according to European views, assumptions and interests (see ibid.: 51). Structuring according to a north-south scheme may create a feeling of togetherness in the north, but it is questionable whether this applies also to the created south. The EMP has at least led to closer cooperation on the Arab side—if only inside the EMP framework. The function of coordinator of the Arab group has been created and consolidated. This alone does not serve as evidence of structural power, but it may be a condition or even the initial expression of such as it creates the feeling of who belongs to whom as a group. This has especially been proven in the framework of security communities that the EMP and the ENP may create. In any case, the south will be looked at in a more consistent way from the northern perspective, and Europe may be also seen as more coherent from the southern perspective. It is doubtful, however, if the so-constructed Mediterranean South will accept this structure and construct itself accordingly in the future.

Content structuring

European policies toward the Middle East build on inclusion-exclusion patterns especially when it comes to economic and migration issues. Economic exchange and common prosperity in a zone of peace are a vital part of European policies towards the Middle East.[4] These inclusive politics stand in direct contrast to the EU's migration politics, which view migration negatively and generally attempt to limit it. By 2020, there will be about another 100 million job seekers in the Arab world. At the same time, perspectives remain limited in most Arab economies. The pressure gets even bigger as Arab societies are becoming fundamentally younger than European ones (see Kühnhardt 2005: 87 et seq.). With some estimations counting twenty million people in North Africa alone who are willing to move to Europe in the search of a better living standard (see Collinson 1996), Europe's efforts generally aim to seal its borders. It is interesting to note that questions of immigration and integration of immigrants who come from the southern shore of the Mediterranean to Europe, is not part of the political agenda in the Euro-Med context—not even in speeches or declarations (see Zapata-Barrero/González 2006: 87). The oft-cited Fortress Europe is a symbol for an exclusive policy, allowing only those across the borders who contribute to economic prosperity (see Calleya 2005: 9; Demmelhuber 2006: 7). The MPCs are very aware of this and complain that the EU "talks

---

[4]   Besides the profit the EU seeks through economic cooperation, it bases its policies on the assumption that economic exchange and the promotion of a free market economy will lead to political reforms and enhance democracy. The author does not share this assumption, but will not further deal with it in the framework of this thesis.

about partnership while building an insurmountable and far from virtual wall in the very heart of the Mediterranean: that of the Schengen area, which makes pariahs of the citizens of the south, as far as freedom of movement is concerned" (Toumi 2005: 98). This goes together with the creation of a security system that is established along a north-south division. The end of the Cold War has created a common European zone but has deepened north-south conflicts. Stephen Calleya even claims that "European and Middle East international region disparities and conflict continue to be the hallmark of Mediterranean interchange" (Calleya 2005: 9).

10.1.2 Structuring via verbal classifications

The EU also classifies its environment verbally. This is a well-known form of exercising power and has become especially famous thanks to the Bush administration in the US. Similar to this administration that constructs a social reality of "good" and "bad" states, the EU also classifies its environment. This can be shown in two exemplary cases: the classification of the international world in terms of good and bad states, and the definition of terrorism.

The classification and distinction of the international scenery as "us" and "them" is based on inclusion-exclusion patterns as much as the political approach of the EMP/ENP is. This way of influencing opinions has gained fame especially through the invention by the Bush administration of the so-called "axis of evil." This is probably more provocative and more polarizing than the EU's attempt to classify into good and bad. Instead of speaking of an "axis of evil," the EU (through Romano Prodi) speaks of a "ring of friends" (see Johansson-Nogués 2004) that would be built around the European states. Criticizing this exercise of power, the EuroMeSCo Report demands in its assessment of the EMP that the partnership should be build on the principles of "inclusion in diversity, which means abandoning the

252

dialogue of civilization approach that establishes a bipolar religious divide that does not correspond to reality, and adopting the notion of 'hospitality' towards an 'other that is not intrinsically different but rather intrinsically similar or equal'" (EuroMeSCo 2005: 10).

Structural power does not only occur when defining the other directly, but also when defining issues that are to be dealt with and that define the opponents less directly. One major issue that has become increasingly relevant in the EMP framework is the definition of terrorism. This definition is highly important as it concerns statements of who is to be fought against, i.e. it defines who is the enemy as well as which actions are to be taken and which are illegitimate.

In the light of the terror attacks in Madrid, the EU adopted a common position at the European Council meeting in Luxembourg in May 2004. Subsequently, one of the main aims of the Barcelona Conference the following November was to secure the approval of a Code of Conduct on Countering Terrorism. The British Presidency pursued the topic as a high priority and made it the number one topic on the agenda.

One can consider the absence of the MPCs' heads of state at the ten-year anniversary of Barcelona as a direct consequence of this priority. Terrorism is a very delicate topic because its definition borders on what many Arabs consider the right to resist foreign occupation. Furthermore, the Arab side had the suspicion that the EMP was being used to align the Arab MPCs behind the American-led so-called war on terror. Even though the heads of state did not come to the conference, the topic remained central during the conference. Not only was it highly controversial regarding the Code of Conduct that the EU tried to reach, it also thwarted the final political declaration of the summit carrying the meaningful name "Common Vision." The EU promoted its working definition of the term terrorism fiercely as it had finally reached an internal agreement. Moreover, Abbas prominently condemned terrorism, and Lebanon and Syria were too divided to find

253

a common position. Israel supported the European position anyway, so that the British Presidency expected a good chance of pushing its version through. This attempt to impose its prerogative of interpretation failed, however, because of the vehement rejection by the moderate Arab states (see Gillespie 2005: 274). The Arab states therefore prevented an agreement on the definition of terrorism and the following commitment to fight against "terrorism" became rather toothless.

10.1.3 Structuring via values

Looking at the way, structures are built up via the promotion of values, one can divide between two main areas in which structuring attempts are taking place. These are the promotion of human rights and the promotion of good governance.

Human rights

The most evident European exercise of structural power may be the attempt not only to include human rights standards in all the major documents and policies of the EMP/ENP (see EC SEC (2003) 1170/COM (2003) 639 final), but to introduce them as a standard on the whole Euro-Mediterranean agenda. The EU points to its principles saying that it "is founded on the values of respect of human dignity, liberty, democracy, equality, the rule of law and respect for human rights. These values are common to the member states in a society of pluralism, tolerance, justice, solidarity and non-discrimination. The Union's aim is to promote peace, its values and the well-being of its peoples. In its relations with the wider world, it aims at upholding and promoting these values" (COM (2004) 373 final: 12). In the same Communication, the EU emphasizes that partner countries are committed to respecting these standards and that the Action Plans are intended to strengthen the commitment to these values (see ibid.: 13).

Human rights are a typical example of what constructivists call social constructions. Despite the fact that they are regarded as values that are universal in and of themselves and refer to humanity as a whole, they are clearly a product of Western history and thinking that dates back to the fights for religious freedom and the secular writings of Kant, Locke and Rousseau (see Schmitz/Sikkink 2002: 517). Human rights only exist as made-up categories that one can refer to because "people believe and act as if they exist" (ibid.). Therefore, already the simple fact that they have become categories and norms on an international level which actors worldwide have to deal with and to justify their actions against, is an expression of structural power. This is especially true for the Euro-Med context as the EU pursues its policies specifically via the spreading of these (Western) values—and not through hard power politics.

This approach has two consequences. First, neighbors are classified as those who share these values and keep to them and those who do not share them (who oppose them at least unofficially) or even violate them. This principle of inclusion and exclusion works in a structuring way. Secondly, it is demanded that neighbors keep to these values and norm standards in order to be accepted as players on an eye-to-eye basis. Here the productive part of power begins. But even if productive power may not reach its aims, the structural power regarding human right norms works well. The highly controversial Barcelona Conference in 2005 did not lead to an agreement concerning the definition of terrorism. None of the countries could withdraw from the commitment to human rights, though. This is not only due to European pressure, but is rather the result of a world-wide campaign which is also led by the United Nations and the Code of Conduct that was signed by all of the participants and binds them to respect human rights.

Good governance

Not only human rights but also good governance is a topic the MPCs cannot avoid for reasons of structural power. This topic has been so well promoted and in such a comprehensive framework that most states must recognize the elements of good governance. Nevertheless, issues have been softened several times during the political process in order to find an agreement (see Gillespie/Whitehead 2002: 198). In the five-year Work Programme that was designed in Barcelona in 2005 in order to give the partnership a new perspective for the coming five years, the British Presidency initially intended to deal with the topics of human rights, democracy, economic growth and reform, and education. During the conference, these were transformed into politically less sensitive and less ambitious objectives. In the case of education, for example, the aims are rather concrete as they are less problematic in political terms. These aims are, among others, the eradication of illiteracy in the region, the enrollment in primary school of all girls and boys, and the elimination of gender disparity at all levels of education by 2015. In contrast, benchmarks for economic reforms remain vague and rather imprecise (see EC Communication/SEC 1521/2005: 11, 6).

Specifically with regard to good governance, the Work Programme dealing with the next five years of the Barcelona Process demands "including the protection of human rights, the empowerment of women, the strengthening of democracy, pluralism, and independent judiciaries" (ibid.: 5), and on the same topic the Chairman's Statement of the Council of the EU calls for "fundamental freedoms, including freedom of expression" (Council 15073/05 (Presse 326) 2005: 2).

10.2 Tracing the exercise of structural power back to the political context

10.2.1 Structuring via the political setup

In structuring the political setup, securitization issues come in once again. Securitization is more than agenda setting in this context. As a means of institutional power, it declares topics as extraordinary and causes them to be dealt with without keeping to the rules and the institutional setting. Working within the framework of structural power, it goes further: the audience is forced to accept these new rules of the game and must deal with the prioritized topics as much as the securitizing actor does. This means, if the EU declares migration as a security issue, puts it on the top of the agenda, and creates special forums and channels of dialogue to deal with it, it exercises institutional power. If the MPCs become part of this new framework of tackling an issue that was not as urgent before and not of their own priority, the EU is exercising structural power (see Jünemann 2003b: 3).

The concept of the EMP is structuralizing insofar as it is based on the very idea of securitization: its aim is to create a security community in regional terms. The concept of regionalism dates back to the 1950s and has seen a revival since the end of the cold war.[5] Today it is discussed against the background of globalization and a weakening of national states facing trans-boundary problems. Regional security communities are based on a basic consent, including agreement on certain basic values. From this perspective it becomes clear why the

---

[5]   It is often divided between the *old regionalism* of the 1950s and 1960s and the *new regionalism* that has emerged after the Cold War. Originally, regionalism was understood as imposed from outside, whereas the current regionalism rather consists of unplanned processes within regions themselves (see Hettne/Söderbaum 1998). For the current debate on regionalism (especially in the Middle East), see Harders/Legrenzi 2008.

EU is promoting its values so eagerly. As most MPCs do not share these values—despite the declarations made in the Barcelona Declaration and the ENP documents—regionalism does not work as a concept that would include the northern and southern Mediterranean states, and therefore a security community does not exist. Creating such a community is the very aim of the EU, though. This goes in line with a current trend: since the 1990s, regionalism has been a common instrument of powerful states to pursue their own interests (see Clark 1997: 1 et seq.). Accordingly, the Helsinki Process was also transformed into the EMP. The EMP is meant to create stability and security through tackling political, economic and social factors that hinder it (see Jünemann 2003b.: 5 et seq.).

In a structural context, securitization also arranges matters according to an inside versus an outside. Based on feelings of threat, it tries to create internal security by delineating regions or actors (see Wæver/Buzan/Kelstrup/Lemaitre 1993: 131 et seq.). This has effects not only for the relationship to MPCs that are regarded as gatecrashers, but also for the inclusion of immigrants and refugees on the European continent (see Huysmans 2000: 753). Besides that, securitization is a structuring principle that defines the way of life of a community. Though it may try to reverse the widely criticized Huntingtonian concept of a *clash of civilizations* into a dialogue between partners or between civilizations, the EU's policies are based on a logic of difference that divides between *them* and *us* as much as Huntington does. While the EMP and the ENP emphasize the "stereotyped 'common history'" (Nicolaïdis/Nicolaïdis 2006: 355), they act on the assumptions of unbridgeable division which therefore even gets deepened by the well-meant effort to understand *the other* (see ibid.). Making the difference between "them" and "us" and declaring the outside as hostile creates an internal unity. Drawing on Carl Schmitt's eminent words that the basis of politics is a thinking which divides the world into friends and enemies (see Schmitt 1996: 26), others have argued that descuritization "unmakes politics which identify the community on the basis of the expectations of hostility"

(Huysmans 1998: 576)[6]. This already has consequences for regional as well as for individual identities which become targets of a whole political schema of identification (see ibid.: 578).

10.2.2 Structuring via verbal classifications and via values

The EU succeeds in implementing a series of its norms and values in the cooperation. It makes clear that they are a must and that the status of a partner, i.e. the possibility of joining the EMP/ENP, is linked to the acceptance of these norms and values. It especially highlights its success in expanding dialogue with Mediterranean countries and creating—for the first time—a subcommittee to launch regular discussions on democracy, human rights and governance (see EC 2005b). This has been widely perceived as another European attempt to control and influence the making and spreading of values. Instead of reaching out to its partners and increasing mutual understanding, the EMP and the ENP are one-way attempts by the EU to introduce its values and norms into the partner countries. In this process, the EU has not questioned its own assumptions and perceptions concerning its partner countries and their values[7] (see Youngs 2001: 45). Nevertheless, there are certain terms that are not amenable to transplantation. Due to its close link to the war in Iraq and its (ab)use in the service of a US-led mission of establishing worldwide democracy, the very term "democracy" has come to be seen rather negatively in the Arab world and therefore is hardly can hardly take root. At the Barcelona summit in 2005, several MPC leaders made it clear that they were not willing to be "lectured on democracy" (Menéndez/Youngs 2006).

---

[6]   Others have argued that it might be more profitable to manage securitized issues than to try to transform them (see Roe 2004).
[7]   This is not a EU policy only, as Andreas Behnke shows in his article on NATO in which he demonstrates how NATO is "inventing the South" (Behnke 2000).

Good governance and human rights are terms that are easier to deal with—but still bear enough explosive potential. A facility for political reform circulated by the Commission in April 2005 lost its original name, "Democracy Facility," in order to make it more acceptable. Instead, it promised financial support to Mediterranean partners that were ready to carry out reforms according to a European perception of civil society development. Nevertheless, Egypt refused to mention the guarantee of judicial independence in the papers worked on in Barcelona 2005, and most Arab delegations resisted any statement that described civil society as independent from the state (see ibid.).

Except for insisting on different, softer sounding names for intentions of promoting democracy, the MPCs have also made it clear that statements cannot be made with them that are more than optional. Cooperating and exchanging experiences in the enforcement of free elections in order to reach better, i.e. more democratic, standards, was an EU idea whose enactment had to remain voluntary.

Neither could the dialogue on human rights be ensured. The attempt to carry out a conference in 2006 especially on this subject failed. The Work Program speaks of the lack of human rights standards, but does not put pressure on regimes to change the situation. Instead, it only gives opportunities for cooperation on a voluntary basis (see Gillespie 2005: 276).

More importantly, even if MPCs sign these declarations, they do not necessarily keep to them. Good governance does not exist, for example, in Egypt, where President Mubarak has prevented several opposition groups from taking part in elections under fair circumstances. Other countries are far away from democratic elections, in any case. The EU may exercise structural power in its interpretation, but it fails to put matters into reality. In addition, human rights standards are not met, as the Egyptian government continues to crack down on Islamist groups such as the Moslem Brotherhood, or on minority groups such as homosexuals. Even severe violations seem

260

not to worsen relations with the EU as a whole (see Menéndez/Youngs 2006).

The EU has also had difficulties enforcing its aims in its agreements with Israel. As with all its partner states, in the case with Israel it has also tried to include issues of democratization and human rights in the Action Plan. In accordance with a recommendation of the European Parliament and of the EMHRN, the EU tried to persuade every ENP country to include in its Action Plan the establishment of a human rights subcommittee. After an intense debate at the EU Israel Association Committee on April 14, 2005, Israel refused to accept such a human rights subcommittee in its Action Plan. It pointed to the fact that it was a democracy and therefore "unlike" its neighboring countries. Instead, Article 73 of the Association Agreement, which provides for the establishment of implementation bodies, set up the following subcommittees: 1) political dialogue and cooperation, 2) economic and financial matters, 3) social and migration affairs, 4) custom cooperation and taxation, 5) agriculture and fisheries, 6) internal market, 7) industry, trade and services, 8) justice and legal matters, 9) transport, energy, and environment, 10) research, innovation, information society, education and culture (see EC 2005/258final). Clearly, the emphasis in the cooperation is on economic and scientific relations and exchange and not on political affairs, as the former have an "enormous potential" (Ferrero-Waldner 2007) for both sides. This had already been the case in the Country Report for Israel. The Report highlights the fact that Israel is a democracy that provides for all the basic freedoms, has an independent system of law that respects international human right standards, and a flourishing and diversified civil society (see EC SEC (2004) 568/COM (2004) 373final).

Therefore, the EU did not insist on a human rights subcommittee. Instead, the subcommittee for political dialogue and cooperation is the only subcommittee authorized to deal with politically sensitive questions. It is led by the EC and Israel with a chairperson from both sides and serves as a forum for discussion, consultation and assessment, and works under the guidance of the Association Committee. Even though it does not have any decision-making power, it may submit proposals in the fields of fighting anti-Semitism and Islamophobia, combating terrorism and illicit trafficking of military equipment, non-proliferation, and the Middle Eastern situation in general (see EC 2005/258final: 7). In its framework, in 2005 principles regarding the Rafah crossing were concluded (see Council 16371/06 ADD 7; EC Commission Staff Working Document/SEC 1507 (2006)).

Though several EU member states made the criticism that the political chapter of the Israel Action Plan was too weak, and that such a human rights concession to Israel would make the EU look double-faced and take credibility away from its policies, the EU did not assert itself and the Action Plan was adopted in this format on April 11, 2005. Instead, the EU came under pressure—and had to make the same concession to the Palestinian Authority in its Action Plan that was adopted on May 4, 2005 (see Council 16371/06 ADD; 5 EC Commission Staff Working Document/SEC 1509 (2006)). Thus, the EU lost a decisive point of civilian influence in the already "law impoverished" (EMHRN 2005: 23) atmosphere of the Middle East peace process. More than that, the EU's declared aim of promoting good governance and a just peace sounds hollow if it steps back in such basic questions. It creates the impression of a weak EU with which one could bargain even about its core values (see ibid.: 23 et seq.).

On the other hand, it is crucial to note that the prime concession of the EU and its stepping back from its demands was corrected in a very subtle way later on: In June 2006, two (Israeli-European) informal working groups on human rights and international organizations met for the first time. Despite the fact that they are not granted the status of a subcommittee and only work on an informal and not institutionalized basis, they nevertheless deal with important issues, such as the "impact of the separation barrier and the restrictions of movement within the Palestinian territories, the extra-judicial killings, and administrative detentions on the one side and on the other the impact of Palestinian Qassam rockets targeting Israel's inhabited areas causing civilian casualties" (Council 16371/06 ADD 5; EC Commission Staff Working Document/SEC 1507 (2006)).

10.3 Conclusion about the exercise of structural power

Structural power works in a more sophisticated way than institutional and compulsory power. It structures a relationship according to patterns of inclusion and exclusion, of classifications, and of values. The EU is the only actor in the analyzed relationship that succeeds in building its relationship on the structural power of the political setup and on the prerogative of interpretation. Its attempt to force MPCs to keep to its values does not completely succeed, though. As in the case of agenda setting, MPCs do not succeed in structuring the relationship according to their own values—but they are successful in fleeing or rejecting the EU's values. More than that, they force the EU to use different terms and to soften its approach. And in the end, it is still doubtful whether they keep to these softened terms. Therefore, neither the EU nor Israel or Egypt succeeds in spreading their values in a structuring way.

In the structural power relationship between the EU and Israel, it is clearly the EU that determines the political setup, verbal classifications, and values. Israel does not have similar power to determine structures. On the other hand, it is not severely affected by the EU's influence. First, it does succeed in refusing certain structuring demands devised by the EU, and second, its values are not very remote from the EU's own.

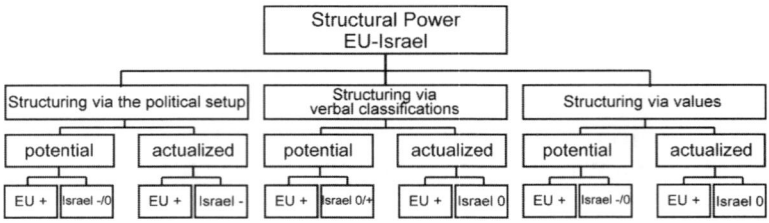

Also in its relations with Egypt, it is only the EU that sets up structures. Compared with Israel, Egyptian values are more remote from the EU's. Egypt therefore senses the EU's structuring ambitions more than Israel does. It is not able to pose anything adequate against this structuring approach, though at the least it may in isolated cases reject a European verbal or value classification. If the EU's classifications are backed by other significant international actors, such as the USA or the UN, it is even less possible for Egypt to escape with its own agenda. This indicates that structural power is more effective if it is supported by a whole environment rather than by one actor only.

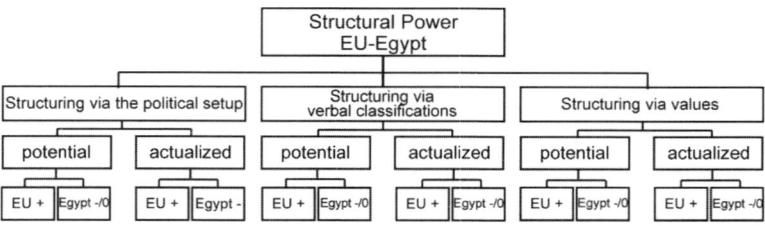

As the example of the informal working groups in Israel has shown, civilian power may not always succeed on the first try and not always on the pursued level, but power may be effective in a slower and subtler way. If the dialogue is already established, it may be easier to find other formats of addressing subjects that were vehemently

264

rejected in a former, more official framework. Civilian structural power therefore takes more time and grinds along more slowly because it has to carve its own ways. In the end, however, it may reach its aims.

11 Analysis of Europe's respective relationships with Israel and Egypt through the focus of productive power

The fourth hypothesis of this paper stated the following: If productive power occurs, then the actors' identities on the governing level, as a society or a community, and as individuals in the Euro-Mediterranean region must have been addressed. That means that in the analyzed elements of the EU-Israel/Egypt relationship, at least one of the three characteristics should appear if productive power was used.

11.1 Evaluation of the analyzed policies regarding productive power

11.1.1 Addressing the actors' identities on the governing level

As a regional approach, the Barcelona Process has the potential to create shared or split identities and thus form new social entities (see Attinà 2006: 242). That means that the EMP and the ENP try to create or at least strengthen group identities in the north and in the south— but not necessarily a comprehensive feeling of belonging together that would include the people of the southern and the northern Barcelona partners. This goes along with questions about how the EU refers to its neighboring countries and peoples. There have been debates, especially in the cases of Morocco and Israel, about whether Southern Mediterranean countries might be potential future candidates for an EU membership, integrating the MPCs as full EU members. This does not seem to be a realistic option right now. On the other hand, the EU can also not afford to regard the Southern Mediterranean as a periphery that needs to be managed successfully in a post-colonial manner. The EMP and ENP are set up between these extremes and

266

therefore do deal with new patterns that go along with the formation of new identities as a Euro-Med region. As the Barcelona process, pointing to alleged common values and interests, rather reflects European norms than the ones of MPCs, the formation of a new identity in which both sides could get closer requires a move in the south rather than in the north. As Joel Peters puts it, to "fulfil the ambitious and wide-ranging agenda laid out in the Barcelona Declaration would require a radical change in the domestic, foreign, and security policies of the southern Mediterranean partner states and the putting aside of long-held rivalries. It also demanded a significant transformation in their domestic and economic policies and in their conception of civil society. It would require a transformation in their perceptions of their own identity and self-definition, in their regional identity, and in their conception of threat and security, as well as the opening up of economic and trade relations with one another" (Peters 2006: 214). The EU thus follows a policy of regionalism through which it promotes identities and behaviors that it perceives as *normal* or as standard (see Bicchi 2006a: 287; Jepperson/Wendt/Katzenstein 1996: 54).

The answer to the question of whether this transformation has actually taken place differs fundamentally between the cases of Egypt and Israel, and also between the micro- and macro-levels. In the examined case the EU is the dominant actor, setting up the norms that the MPCs are browbeaten in order to achieve and to assimilate to. Both Israel and Egypt had to sign these norms, but the EU's productive power still developed different strength in each case. This came especially to light in the field study conducted.

Based on the assumption that both cases are of the same type because they are parts of exactly the same political programs, the EMP and ENP, and therefore both are subject to the according policies and guidelines and have signed the same basic agreements, the interviews were planned in the same way for both cases. In Israel, as well as in Egypt, the responsible EU official as well as his/her Israeli or

Egyptian counterparts were to be interviewed on the planning and on the operational level.

The first set of interviews was conducted on the operational level, i.e. in Tel Aviv and in Cairo. Alexandra Meir in Tel Aviv, representing the EU Partnership for Peace Programme, was the first interviewee. She graciously provided information about the civil society projects the EU supports in Israel, the Palestinian territories and Jordan. However, when asked who was her Israeli counterpart, she answered that there was none. This means that the EU and Israel reach their agreements and sign the according documents in Brussels, but on the operational level the Israeli government is not integrated in the civil society promotion upon which both partners agreed their accords. The EU issues calls for potential civil society groups and projects to be promoted in Israel without asking the Israeli government for permission in concrete cases. Institutionally, this can be explained by the fact that civil society promotion is based on the Barcelona Process, but not directly on the Action Plan. According to Christian Berger, who was interviewed for the EU on the planning level in Brussels later on, the cooperation with partner governments on the operational level is therefore desirable but not necessary. This strategy, promulgated throughout the complete EMP and ENP, comes to light as somehow ambivalent—or, as Mr. Berger hinted, the EU does have a clear interest in spreading its values and does try to plant them into the MPCs, but rather in a cooperative process. He emphasized that the spreading of European values is an end in itself, and they were therefore included in every single agreement, no matter which specific state and constellations the EU was dealing with.

As the case study was originally designed to also interview the EU's counterparts in order to take the relationality of power into account, the fact that there is no counterpart in the Israeli government was already surprising and meaningful for the course and the results of the study. The expert interview therefore developed in an unforeseen direction—a fact that validated the decision to use expert interviews as a rather open and flexible tool to conduct the research. Asked for any possible interactions or reactions of the Israeli government regarding the EU's civil society promotion on site, Mrs. Meir pointed to the fact that there was hardly any reaction. Mr. Berger confirmed this assessment but said that opposition did take place while the Barcelona documents were negotiated, i.e. on the planning level. Depending on the government the EU was dealing with, negotiations took different forms. With Israeli governments led by the labor party *Avoda*, issues including civil society promotion could mostly be agreed upon without serious conflicts. On the contrary, the rather right-wing *Likud* government was opposed to many issues, and negotiations were difficult. The *Likud* was principally opposed to the EU's acting inside Israel and supporting certain groups. It emphasized that Israeli identity as a Jewish state and society were not the EU's business at all and that the EU's intentions were latently anti-Semitic. Even though right-wing Israeli governments were not opposed to principles of democracy or to a market economy, they did not want the EU to interfere in Israeli identity affairs on the ground.

One can conclude that during basic political negotiations, the parties did try to pursue their wills. In the end, all basic agreements were concluded, so that the EU basically took hold on the planning level. That means that the European strategy has been successful not only in addressing but also in planting its perceptions and notions into the Euro-Mediterranean dialogue. MPC officials have not been able to avoid the European rhetoric on values and norms noted and signaled in the various EMP and ENP documents. More than that, they had to make this rhetoric their own, at least in an artificial way, in order to remain part of the discourse. The EU also states with satisfaction that, "Member States are increasingly addressing the same reform priorities in their own bilateral assistance programmes" (EC 2005b) and that international financial institutions "are beginning to take the ENP Action Plans as the basis of their strategic agenda for operations with partner countries" (ibid.). As has been shown in the case of Egypt, MPC governments are very aware of the fact that cooperation with the

EU depends on their willingness to allow at least a certain degree of democratic activity. Even though concepts such as the idea of a vibrant civil society may remain unacceptable, declarations are made in a Western style (see Grünert 2003: 150 et seq.). As most southern elites try hard to be players in the game, this discursive socialization (see Youngs 2002: 46 et seq.) has worked at least when it comes to making declarations. A look at the ministerial meetings in Naples, Dublin and Luxembourg is especially enlightening in this regard. The most famous example is probably the Tunis Declaration by the Arab League of 2004, which does not only call for democratic practice but even for a lively civil society and the active participation of women in public life (see Arab League Council 2004: http://www.arabsummit.tn/en/tunis-declaration.htm). Obviously, the declaration reflects Western demands in such an over-exemplary way that it may rather be considered as a kneeling down to Western financial donors than as an honest avowal. In any case, it shows that Western rhetoric is used and may gradually be internalized on government levels.

11.1.2 Addressing the actors' identities as a society or a community

The political strategy of addressing identities is also visible in the attempt to create civil societies in Mediterranean countries. The concept of civil society already has a very high normative valance (see Feliu 2005: 372), even more when it is connected to the promotion of values and of democratization. As Laura Feliu argues, it "owes itself more to will than to reality, and it distorts a situation of predominantly local ties with a partial international dimension" (ibid.: 381). It can be considered as a political discourse that has been created and that "has generated its own dynamic and created other realities" (ibid.). Supporting civil society as a concept is "a political act, a description of what is and a desire for the arrival of something that has yet to

270

exist" (ibid.). The EU's policy is built upon the assumption that the path towards democracy and towards peace is essentially linked to the existence of a civil society and to the degree of its prosperity. This assumption leads to a policy that pursues gradual transformations and a mentality change through dealing with societies—instead of pressuring regimes directly (see ibid.: 368).

It is therefore interesting to see how the EU's policy is carried out on the operational level. As stated above, the Israeli government does not interact with the EU on an operational level at all. The question is, then, who is the European counterpart on the operational level if Israeli governments and politicians remain silent. Both Mrs. Meir and Mr. Berger stated that Israeli society itself is the actor B in the game of productive power. Strong opposition against EU civil society promotion comes from Israeli rightwing groups. The Jerusalem-based group *NGO-Monitor* is especially active in running down civil society promotion by external donors, claiming that these do not have humanitarian goals but rather pursue anti-Israeli policies. It tries to beat the EU at its own game, claiming that the promotion of NGOs is not a democratic measure itself as NGOs are not subject to accountability or transparency. NGO-Monitor claims that supporting civil society groups is against democratic principles as they are funded by taxpayer money and have a great influence in society, but are not elected and cannot be controlled as democratic institutions. Moreover, NGO Monitor takes offense at the fact that the EU interferes in the Arab-Israeli conflict by supporting NGOs that deal with related matters. It claims that this "demonstrates a clear and consistent bias in EU funding for politicized NGOs that ignore the context of terrorism and conflict, and are among the leaders in the demonization and delegitimation of Israel" (NGO Monitor 2007: http;//ngo-monitor.org/issues/eu.htm). Thus, the EU ignores hate against Israel and against Jews and even supports the "new anti-Semitism" (ibid.) through its policy of supporting the "standard Palestinian position in the conflict with Israel" (ibid.) and through ignoring Arab violence against Israel. NGO Monitor comes up with a list of examples: the

271

EMHRN and EIDHR especially are regarded as biased and even anti-Israeli.

The broader society also regularly voices its opposition to European policies and projects. In general, the EU does not hold great value in Israeli society, and its policies are rather regarded with suspicion. Many Israelis have a very ambiguous view of Europe. They still associate it clearly with anti-Semitism and allege that its policies are pro-Arab. On the other hand, there is also a certain longing or nostalgia for Europe that often results in a feeling of opposition, as Europe often did not reciprocate this feeling of affection. Therefore, many Israelis are very distant when Europe tries to interfere in their issues and regard it as rubbing salt in the wounds of their society, with its manifold cleavages.

In the end, Israeli society is very used to loud and sharply led discussions. It is a pluralistic society that has gotten used to its heated debates and that knows the different facets of its opinions. The EU does support certain opinions or groups in the colorful landscape of Israeli society; it does not add a completely new shade or element to it, however. Moreover, the foreign financing of projects is customary. A great part of organizations, no matter whether leftist or rightist or with which aims, are financed by American or European donors, so that the EU's civil society promotion also does not represent an extraordinary policy. Therefore, even if there were debates about certain policies, EU projects are always accepted in the end and in any case take place and function.

The interview in Cairo was subsequently conducted with the insight that productive power is more relevant on the ground as it aims at the identity of societies. The interviewee was Nicola Bellomo, the EU's counselor for human rights and non-governmental organizations in the Delegation to Egypt. As both examined cases belong to the same type, it was expected that also with Egypt, agreements are made in Brussels, but when it comes to their realization on the ground, the Egyptian government would not be included. Instead, the actor at whom the projects aimed at—society itself—would become active.

This did not prove to be true, however. Instead, things in Egypt are rather the opposite. The Egyptian government cannot elude the EU's pressure concerning the formal commitment to democracy and good governance. Because of political and financial dependencies and conditionality, which have been explained before in the context of compulsory power, Egypt does not resist signing the EU's catalogue of norms. It rather tries to create the impression that it is a country that fulfils or at least does not reject norms, in order to be accepted in western political spheres and to guard its position as a key Middle Eastern player with whom the west can easily deal.

However, things look different when it comes to civil society promotion on the ground. The EU negotiates with Egyptian government officials in detail and over several months regarding the civil society projects it wants to carry out. These negotiations are highly complicated and are conducted in small circles and behind closed doors. The interviewee did not give more information about these talks with the explanation that negotiations had been so tense that he did not want to put the final agreement at risk by revealing the details. This shows already what importance is attached to this issue on the Egyptian side and how much it touches its concerns about social movements.

When the EU delegation in Cairo finally reaches an agreement with the Egyptian authorities about which projects can be run, things become significantly easier. There are no political wings, as in Israel, that could oppose a project, and no part of society comments on or rejects the projects. Egyptian society is used to having projects implemented by a top-down approach, rather than to voicing its own opinions and ideas. Public debates differ fundamentally from discussions in Israel. They are limited not only because the government restricts them but also because society itself is not used to sharp and open debates that might also touch political or social taboos. The lack of democracy becomes obvious here. Also the government itself does usually not interfere directly in projects after they have been approved. There have been certain exceptions, though. In this context especially the aforementioned case of the "Ibn Khaldun Center for Development Research" became famous. This Center was led by Saad Eddin Ibrahim and supported by the EU. The goal of the project was to inform women about their rights as citizens and encourage them to vote. The Egyptian government was opposed to this NGO and imprisoned Ibrahim from 2000 to 2003. As it had agreed to the EU's norms and to the EU's promotion of Egyptian civil society beforehand, though, the government could not prosecute him for political agitation. Thus, it transformed the political accusation into an economic one and claimed that Ibrahim had embezzled money.

One can conclude that there are counterparts, i.e. that there is reciprocity in the EMP/ENP game of productive power, but that this actor B is not necessarily the government. Whereas in Egypt it is the government, in Israel it is the civil society. It is also important to note that these counterparts try to resist European productive power. However, they do not exercise productive power themselves in a way that would aim to address European identity characteristics.

11.1.3 Addressing the actors' identities as individuals in the Euro-Mediterranean region

Productive power is also exercised when it addresses the identities of individuals as members of a region or a group. Shared identities are the basis of every group and of every state, keeping them together by creating and employing historical and symbolic narratives and by delineating them against other units, and thereby legitimizing their existence in a broader political and social arena.[1] That means that

---

[1]   On collective identities see Anderson 1991; Diez/Whitman 2002: 58;

identities are responsible for how reality is perceived and thus how it is manifested. As identities are not given facts but rather historically, culturally and socially created crystallizations, they may change and may be changed and are therefore subject to internal and external attempts at alteration.[2]

Also in the context of the ENP and especially the EMP, the definition of a group has been understood as a European attempt at creating a regional identity, i.e. the identity of individuals as Euro-Mediterraneans with a strong identification with their region as either Europeans or Southern Mediterraneans or as Euro-Mediterraneans (see Christiansen/Jørgensen/Wiener 2001; Wæver 1996; Wintle 1996). Raffaella A. Del Sarto even speaks of "attempted 'identity manipulation'" (Del Sarto 2006a: 296) in the context of Euro-Mediteranean region building. She highlights that by aiming at (national) identities, productive power touches the very core of a state, the legitimization of its existence as well as its internal and foreign policies. As this is comprises not only region-building and the promotion of security and peace, it goes significantly further than structural power does. It touches not only relations among southern MPCs, but also the identity connected to the constructed geographical patterns as well as values and norms of the southern partners. Del Sarto considers these attempted manipulations of existing identities to be so severe that she predicts resistance by the southern states (see ibid. 2003; ibid 2006: 300 et seq.).

If this assumption is true, it must be analyzed later on. In any case, it is also possible that not only is the south influenced by the EU's attempts to change its identity, but also the other way round. Frédéric Volpi believes that in the "current international climate, even well-entrenched European democracies are facing what may be likened to an identity crisis, and some well-established liberal-democratic norms

Norton 1988; Wendt 1994; Whitman 1997.

[2]   On processes of collective identity formation and alteration see Berger/Luckmann 1966; Hogg/Abrams 1993; Sherif 1966.

275

and practices appear to be if not up for grabs, at least under serious considerations. Thus, the regional security community that can be created in the Mediterranean may not necessarily be constructed via the accretion of the more supple political norms of the EU, but it could also be built on a set of basic insecurities (and associated security practices) that are increasingly shared by states, and to some extent populations, on both shores of the Mediterranean" (Volpi 2006: 120 et seq.).

11.2 Tracing the exercise of productive power back to the political context

11.2.1 Addressing the actors' identities on the governing level and as a society or a community

The EU's strategy in addressing Israel's and Egypt's identities as states and as societies is split. On the one hand, it keeps to the rules of the liberalized autocratic Egyptian state and disregards civil society itself as the first actor to turn to—as it does in its relations with the democratic Israeli environment. By passing over the civil society in issues that concern civil society itself and turning to the Egyptian government instead to ask for allowance, it does not act according to the rules of democracy, i.e. the empowerment of the people as a sovereign, that it tries to promote. The projects it asks to be permitted to carry out are parts of its normative conviction, however. Kalypso and Dimitri Nicolaïdis even maintain the opinion that productive power is expressed through the EU's bribing the non-democratic EMP states to accept interference in their internal affairs (see Nicolaïdis/Nicolaïdis 2006: 364). Therefore, the EU tries to exercise productive power in its relationship with the Egyptian state, but remains surprisingly weak in its interaction with the Egyptian state and loses credibility among civil society actors.

On the other hand, the EU does exercise a decisive productive power policy when it comes to projects on the ground. Even though it claims that its promotion of civil society "is not a machine for proselytizing or peddling propaganda, but more an effort to engage the various stakeholders in discussions about the further evolution of the Partnerships" (Leffler 2005: 3), it does exercise productive power determinedly. All of the projects clearly reflect European interests and norms. They do not take into account the expressed wishes and needs of Egyptian civil society, but rather European ones (which from a European perspective should also be Egyptian ones). Regarding this, some analysts claim that the gaps between Europe and the Mediterranean persist and fear they might even deepen into a chasm (see Buzan/Robertson 1993).

By choosing and contracting with certain groups in Israeli and Egyptian societies, the EU produces a civil society with a highly "imaginary character" (Kühnhardt 2005: 85), a civil society that is promoted according to the European notion of what a civil society should be like. In Israel only groups that are regarded as leftist inside Israeli society are promoted. As Israeli society is pluralistic in itself and has always included rightist groups as well as leftist ones, the European program does choose a political direction; it does not create something that has not been there before. In contrast, in Egypt there is no vibrant civil society as there is in Israel. Therefore, European influence plays an even more guiding role and tries to a greater extent to establish structures according to the European idea of civil society. It also becomes obvious that the EU (like different development aid organizations as well) especially promotes groups in which it recognizes itself. For instance, Christian groups tend to be promoted over Moslem groups.

In addition, previous conferences with Egyptian civil society leaders do not change this matter crucially because—as has been shown

277

before—agenda setting for these conferences is in European hands. Topics such as religion which are essential for the identity and the self-perception of Egyptian society are left out, and even moderate groups that deal with these topics or define themselves as religious are excluded from the Democratisation, Human rights and Civil Society Programme. Instead, Western topics that go along with democracy, such as pluralism and gender issues, are strongly promoted. The practice of taking the autonomy of determining topics and issues away from civil society, and keeping it on the European side (with a de facto veto over the Egyptian government), the EU contradicts its very own aim, namely empowering populations (see ibid.: 349).

One can conclude that negotiations about European influence were much more difficult with Egyptian than with Israeli authorities and not only took place in Brussels but also had to be repeated in Cairo regarding the single projects. On the contrary, Egyptian civil society remained silent, whereas opposition against EU projects was loudly voiced in Israeli society and campaigns run against them.

At first glance, it might seem that the EU's productive power was greater in the relationship with Israel than with Egypt because it had an easier time in the negotiations with Israel. However, that would be a hasty conclusion. In analyzing productive power, a careful differentiation must be made that matches the complexity and subtlety of the issue.

The EU provoked more resistance in Israeli society, but (except with the Netanyahu government) had a rather easy time negotiating agreements with the Israeli authorities in Brussels. This can be explained by the fact that Israel and the EU agree about basic (Western) norms and values that are linked to democracy and good governance. Therefore, they do not have significant arguments concerning the conclusion of EMP and ENP framework agreements. The political circumstances of single governments may play a certain role, but they will not prevent framework agreements that reflect

Western norms and the support of democratic and capitalist systems. That means that due to these basic agreements between the EU's perception of democracy and good governance and Israel's, the EU's potential is rather small when it comes to spreading its norms. Or, to put it the other way round, on the governing level Israel presents rather a narrow flank when its (already democratic) identity is addressed. That means, that the EU's productive power is rather limited in this case.

The flipside of this coin is Israel's very active and involved civil society. As the situation here is rather opposite to smooth interaction on the planning level, one might assume that here, the EU does exercise strong productive power. But again, this would be a misinterpretation. An active civil society that voices its opinions and also campaigns for or against certain policies is one sign of a functioning democracy. It does not mean that the EU exercises especially great influence. Rather, the opposition that comes up is part of the normal process. More than that, Israelis are well informed about political matters and are very strong in their opinions. Thus, the EU projects do not present anything completely new for them, but are rather part of the political and social game that people are already used to. Consequently, in this case it is very hard to fundamentally influence people. In the end, both governments and society know that civil society is part of the democratic game and do not feel threatened in their identity by the EU's projects. They thus present a very narrow flank for addressing their identity, and the EU's productive power remains limited.

In the Euro-Egyptian relationship, things are fundamentally different. Negotiations were harder due to the fact that Egypt has greater problems than Israel in signing agreements that call for democracy and good governance. In the end, however, they were signed. One may therefore conclude that the EU went further with Egypt than with Israel, which had no major problems saying yes to good governance even if it did not agree with the EU's civil society promotion. The

EU's policy of democracy promotion must also be understood in light of European history. European policy makers are convinced that security and peace in Europe are built on shared values between democracies. Nevertheless, democratization and security are not at ease with each other in the short-term; that is, promoting democracy involves instability at least in the transition phase (see Gillespie 2004; Haddadi 2006; Joffé 2001: 48; Solingen 1998). These Western fears of instability have been fueled by the start of democratic election processes in the Palestinian Authority and in Egypt, which have brought to light the strength of non-moderate Moslem parties (see Nicolaïdis/Nicolaïdis 2006: 349). In the investigation at hand, the EU therefore does not follow a clear line and loses parts of its normative credibility. At the same time, the MPCs do not address European identities as a governing system or as a community at all. Thus they remain incomparably weaker than the EU in the game of productive power.

11.2.2 Addressing the actors' identities as individuals in the Euro-Mediterranean region

Productive power is exercised in the framework of the EMP and the ENP when it addresses the self-image of Europeans, Israelis and Egyptians as regional identities, i.e. when it tries to create a *homo Euro-Mediterraneus*. As the case study and especially the interviews have shown, productive power is active in one way only: it is the EU that tries to alter identities whereas it itself is rather inflexible in its internal debates on Euro-Mediterraneanness. It is clear that Israel and Egypt are subject to productive power. Interestingly enough, this works significantly differently in each case.

Israeli society is very fragmented and has to deal with internal conflicts on an everyday basis.[3] Identity topics that are essential for

---

[3]   For detailed studies on cleavages in Israeli society see Elazar/Sandler 1997;

Israel as a society and as a state especially revolve around the relationship between ethnicity, nation and religion. Among the main questions are how to deal with the controversy of a Jewish *and* a democratic state, how to delineate Jewishness and Israeliness, that is how to deal with secular and religious demands, and how to deal with Jewish and non-Jewish populations. This includes inter-religious conflicts as well as tensions between Jews, Moslems and Christians.[4] Also heavily disputed is the question of whether to define Israel in biblical terms as *eretz Israel*—"the land of Israel," which would include the West Bank—or as a non-religious and politically moderate *medinat Israel*—a "state of Israel" which would have it borders at the green line.[5] This borders on questions of Zionism and post-Zionism as well as historical feelings of togetherness that were created throughout hundreds of years of persecution in the Jewish case and through the experience of expulsion in the Palestinian case. Lastly, tensions between *ashkenazim* and *sfaradim* still prevail with discrimination against Ethiopians being especially serious.

Israelis know the cleavages that run through their society very well, and the predominant majority of them are clearly decided about where they stand in the public discourse. It is therefore almost impossible to address the identity of the Israeli people as a whole. The EU's projects mostly have a very limited scope. They only take in people who are already close to the issues the EU addresses. Peace projects are mostly carried out in populations that are already affined and therefore neither lead to tensions with the EU nor bring up fundamental questions of identity. Also, if there is opposition from other groups (such as NGO-Monitor) to certain projects that are considered leftist, it is an opposition not only against the EU but would apply to other

Evron 1995; Hofmann 1999; Kimmerling 1998; Klein 1998; Sandler 1993; Sprinzak/Diamond 1993; Zimmermann 1998.
[4]   For analyses of the development of religion and the struggle between secular and different religious populations see Hazan/Rahat 2000; Peretz/Doron 2000.
[5]   For studies dealing with challenges to Israeli identity occasioned by peacemaking see, for example, Alpher 1995/1996; Hermann/Yuchtman-Yaar 1997; Newman 1997; Weissbrod 1997.

organizations or projects as well. Opposition is certainly a reaction to the feeling that the EU aims at identities in the region with its projects. This does not mean, however, that the EU succeeds in changing these identities.

Another important element is the fragmentation of Israeli society. As Alfred Tovias points out, the "option of being part of the Mediterranean had never been seriously considered in Israel" (Tovias 2003: 217). He argues that the Israeli elite is still mostly Ashkenazik and feels closer to Europe in terms of identity, political and socio-economic patterns than it feels to its Arab neighbors. Even for many Sephardic Jews, Europe feels closer than their countries of origin due to continuing conflicts and wars. Tovias assumes that the Barcelona Process with its regional approach may contribute to a change in these perceptions and lead to a new identity that locates itself in the Mediterranean (see ibid. et seq.). He even claims with a certain enthusiasm that "given the uneasy co-existence of 'European' and 'Oriental' patterns within Israeli culture, the ambiguity of the Mediterranean idea is undoubtedly an asset, since it accommodates different interpretations of Israeli identity and may 'over-arch' different sub-identities. At the same time, a Mediterranean identity has the potential to bridge East and West, North and South, and may thus create and promote common themes and values between Israel and its Mediterranean neighbours, on the one hand, and between the EU and its southern periphery on the other" (ibid.: 219).

Tovias may be right about the potential he sees in the concept of a *homo Euro-Mediterraneus* for Israel. However, he underestimates the extent to which Israeli society feels threatened from outside as well as from inside. Due to its numerous and broad ethnic, religious, cultural and social frictions, it is not open to changing its identity as a whole, but rather every single group tries to maintain or increase its influence in the given constellation. The EU may support certain groups, but it does not succeed in changing the game as a whole or in making a significant difference. As other elements of society also have other

282

supporters, it does not make much of a difference. Because Israelis also feel threatened in the regional context, EU policies aiming at the creation of a Euro-Med identity do not work in Israel. The conflict with neighboring countries and between Jews and Arabs inside Israel is too strong to make possible a Euro-Mediterranean feeling of togetherness. Lastly, historical reasons cause Israelis not to trust the EU enough to let it gain significant influence.

With Egypt, things are fundamentally different. Identity-wise, Egypt is a hard-and-fast society and state. Internal cleavages are not as numerous and not as deep as in Israel. Even if tensions between Moslems and Copts may arise from time to time, both have a strong identity of being Egyptian and to belong to a great and ancient nation. The same is true for Egypt as a state and a people in the region. It has a noticeable political and cultural influence and enjoys respect among its neighbors. In such a self-assured society, influences from outside draw greater attention as the society is not too occupied with itself. This is especially true if several external actors, such as the EU and the US, pursue similar policies.

The EU's projects also come up against a rather uninformed society. Illiteracy is still widespread, and most Egyptians do not have access to the Internet. Egyptians are not used to open and controversial debates in public mediums, as Israelis are. Even if the government may be criticized in the streets of Cairo, the media remains rather silent. Lastly, Egyptians are less critical of Europe than Israelis are. They would rather welcome Europeans and their projects than watch and monitor them critically. Therefore, Egyptian society receives Europeans more readily and openly than Israelis do. As long as it does not feel attacked and as long as its basic religious and national identity is not in question, it is rather interested or even welcoming to European ideas than critical. The appreciation for Europe goes so far that the creation of a Euro-Med-identity, a *homo Euro-Mediterraneus*, also falls onto fruitful ground.

In any case, civil society promotion can be perceived here as a direct and determined exercise of Western (productive) power—and not as a different, soft and possibly even altruistic approach that would be far away from exercising one's will and interests over another actor, as the EU itself and many supporters of the "EU as a civilian power"-concept see it. In the context of civil society promotion, EU policies aim at changing the (Islamic) identity of Arab societies (see Gillespie 2004) and therefore are a clear expression of productive power. As by pursuing its normative interests, it undermines empowerment of societies as a key to democratization and causes the opposition of people who consider EU norms to be an interference in their own identities, it is however doubtful how effective this productive power will be in the long run. Consequently, it is clear that the EU exercises strong productive power, but it remains doubtful whether this power will reach its aims for the future.

The assumption that shared problems create common identities may well be true, but in the cases at hand existing problems seem not to be perceived as of common interest. Instead, one can conclude that the EU has a greater power in addressing identity issues of Egypt's society and state than it has with Israel, as the creation of a *homo Euro-Mediterraneus* requires a fundamentally greater change in Israeli identity and self-perception than in the Egyptian case. Paradoxically enough, *because* Israeli and European cultures are closer to each other, it is harder for the EU to influence Israeli patterns of thinking, as Israelis already know the game. Moreover, the EU's policy requires a redefinition of Israel's place in the region and the relationship towards its neighbors that goes along with internal identity problems, as well as a change in Israel's cultural and historical narrative. Moreover, it requires better, i.e. more trustful relationships with Europe, which is traditionally hard for Israelis who have a historically reasoned suspicion that Europe acts in an anti-Israeli or at least pro-Arab manner (see Del Sarto 2006a: 302; ibid. 2006b). By contrast, Egyptians are more open and friendlier towards European policies, not only because they appreciate its policies more but also because they are internally more stable than Israeli society and thus feel less threatened when their identity in a Euro-Mediterranean context is addressed.

11.3 Conclusion about the exercise of productive power

It has become clear that productive power is a delicate matter that is hard to grasp because it involves complex matters of identities on different levels. As multifaceted structures of society and of the identities of individuals have to be taken into account, a closer look at circumstances and the social and political environment has proven helpful. Here, the importance of process-tracing with the asset of conducting interviews with involved actors has become especially obvious. As stated above, the EU is the only actor in the game that exercises significant productive power. Egypt and Israel do not do so but are rather targeted by the EU's power. This turned out very differently in each case. When it came to reaching the governments' agreements, it was considerably easier for the EU to implement its projects in Israel than in Egypt; it even did not (have to) ask the Israeli government for allowances concerning the projects on the ground. On the societal and individual level, however, the opposite was the case.

In the case of Israel, the EU's potential power is greater than Israel's. It has a greater potential than it could actualize, though. Israel itself was not successful in exercising productive power towards the EU, but was not severely affected by the EU's productive power, as its own societal structure regularly fields strong and differing opinions and is thus hard to influence as a whole. The Israeli state obviously considers the European influence so relatively non-threatening to its identity that the government does not insist on checking projects on the ground in advance.

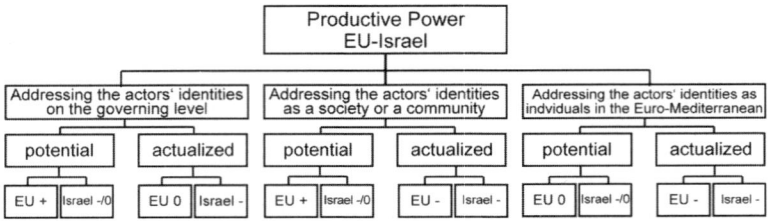

In contrast, the EU realized its potential power with Egypt, an actor that does not succeed in exercising productive power itself. Though Egypt tries to resist the EU's attempts on a government level, the EU does succeed in realizing its projects after receiving the Egyptian government's assent in rather complicated negotiations. On a societal level, people are ready and open to receive the EU's approaches, so that its productive power is effective here. Whether Egyptians' individual perceptions of themselves are changed as a result of the EU's projects is hard to say. Egyptians at least are open to the perceptions conveyed by the EU's projects.

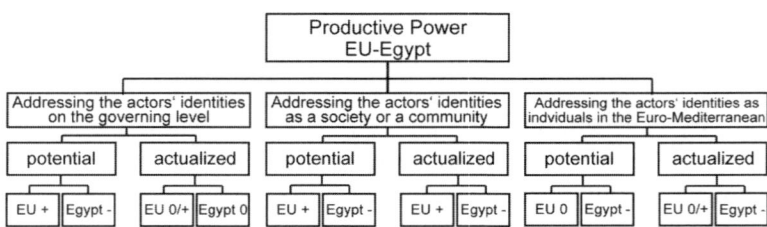

The Israeli and Egyptian constellations differ significantly. Here, possible intervening variables become clear. Three main characteristics are especially decisive if productive power is exercised: first of all, the similarity between the actors in culture and norms; secondly, their inner stability and consistency; and thirdly, the degree of their rigidity in a regional context.

12 Readdressing the initial questions: differences between the cases

The initial interest of this study was specified by asking whether the relationships were characterized by a certain type of power or by no power at all, whether the two observed cases differed from each other, and how this could be possibly explained. Looking at these results, one cannot say that the analyzed relationships of the EU with Israel and Egypt (respectively) are characterized by one of the four types of power especially. Rather, all four types appear and are active. Clearly, the EU is the dominant actor in both relationships, even if Israel or Egypt succeeds in rejecting its influence in isolated cases. Concerning institutional power, Israel and Egypt are in similar positions regarding the EU, as the institutional setup determines follow-up processes and has effects on related fields. With the exception of institutional power relations, though, both cases differ significantly from one another. This result is surprising insofar as the cases of Egypt and Israel are two instances of the same policy. In both cases, the EU's policy is a typical civilian power policy. In both cases, it is based on the same assumptions (i.e. that change may be fostered through civil society promotion), is embedded in the same policy framework (EMP and ENP), uses the same formal documents (Association Agreements and Action Plans), is active in the same fields of policy, and has similar aims. Therefore, one would expect a similar outcome in both cases.

Consequently, these differences might be explained using intervening factors. In the case of compulsory power, for example, differences between the cases emerge because Israel's and the EU's interests and values overlap at least to a certain degree, whereas Egyptian interests and (human rights) standards differ more clearly from Europe's. Israel's advanced economic level compared to Egypt's position as a developing country also creates differences. With reference to structural and productive power, the differing compositions of Israeli and Egyptian society appear to be significant. This is connected to the respective stability of their perceived identities in the regional context and to their different forms of government.

If one considers why the examined types of power differ, one can probably sum up the following intervening factors: 1) the form of government, 2) connected to that, the composition of societies, 3) the social stability internally and in the regional context, 4) cultures and norms, 5) economic and political dependencies, 6) the broader political environment, and 7) the consistency of strategies.

The form of government influences the way power is exercised and how permeable the state is to the influence of other actors. It certainly makes a difference for international power relations whether a state is a democracy, like Israel, or an autocratic regime, like Egypt. As the case study shows, the EU met different demands when it tried to implement its policies in Egypt than in Israel. Moreover, it may make a difference if a democracy has a rather leftist or a rather rightist government, i.e. if the government more or less agrees ideologically with the influencing actor. This is also true for autocratic regimes, where a lot may depend on the specific (group of) leader(s). Nevertheless, the main difference concerns the forms of government and not so much the group of political leaders. This goes along with the setup of societies. A vivid and pluralistic civil society may be more open to receiving foreign influences, but it also may be stronger in resisting them or at least in integrating them into its own pluralistic structures. Less democratically trained societies may have a harder time doing so, as they are less used to discussing political positions and because they do not have the structures and institutions that might be able to absorb foreign influence as just one part of the political discussion without causing greater attention. This goes together with the stabilities and rigidities of societies internally and in a regional context. For Israel, the EMP framework is difficult due to its politically and socio-economically singular position in the region. Therefore, it adopted a rather defensive position in the beginning of the EMP. With the years, interest in a more intensive relationship with Europe prevailed, and Israel became more active in the EMP framework, especially as it sees itself economically as similar to Europe (see Tovias 2003: 214). Israel differs significantly from its Arab neighbors in terms of its socio-economic features. It is a lot closer to Europe than to its own region and economically even outnumbers the new Eastern European EU member states, each of which has a GDP per capita below the Israeli level. Moreover, it has never relied on regionalism as a strategy to gain security. Its own policies are bilateral rather than multilateral. Thus, the ENP suits its aims better. Nevertheless, the proclaimed aim of the EMP to create a region of peace and stability is without doubt in Israel's interest. Therefore, it supports the concept as a whole, even if it may not immediately find itself in the EMP framework and may reject certain attempts at identity or region building. This is easier for Egypt, on the other hand. The society is not as split internally and regionally; Egypt has an easier time due to the fact that the EMP comprises mostly Arab and Moslem countries. Egypt is also less fragile identity-wise and has fewer existential fears than Israel does, so that productive power may work more easily here.

If one imagines the case that two actors with the same forms of government may still exercise structural or productive power towards each other, and if one considers that democratically untrained societies may still strongly resist foreign projects, it becomes clear that the fourth factor, cultures and norms, could be even more decisive. Culture and norms are also connected to historical experiences. Both Egyptian and Israeli societies have objections against European policies for historical reasons. The Holocaust is still a very present matter in Israeli politics, and Egyptians are influenced by the memory of colonialism. Nevertheless, Israeli norms and values are a lot closer to European ones than are Egypt's. No matter whether the EU is dealing with the Egyptian elite and its officials or with the Egyptian people, it is always confronted with a resistance that stems from a cultural and religious background. Historio-culturally, the situation in Egypt cannot be compared to the one in Israel—and also not to the one in Central and Eastern Europe of the early 1990s. The emergence of a civil society movement that was crucial in the democratization process in Eastern Europe was not a completely new appearance but rather has its roots in Western history. In Egypt, however, there are different historical patterns and different culturally and religiously determined patterns of society. Some claim that family, clans and religious references are the points that would lead to change inside Egyptian society—and not a Western-imported concept of civil society (see Baroudi 2004). From an Egyptian standpoint, the European concept of civil society promotion and of spreading "good" values becomes a threat to Egypt's own culture. It reminds many of the times of colonialism and creates a fear of being forced into new forms of dependency.

The fact that the EU shies away from promoting religious organizations—be it out of uncertainty about their status in Egyptian society or even out of suspicion regarding their aims—also makes it lose attraction in Egyptian eyes. Egyptians find the EU's policies suspicious in great part due to the fact that there is "a widespread suspicion that EU democracy and human rights promotion has a subtext in the Mediterranean of undermining the Islamic identity of societies" (Gillespie 2004: 6). As the EU has frequently been seen as "pushing Europeanness and Euro-centric structures and values too openly and in scant respect of local societal and identitarian constructions" (Johansson-Nogués 2006: 12), productive power does not work to a full extent. It is nevertheless more successful than in Israel, where similar norms and values offer a smaller potential for influence and where EU strategies are seen through more easily.

Moreover, the outcome of power relations may be influenced by economic and political dependencies. For both Israel and Egypt, a good European political and economic disposition is crucial. As Israel is economically stronger than Egypt, the EU is more interested in cooperation with Israel, which gives Israel more power in this field than Egypt. Furthermore, the broader political environment is significant in the cases of structural and productive power. This was not a focal point of this study, but deserves attention as a side-note. Whenever there has been additional pressure from other actors, such as the US or the United Nations, standards have been easier to press for and have awarded the EU greater power. This has been especially obvious in the case of internationally agreed-upon human rights standards and also in the avowal of peace in the Israeli case. Finally, the consistency of strategies is decisive in how power works. As the EU's policies concerning democracy promotion and presumed security are not consistent, its policies lose credibility and allow its counterparts to torpedo its programs. Again, this is more significant with Egypt than with Israel.

13 Conclusion

The goal of the present study was to gain a more refined picture concerning the appearance of civilian power in two concrete cases of Euro-Mediterranean politics. To achieve this goal, two main steps of research were taken. First, the four main existing types of power were developed into statements about power that is civilian and that takes place between actors on an international level. For each of the four types a hypothesis was formulated. Then, the three most significant civilian characteristics were worked out and sub-hypotheses were formulated accordingly, so that the existing four-limbed tree of power could be further differentiated. Secondly, for each type of power, its hypothesis as well as its three sub-hypotheses were analyzed in two typical cases of civilian power. The study thus came up with statements about how each of the four types of power works in the specific Euro-Mediterranean relationships, i.e. which of its three according characteristics appeared, and which of the actors was dominant in each one of the twelve characteristics.

The result shows that the EU was dominant in most of the twelve characteristics of civilian power, but could nevertheless not always reach its mid-term aims. In certain aspects, Israel or Egypt also had the upper hand. The study also shows that the relationships are significantly different, even though they present two examples of the same policies, i.e. case. By examining the specific situations and tracing the actors' strategies back to the regional and socio-political environment, the study has tried to come up with possible explanations for these differences.

Thus, the study contributes to academic research in two ways. First, it adds to the research of civilian power by further refining the existing types of power and developing criteria for each of them to analyze power relationships. This effort to direct the unstructured power debate into criteria and sub-hypotheses might help to systematize the discussion about civilian power. It excludes questions about the relationship between military and ethical power (and thus also about human security) by concentrating only on civilian power. By taking the four main characteristics of power as such as a basis, it avoids dealing with ethical, normative or aspects of power only—without, however, neglecting them. These aspects are mostly included in the third and fourth type of power, i.e. structural and productive power. Going beyond that, the two other types of power, i.e. compulsory and institutional aspects, are equally taken into account. This helps to present an academically rooted picture of power that does not neglect important aspects of power, while maintaining a sharp focus on civilian forms of power only. It thus might help to contribute to the "systematic empirical study of power relations" (Dahl 1968: 414) whose development is still going on.

Secondly, the study contributes to the debate concerning the EU's civilian power policies, i.e. its foreign policy in the Middle East. It dismantles the common equalization of civilian power as an actor. Instead, it looks at how an actor that typically uses civilian power policies acts in relationship to his counterparts. Thus, this study not only achieved insights about how civilian power worked in the case study, but also provides an added benefit for research concerning European foreign policies in the Middle East: the study presents two cases in detail, with which further research dealing with strategies of the EMP and the ENP, as well as with Euro-Israeli or Euro-Egyptian relations, might connect.

At the same time, the study does have its limits. It could not come up with general statements about civilian power that would go beyond the analyzed cases. We could show that the four types of civilian power did appear in the examined cases. However, their appearance differed between the two cases, and their effectiveness depended on intervening factors. Further building block studies should therefore not only examine power relationships between the EU and other countries but also focus on one or more of these possibly intervening factors to test the results gained here. It also would be interesting to compare civilian power in two non-democratic countries. A comparison between a full autocracy and a liberalized autocracy with different levels of freedom and of civil society activity, for example, could offer further insights about how civilian power differs in the case of non-democratic countries.

This study adds a brick to the building of civilian power research. As much as it showed how civilian power works in a certain case, it also brought up new questions. Civilian power thus remains an exciting matter that we will continue to hear of in the coming years while watching the EU develop its foreign policies.

Bibliography[1]

Abbott, Kenneth W./Snidal, Duncan: "Why States Act through Formal International Organizations," in *Journal of Conflict Resolution*, Vol. 42, No. 1, February 1998, pp. 3 – 32.

Abouyoub, Hassan: "Barcelona II: towards a Renewed Commitment?" publication information unavailable: *Dossier. Ten Years after the Barcelona Process: Assessment and Perspectives*. s.l. 2005, pp. 66 – 71, http://www.gencat.net/relacions_exteriors/bcn10/eng/pdf/dossier.pdf, 04/08/2007.

Achen, Christopher/Snidal, Duncan: "Rational Deterrence Theory and Comparative Case Studies," in *World Politics*, Vol. 41, No. 2, January 1989, pp. 143 – 169.

Adler, Emanuel/Barnett, Michael: "Security communities in theoretical perspectives," in Adler, Emanuel/Barnett, Michael (eds.): *Security Communities*. Cambridge 1998a, pp. 3 – 28.

Adler, Emanuel/Barnett, Michael: "A framework for the study of security communities," in Adler, Emanuel/Barnett, Michael (eds.): *Security Communities*. Cambridge 1998b, pp. 29 – 65.

Adler, Emanuel/Bernstein, Steven: "Knowledge in power: the epistemic construction of global governance," in Barnett, Michael/Duvall, Raymond (eds.): *Power in Global Governance*. Cambridge 2005, pp. 294 – 318.

Adler, Emanuel/Crawford, Beverly: "Normative power: the European Practice of Region-Building and the Case of the Euro-Mediterranean Partnership," in Adler, Emanuel/Bicchi, Federica/Crawford,

---

[1]   European Commission-related documents appear according to the years in which they were published and, within the years, according to the offical nummeration of the document.

Beverly/Del Sarto, Raffaella A. (eds.): *The Convergence of Civilizations. Constructing a Mediterranean Region.* Toronto/Buffalo/London 2006, pp. 3 - 47.

Aggestam, Lisbeth: "Introduction: ethical power Europe?" in *International Affairs*, Vol. 84, No. 1, 2008, pp. 1 – 11.

Aggestam, Lisbeth/Hill, Christopher: "The challenge of multiculturalism in European foreign policy," in *International Affairs*, Vol. 84, No. 1, 2008, pp. 97 – 114.

Albert, Mathias/Walter, Jochen: "Die Intelligenzfunktionen der Politik," in Baecker, Dirk (ed.): *Schlüsselwerke der Systemtheorie.* Wiesbaden 2005, pp. 95 – 106.

Aliboni, Roberto: "Re-Setting the Euro-Mediterranean Security Agenda," in *The International Spectator*, Vol. 33, No. 4, October-December 1998, pp. 11 – 15.

Aliboni, Roberto/Guazzone, Laura: "Democracy in the Arab Countries and the West," in *Mediterranean Politics*, Vol. 9, No. 1, Spring 2004, pp. 82 – 93.

Alpher, Joseph: "Israel. The Challenges of Peace," in *Foreign Policy*, No. 101, Winter 1995/1996, pp. 130 – 145.

Anderson, Benedict: *Imagined Communities: Reflections on the Origins and Spread of Nationalism*, 2nd edition. London 1991.

Arab League Council: *Tunis Declaration issued at the 16th session of the Arab Summit,* held in Tunis on May 22-23, 2004; http://www.arabsummit.tn/en/tunis-declaration.htm, 21/02/08.

Arendt, Hannah: *On Violence.* San Diego/New York/London 1970.

Armstrong, David: *The Rise of the International Organisation. A Short History.* London/Basingstoke 1982.

Armstrong, David/Lloyd, Lorna/Redmond, John: *From Versailles to Maastricht. International Organisation in the Twentieth Century.* Houndmills et al 1996.

Art, Robert J./Waltz, Kenneth N. (eds.).: *The Use of Force. International Politics and Foreign Policy*, 2nd edition. London 1983.

Attinà, Fulvio: "The Euro-Mediterranean Partnership assessed: the realist and liberal views," in *European Foreign Affairs Review*, Vol. 8, No.2, 2003, pp. 181 – 200.

Attinà, Fulvio: "The Building of Regional Security Partnership and the Security-Culture Divide in the Mediterranean Region," in Adler, Emanuel/Bicchi, Federica/Crawford, Beverly/Del Sarto, Raffaella A. (eds.): *The Convergence of Civilizations. Constructing a Mediterranean Region.* Toronto/Buffalo/London 2006, pp. 239 - 265.

Axelrod, Robert: *The Evolution of Cooperation.* New York 1984.

Bachrach, Peter/Baratz, Morton S.: "Two Faces of Power," in *The American Political Science Review*, Vol. 56, No. 4, December 1962, pp. 947 – 952.

Bachrach, Peter/Baratz, Morton S.: "Decisions and Non-decisions: An Analytical Framework," in *American Political Science Review*, Vol. 57, No. 3, September 1963, pp. 632 – 642.

Bachrach, Peter/Baratz, Morton S.: *Power and Poverty: Theory and Practice.* New York 1970.

Bachrach, Peter/Baratz, Morton S.: "Power and its Two Faces Revisited: A Reply to Geoffrey Debnam," in *American Political Science Review*, Vol. 69, No. 3, September 1975, pp. 900 – 904.

Bahr, Egon: "Europas strategische Interessen," in *Internationale Politik*, April 2007, pp. 86 – 97.

Bailes, Alyson J. K.: "The EU and a 'better world': the role for the European Security and Defence Policy?" in *International Affairs*, Vol. 84, No. 1, 2008, pp. 115 – 130.

Bailey, Kenneth D.: "Polythetic Reduction of Monothetic Property Space," in *Sociological Methodology*, Vol. 4, 1972, pp. 83 – 111.

Bailey, Kenneth D.: *Typologies and Taxonomies: An Introduction to Classification Techniques*. London 1994.

Baldwin, David A.: "Power and International Relations," in Carlsnaes, Walter/Risse, Thomas/Simmons, Beth A. (eds.): *Handbook of International Relations*. London/Thousand Oaks/New Delhi 2002, pp. 177 - 191.

Barbé, Esther/Johansson-Nogués, Elisabeth: "The EU as a modest 'force for good': The European Neighbourhood Policy," in *International Affairs*, Vol. 84, No. 1, 2008, pp. 81 – 96.

Barnavi, Elie: "L`Europe et le conflit du Proche Orient," in *Le Forum Franco-Allemand*, Numéro spécial 2006/07, pp. 83 – 87.

Barnett, Michael/Duvall, Raymond: "Power in Global Governance," in Barnett, Michael/Duvall, Raymond (eds.): *Power in Global Governance*. Cambridge 2005, pp. 1 - 32.

Barnett, Michael/Finnemore, Martha: "The Power of liberal international organizations," in Barnett, Michael/Duvall, Raymond (eds.): *Power in Global Governance*. Cambridge 2005, pp. 161 – 184.

Baroudi, Sami E.: "The 2002 Arab Human Development Report: Implications for Democracy, in *Middle East Policy*," Vol. XI, No. 1, Spring 2004, pp. 132-141.

Barry, Brian (ed.): *Power and Political Theory. Some European Perspectives*. London 1976.

Bartels, Lorand: "A Legal Analysis of Human Rights Clauses in the European Union's Euro-Mediterranean Association Agreements," in *Mediterranean Politics*, Vol. 9, No. 3, Autumn 2004, pp. 368 – 395.

Barton, Allen H.: "The concept of property-space in social research," in Lazarsfeld, Paul/Rosenberg, Morris (eds.): *The Language of Social Research*. New York 1955, pp. 40 – 53.

Bauer, Martin W.: "Classical Content Analysis: A Review," in Bauer, Martin W./Gaskell, George (eds.): *Qualitative Researching with Text, Image and Sound – A Handbook*. London et al 2000, pp. 131-150.

Behnke, Andreas: "Inscriptions of Imperial Order: NATO's Mediterranean Initiative," in *The International Journal of Peace Studies*, Vol. 5, No. 1, January 2000, pp. 61 – 83.

Benington, John: "New Paradigms and Practices for Local Government: Capacity Building Within Civil Society," in Rietdorf, Werner/Hewitt, Patricia (eds.): *The Politics of Attachment. Towards a Secure Society*. London et al 1996, pp. 152 – 168.

Benn, Stanley I.: "Power," in *The Encyclopedia of Philosophy*, Vol. 6. New York/London 1967, pp. 424 – 427.

Berenskoetter, Felix: "Thinking about power," in Berenskoetter, Felix/Williams, Michael J. (eds.): *Power in World Politics*. London/New York 2007, pp. 1 – 22.

Berger, Peter L./Luckmann, Thomas: *The Social Construction of Reality. A Treatise in the Sociology of Knowledge*. New York 1966.

Bhaskar, Roy: *The Possibility of Naturalism: A Philosophical Critique of the Contemporary Human Sciences*. Atlantic Highlands 1979.

Bially Mattern, Janice: "Why 'soft power' isn't soft: representational force and attraction in world politics," in Berenskoetter, Felix/Williams, Michael J. (eds.): *Power in World Politics*.

299

London/New York 2007, pp. 98 – 119.

Bicchi, Federica: "'Our size fits all': normative power Europe and the Mediterranean," in *Journal of European Public Policy*, Vol. 13, No. 2, March 2006a, pp. 286 – 303.

Bicchi, Federica: "The European Origins of Euro-Mediterranean Practices," in Adler, Emanuel/Bicchi, Federica/Crawford, Beverly/Del Sarto, Raffaella A. (eds.): *The Convergence of Civilizations. Constructing a Mediterranean Region.* Toronto/Buffalo/London 2006b, pp. 137 – 167.

Bierstedt, Robert: "An Analysis of Social Power," in *American Sociological Review*, Vol. 15, No. 6, December 1950, pp. 730 – 738.

Birnbaum, Robert: *How Colleges Work: The Cybernetics of Academic Organization and Leadership.* San Francisco 1988.

Blanc, Frédéric: "An Assessment of the Economic Aspects of the Barcelona Process on the Occasion of its 10th Anniversary," publication information unavailable: *Dossier. Ten Years after the Barcelona Process: Assessment and Perspectives.* s.l. 2005, pp. 76 – 77,
http://www.gencat.net/relacions_exteriors/bcn10/eng/pdf/dossier.pdf, 04/08/2007.

Blau, Peter Michael: *Exchange and Power in Social Life.* New York/London/Sydney 1964.

Bliss, Frank: "What is civil society? Too little attention to the aspect of legitimacy," in *Development and Cooperation*, Vol. 30, No. 5, May 2003, pp. 195 – 199.

Blondel, Ylva Isabelle: *The Power of Symbolic Power: An Application of O'Neill's Game of Honour to Asymmetric Internal Conflict.* Uppsala 2004.

300

Bodin, Jean: *On sovereignty: four chapters from the six books of the commonwealth*, (ed. and trans. Franklin, Julian H.). Cambridge 1992.

Boli, John/Thomas, George M.: „World Culture in the World Polity: A Century of International Non-Governmental Organization," in *American Sociological Review*, Vol. 62, No. 2, April 1997, pp. 171 – 190.

Bourdieu, Pierre: *Language and Symbolic Power*. Cambridge 1993.

Börzel, Tanja: "Member State Responses to Europeanization," in *Journal of Common Market Studies*, Vol. 40, No. 2, June 2002, pp. 193 – 214.

Bradshaw, Alan: "A Critique of Steven Lukes' Power: A Radical View," in *Sociology*, Vol. 10, No. 1, January 1976, pp. 129 – 132.

Bremer, Stuart A.: "Dangerous Dyads, Conditions Affecting the Likelihood of Interstate War, 1816-1965," in *Journal of Conflict Resolution*, Vol. 36, No.2, pp. 309-341.

Brock, Lothar: "Triangulating War: the Use of Force by Democracies as a Variant of Democratic Peace," in Brock, Lothar/Geis, Anna/Müller, Harald (eds.): *Democratic Wars. Looking at the Dark Side of the Democratic Peace*. Houndmills 2006, pp. 90 – 119.

Brown, Michael E./Lynn-Jones, Sean M./Miller, Steven E. (eds.): *Debating the Democratic Peace*. Cambridge 1996.

Brownlee, Jason: "The Decline of Pluralism in Mubarak`s Egypt," in Diamond, Larry/Plattner, Marc F./Brumberg, Daniel (eds.): *Islam and Democracy in the Middle East*. Baltimore/London 2003, pp. 48 – 57.

Brynen, Rex/Korany, Bahgat/Noble, Paul (eds.): *Political Liberalization and Democratization in the Arab World. Theoretical Perspectives*, Vol. 1. Boulder 1995.

Bueno de Mesquita, Bruce/Stokman, Frans N. (eds.): *European Community Decision Making. Models, Applications, and Comparison.* New Haven 1994.

Bull, Hedley: *The Control of the Arms Race. Disarmament and Arms Control in the Missile Age*, The Institute for Strategic Studies. London 1961.

Bull, Hedley: "Civilian Power Europe: A Contradiction in Terms?" in *Journal of Common Market Studies*, Vol. 21, No. 2, December 1982, pp. 149 – 164.

Butler, Judith: *Gender Trouble. Feminism and the Subversion of Identity.* New York/London 1990.

Buzan, Barry: *People, States and Fear. An Agenda for International Security Studies in the Post-Cold War Area*, 2nd edition. New York et al 1991.

Buzan, Barry/Robertson, Roland: "Europe and the Middle East: Drifting towards Societal Cold War?" in Waever, Ole/Buzan, Barry/Kelstrup, Morten/Lemaitre, Pierre (eds.): *Identity, Migration and the New Security Agenda in Europe.* London 1993, pp. 131 – 147.

Buzan, Barry/Wæver, Ole: *Regions and Powers. The Structures of International Security.* Cambridge 2003.

Buzan, Barry/Wæver, Ole/de Wilde, Jaap: *Security: A New Framework for Analysis.* Boulder 1998.

Calleya, Stephen C.: "The Euro-Mediterranean Partnership and the Concept of the Greater Middle East," in Marchetti, Andreas (ed.): *Ten Years Euro-Mediterranean Partnership. Defining European Interests for the Next Decade*, Discussion Paper C 154, Zentrum für Europäische Integrationsforschung. Bonn 2005, pp. 7 – 23.

Calleya, Stephen C.: "The Euro-Mediterranean Partnership and Sub-

Regionalism: A Case of Region-Building?" in Adler, Emanuel/Bicchi, Federica/Crawford, Beverly/Del Sarto, Raffaella A. (eds.): *The Convergence of Civilizations. Constructing a Mediterranean Region.* Toronto/Buffalo/London 2006, pp. 109 – 133.

Caporaso, James: "International Relations Theory and Multilateralism: The Search for Foundations," in *International Organization*, Vol. 46, No. 3, 1992, pp. 599 – 633.

Carothers, Thomas: "Civil Society," in *Foreign Policy*, No. 117, Winter 1999/2000, pp. 18 – 29.

Carr, Edward Hallett: *The Twenty Years` Crisis 1919 – 1939. An Introduction to the Study of International Relations*, 2nd edition. London/Toronto/New York 1946.

Cartwright, Dorwin: "Influence, Leadership, Control," in March, James (ed.): *Handbook of Organizations.* Chicago 1965, pp. 1 – 47.

Catlin, George Edward Gordon: *The Science and Method of Politics.* Hamden 1964.

Chartouni-Dubarry, May: "Political Transition in the Middle East," in *Mediterranean Politics*, Vol. 5, No. 1, Spring 2000, (Vasconcelos, Álvaro/Joffé, George (eds.): "Special Issue on the Barcelona Process. Building a Euro-Mediterranean Regional Community"), pp. 53 – 76.

Chenal, Odile: "The Euro-Mediterranean Partnership, Civil Society and Cultural Co-operation: an Uncertain Triangle," publication information unavailable: *Dossier. Ten Years after the Barcelona Process: Assessment and Perspectives.* s.l. 2005, pp. 87 – 89, http://www.gencat.net/relacions_exteriors/bcn10/eng/pdf/dossier.pdf, 04/08/2007.

Chojnacki, Sven: *Demokratien und Krieg. Das Konfliktverhalten demokratischer Staaten im internationalen System, 1946-2001*, Discussion Paper P 2003-304, Wissenschaftszentrum Berlin für

Sozialforschung (WZB). Berlin 2003.

Chojnacki, Sven: "Wandel der Kriegsformen? Ein kritischer Literaturbericht," in *Leviathan. Zeitschrift für Sozialwissenschaft*, Vol. 32, No. 3, 2004, pp. 402 – 424.

Chojnacki, Sven: *Wandel der Gewaltformen im internationalen System, 1946-2006*, Deutsche Stiftung Friedensforschung, Nr. 14. Osnabrück 2008.

Chourou, Béchir: "Arab Regional Integration as a Prerequisite for a Successful Euro-Mediterranean Partnership," in *Mediterranean Politics*, Vol. 8, No. 2, Summer 2003, pp. 194 – 213.

Christiansen, Thomas/Jørgensen, Knud Erik/Wiener, Antje (eds.): *The Social Construction of Europe*. London 2001.

Clark, Ian: *Globalisation and Fragmentation: Internatioal Relations in the Twentieth Century*. Oxford 1997.

Claude, Inis L.: *Power and International Relations*, 5th edition. New York 1965.

Clegg, Stewart: *Frameworks of Power*. London/Newbury Park/New Delhi 1989.

Colás, Alejandro: *International Civil Society. Social Movements in World Politics*. Oxford/Malden 2002.

Collard-Wexler, Simon: "Integration Under Anarchy: Neorealism and the European Union," in *European Journal of International Relations*, Vol. 12, No. 3, 2006, pp. 397 – 432.

Collinson, Sarah: *Shore to Shore: The Politics of Migration in Euro-Maghreb Relations*, The Royal Institute for International Affairs. London 1996.

Connolly, William E.: *Identity/Difference. Democratic Negotiations of*

Political Paradox. Ithaca/London 1991.

Connolly, William E.: *The Terms of Political Discourse*, 3rd edition. Oxford 1993.

Cooper, Richard: *The Economics of Interdependence: Economic Policy in the Atlantic Community*. New York 1968.

Council of the European Union (Council 1488/96, amended by EC 780/98): *Council Regulation on financial and technical measures to accompany (MEDA) the reform of economic and social structures in the framework of the Euro-Mediterranean partnership*, amended by Council Regulation (EC) No. 780/98. Brussels 2000.

Council of the European Union (Council 2698/2000): "Council Regulation of 27 November 2000 amending Regulation No 1488/96 on financial and technical measures to accompany (MEDA) the reform of economic and social structures in the framework of the Euro-Mediterranean Partnership," in *Official Journal of the European Communities*, L311/1. Brussels 2000.

Council of the European Union (Council 15073/05 (Presse 326)): *10th Anniversary Euro-Mediterranean Summit*, Barcelona, 27 and 28 November 2005. Chairman's Statement. Brussels 2005.

Council of the European Union (Council 14087/06 (Presse 292)): *Council approves financing instrument to provide more than EUR 11 billion for European Neighbourhood policy*. Luxembourg 2006.

Council of the European Union (Council 16371/06 ADD 5): *Commission staff working document accompanying the Communication from the Commission of the Council and the European Parliament on strengthening the European Neighbourhood Policy – ENP Progress Report on the Palestinian Authority*. Brussels 2006.

Council of the European Union (Council 16371/06 ADD 7):

Commission staff working document accompanying the Communication from the Commission of the Council and the European Parliament on strengthening the European Neighbourhood Policy – ENP Progress Report on Israel. Brussels 2006.

Daase, Christopher: "Democratic Peace – Democratic War: Three Reasons Why Democracies Are War-prone," in Brock, Lothar/Geis, Anna/Müller, Harald (eds.): *Democratic Wars. Looking at the Dark Side of the Democratic Peace.* Houndmills 2006, pp. 74 – 89.

Dahl, Robert: "The Concept of Power," in *Behavioral Science*, Vol. 2, No. 3, July 1957, pp. 201 – 215.

Dahl, Robert: "A Critique of the Ruling Elite Model," in *The American Political Science Review*, Vol. 52, No. 2, June 1958, pp. 463 – 469.

Dahl, Robert: *Who Governs? Democracy and Power in an American City.* New Haven/London 1961.

Dahl, Robert: *Modern Political Analysis.* Englewood Cliffs/New York 1963.

Dahl, Robert: "Cause and Effect in the Study of Politics," in Lerner, Daniel (ed.): *Cause and Effect.* New York 1965, pp. 75 – 98.

Dahl, Robert: "Power," in *International Encyclopedia of the Social Sciences*, Vol. XII. New York 1968, pp. 405 - 415.

Dahl, Robert: *Democracy and Its Critics.* New Haven 1989.

Dam, Rijk van: "Anti-Israel Bias in the European Parliament and Other EU Institutions," in Gerstenfeld, Manfred (ed.): *European-Israel Relations: Between Confusion and Change?* Jerusalem Center for Public Affairs/Adenauer Foundation, Jerusalem 2006, pp. 79 – 90.

Davis, Kingsley: "The Demographic Foundations of National Power," in Berger, Morroe/Abel, Theodore/Page, Charles H. (eds.): *Freedom and Control in Modern Society*. New York 1954, pp. 206 - 242.

Del Sarto, Raffaella A.: "Israel's Contested Identity and the Mediterranean," in *Mediterranean Politics*, Vol. 8, No. 1, Spring 2003, pp. 27 – 58.

Del Sarto, Raffaella A.: „Region-Building, European Normative Power, and Contested Identities: The Case of Israel," in Adler, Emanuel/Bicchi, Federica/Crawford, Beverly/Del Sarto, Raffaella A. (eds.): *The Convergence of Civilizations. Constructing a Mediterranean Region*. Toronto/Buffalo/London 2006a, pp. 296 - 333.

Del Sarto, Raffaella A.: "The EU and Israel: An Enhanced Political Cooperation? An Assessment of the Bilateral ENP Action Plan," in Nathanson, Roby/Stetter, Stephan (eds.): *The Israeli European Policy Network. The Monitor of the EU-Israel Action Plan. Friedrich-Ebert-Stiftung*. Tel Aviv/Vienna 2006b.

Del Sarto, Raffaella A./Schumacher, Tobias: "From EMP to ENP: What's at Stake with the European Neighbourhood Policy towards the Southern Mediterranean?" in *European Foreign Affairs*, Vol. 10, No. 1, Spring 2005, pp. 17 – 38.

Dembinski, Matthias: *Kein Abschied vom Leitbild „Zivilmacht". Die Europäische Sicherheits- und Verteidigungspolitik und die Zukunft Europäischer Außenpolitik*, HSFK-Report 12/2002. Frankfurt am Main 2002.

Dembinski, Matthias: "Die Europäische Sicherheits- und Verteidigungspolitik: Abschied vom Leitbild 'Zivilmacht Europa'?" in Schlotter, Peter (ed.): *Europa – Macht – Frieden? Zur Politik der „Zivilmacht Europa."* Baden-Baden 2003, pp. 72 – 100.

Demmelhuber, Thomas: *The Euro-Mediterranean Space as an Imagined (Geo-)political, Economic and Cultural Entity*, Discussion

Paper C 159, Zentrum für Europäische Integrationsforschung. Bonn 2006.

Denzin, Norman K.: *The Research Act: A Theoretical Introduction to Sociological Methods*, 3rd edition. Englewood Cliffs 1989.

Deutsch, Karl W. et al: *Political community and the North Atlantic area: international organization in the light of historical experience.* Princeton 1957.

Deutsch, Karl W.: *The Nerves of Government. Models of Political Communication and Control.* New York 1963.

Deutsch, Karl W.: *The Analysis of International Relations*, 2nd edition. Englewood Cliffs 1978.

Diamond, Larry: "Rethinking Civil Society: Toward Democratic Consolidation," in *Journal of Democracy*, Vol. 5, No. 3, July 1994, pp. 4 – 18.

Diesing, Paul: *Patterns of Discovery in the Social Sciences.* Chicago 1971.

Digeser, Peter: "The Fourth Face of Power," in *Journal of Politics*, Vol. 54, No. 4, November 1992, pp. 977 – 1007.

Diez, Thomas/Manners, Ian: "Reflecting on normative power Europe," in Berenskoetter, Felix/Williams, Michael J. (eds.): *Power in World Politics.* London/New York 2007, pp. 173 – 188.

Diez, Thomas/Whitman, Richard G.: "Analysing European Integration: Reflecting on the English School – Scenarios for an Encounter," in *Journal of Common Market Studies*, Vol. 40, No. 1, 2002, pp. 43 – 67.

Dixon, William J.: "Democracy and Peaceful Settlement of International Conflict," in *American Political Science Review*, Vol. 88,

308

No. 11, March 1994, pp. 14 – 32.

Dosenrode, Søren/Stubkjær, Anders: *The European Union and the Middle East*. London 2002.

Doty, Roxanne L.: *Imperial Encounters: The Politics of Representation in North-South Relations*. Minneapolis 1996.

Dûchene, François: "Die Rolle Europas im Weltsystem: Von der regionalen zur planetarischen Interdependenz," in Kohnstamm, Max/Hager, Wolfgang (eds.): *Zivilmacht Europa – Supermacht oder Partner?* Frankfurt am Main 1973, pp. 11 - 35.

Dunne, Tim: "Good citizen Europe," in *International Affairs*, Vol. 84, No. 1, 2008, pp. 13 – 28.

Duyvesteyn, Isabelle: *The Political Dynamics of Civil War*. London 2002.

Eckstein, Harry: "Case Study and Theory of Political Science," in Greenstein, Fred I./Polsby, Nelson W. (eds.): *Handbook of Political Science*. Reading 1975, pp. 79 – 137.

Edwards, Michael/Hulme, David: *Non-Governmental Organisations - Performance and Accountability beyond the Magic Bullet*. West Hartford 1995.

Eisenhardt, Kathleen M.: "Building Theories from Case Study Research," in Huberman, A. Michael/Miles, Matthew B. (eds.): *The Qualitative Researcher's Companion: Classic and Contemporary Readings*. London 2002, pp. 5 – 36.

Elazar, Daniel J./Sandler, Shmuel: "The Battle over Jewishness and Zionism in the Post-Modern Era," in *Israel Affairs*, Vol. 4, No. 1, Autumn 1997, pp. 1 – 29.

Emerson, Michael/Noutcheva, Gergana: "From Barcelona Process to

Neighbourbood Policy," publication information unavailable: *Dossier. Ten Years after the Barcelona Process: Assessment and Perspectives.* s.l. 2005, pp. 92 – 97, http://www.gencat.net/relacions_exteriors/bcn10/eng/pdf/dossier.pdf, 04/08/2007.

EU/Egypt Association Agreement (EU/Egypt AA): *Euro-Mediterranean Agreement Establishing an Association between the European Communities and their Member States, of the one part, and the Arab Republic of Egypt, of the other part.* Brussels 2004.

EU/Israel Association Agreement (EU/Israel AA): "Euro-Mediterranean Agreement Establishing an Association between the European Communities and their Member States, of the one part, and the State of Israel, of the other part," in *Official Journal of the European Communities*, L 147/3. Brussels 2000.

European Commission (COM (1995) 216 final): *Communication from the Commission on the Inclusion of Respect for Democratic Principles and Human Rights in Agreements between the Community and Third Countries.* Brussels 1995.

European Commission (EC): *The EU`s People to People Programme.* Tel Aviv 2000.

European Commission (COM (2001) 252 final): *Communication from the Commission to the Council and the European Parliament. The European Union`s Role in Promoting Human Rights and Democratisation in Third Countries.* Brussels 2001.

European Commission (EC): *The EU Partnership for Peace Programme.* Tel Aviv 2003a.

European Commission (EC): *A Secure Europe in a Better World. European Security Strategy.* Brussels 2003b.

European Commission (COM (2003) 104 final): *Communication from the Commission to the Council and the European Parliament. Wider Europe – Neighbourhood: A New Framework for Relations with our Eastern and Southern Neighbours..* Brussels 2003.

European Commission (COM (2003) 294 final): *Communication from the Commission to the Council and the European Parliament. Reinvigorating EU actions on Human Rights and democratization with Mediterranean partners. Strategic guidelines.* Brussels 2003.

European Commission (COM (2003) 393 final): *Communication from the Commission. Paving the way for a New Neighbourhood Instrument.* Brussels 2003.

European Commission (EC SEC (2003) 1170/COM (2003) 639 final): *Proposal for a Regulation of the European Parliament and of the Council amending Regulation (EC) No 975/1999 laying down the requirements for the implementation of development cooperation operations which contribute to the general objective of developing and consolidating democracy and the rule of law and to that of respecting human rights and fundamental freedoms and Regulation (EC) No 976/1999 laying down the requirements for the implementation of Community operations, which within the framework of Community cooperation policy, contribute to the general objective of developing and consolidating democracy and the rule of law and to that of respecting human rights and fundamental freedoms in third countries.* Brussels 2003.

European Commission (EC): *Aid Delivery Methods. Project Cycle Management Guidelines.* Brussels 2004a.

European Commission (EC): *EU Partnership for Peace. Guidelines for grant applicants responding to the call for proposals for 2004.* Tel Aviv 2004b.

European Commission (EC): *The Partnership for Peace Programme.* Tel Aviv 2004c.

European Commission (COM (2004) 790 final): *Proposal for a Council Decision on the position to be adopted by the Communities and their Member States within the Association Council established by the Euro-Mediterranean Agreement establishing an association between the European Communities and their Member States, of the one part, and the State of Israel, of the other part, with regard to the adoption of a Recommendation on the implementation of the EU-Israel Action Plan*. Brussels 2004.

European Commission (COM (2004) 373 final): *Communication from the Commission. European Neighbourhood Policy*. Strategy Paper. Brussels 2004.

European Commission (EC 2004/0219 COD/628 final): *Proposal for a Regulation of the European Parliament and of the Council laying down general provisions establishing a European Neighbourhood and Partnership Instrument*. Brussels 2004.

European Commission (EC SEC (2004) 568/COM (2004) 373 final): *Commission Staff Working Paper. European Neighbourhood Policy. Country Report Israel*. Brussels 2004.

European Commission (EC): The EU Partnership Programme. Tel Aviv 2005a.

European Commission (EC): *European Neighbourhood Policy: A year of progress*. Press Release (IP/05/1467). Brussels 2005b.

European Commission (EC COM (2005) 72 final): *Communication from the Commission to the Council. European Neighbourhood Policy. Recommendations for Armenia, Azerbaijan, Georgia and for Egypt and Lebanon*. Brussels 2005.

European Commission (EC Communication): *Communication from the Commission to the Council and the European Parliament. Tenth Anniversary of the Euro-Mediterranean Partnership: A work*

312

programme to meet the challenges of the next five years. Brussels 2005.

European Commission (EC 2005/258 final): *Proposal for a Council Decision on a Community position in the Association Council on the implementation of Article 73 of the Euro-Mediterranean Agreement establishing an association between the European Communities and their Member States, on one part, and the State of Israel, of the other part*. Brussels 2005.

European Commission (EC Communication/SEC 1521/ 2005): *Communication to the Commission. Implementing and promoting the European Neighbourhood Policy*. Brussels 2005.

European Commission (EC SEC (2005) 287/3/COM (2005) 72 final): *Commission Staff Working Paper. Annex to: European Neighbourhood Policy. Country Report Egypt*. Brussels 2005.

European Commission (EC COM (2006) 23 final): *Communication from the Commission to the Council and the European Parliament. Thematic Programme for the promotion of democracy and human rights worldwide under the future Financial Perspectives (2007 – 2013)*. Brussels 2006.

European Commission (EC COM (2006) 282 final): *Proposal for a Council Decision on the position to be adopted by the European Community and its Member States within the Association Council established by the Euro-Mediterranean Agreement establishing an association between the European Communities and their Member States, of the one part, and the Arab Republic of Egypt, of the other part, with regard to the adoption of a Recommendation on the implementation of the EU-Egypt Action Plan*. Brussels 2006.

European Commission (EC COM (2006) 354 final/2006/0116 (COD)*)): Proposal for a Regulation of the European Parliament and the Council on establishing a financing instrument for the promotion* *of democracy and human rights worldwide*. (European Instrument for Democracy and Human Rights). Brussels 2006.

European Commission (EC COM (2006) 726 final): *Communication from the Commission to the Council and the European Parliament on strengthening the European Neighbourhood Policy*. Brussels 2006.

European Commission (EC Commission Staff Working Document/SEC 1504/2 (2006)): *Accompanying the Communication from the Commission to the Council and the European Parliament on Strengthening the European Neighbourhood Policy. Overall Assessment. COM (2006)726 final*. Brussels 2006.

European Commission (EC Commission Staff Working Document/SEC 1507 (2006)): *Accompanying the Communication from the Commission to the Council and the European Parliament on Strengthening the European Neighbourhood Policy. ENP Progress Report Israel. COM (2006)726 final*. Brussels 2006.

European Commission (EC Commission Staff Working Document/SEC 1509 (2006)): *Accompanying the Communication from the Commission to the Council and the European Parliament on Strengthening the European Neighbourhood Policy. ENP Progress Report Palestinian Authority. COM (2006)726 final*. Brussels 2006.

European Commission (EC Commission Staff Working Document/SEC 1512/2 (2006)): *Accompanying the Communication from the Commission to the Council and the European Parliament on Strengthening the European Neighbourhood Policy. Sectoral Progress Report. COM (2006)726 final/SEC 1512/2*. Brussels 2006.

European Commission/Directorate-General for Economic and Financial Affairs (EC/EFA): *European Neighbourhood Policy: Economic Review of the ENP Countries*. Occasional Papers, No. 25. Brussels 2006.

European Commission (EC/Eurobarometer): *The European Union and its Neighbours*. Special Eurobarometer 259/Wave 65.3. TNS Opinion and Social. Brussels 2006.

European Commission (EC/Euromed): *European Neighbourhood and Partnership Instrument (ENPI): Regional Strategy Paper (2007-2013) and Regional Indicative Programme (2007-2010) for the Euro-Mediterranean Partnership*. Brussels 2006.

European Commission (EC/IP/06/1676 (2006)): *Strengthening the European Neighbourhood Policy*. Brussels 2006.

European Commission (EC): *European Neighbourhood Policy*, http://ec.europa.eu/world/enp/index_en.htm, 12/01/2007.

European Commission (EC/Egypt): *Egypt. Country Strategy Paper 2007 - 2013.* Brussels 2007.

European Commission (EC/Israel): *Israel. Strategy Paper 2007 – 2013 & Indicative Programme 2007 - 2010*. Brussels (without date).

European Commission (EC): *Barcelona Declaration. Adopted at the Euro-Mediterranean Conference 27-28/11/1959*, http://ec.europa.eu/external_relations/euromed/bd.htm, 30/05/2008.

European Commission`s Delegation to Egypt: *EU-Funded Cooperation Programmes*, http://www.delegy.ec.europa.eu/en/eu_funded_programmes/program mes3.htm, 01/07/2008.

European Communities (EC 2000/C 364/1): "Charter on Fundamental Rights of the European Union," in *Official Journal of the European Union L 310*. Brussels 2000.

European-Mediterranean Human Rights Network (EMHRN): *A Human Rights Review on the EU and Israel. Mainstreaming or Selectively Extinguishing Human Rights?* Copenhagen 2005a.

European-Mediterranean Human Rights Network (EMHRN): *European Neighbourhood Policy: Human Rights in EU-Egypt Relations. Recommendations of Egyptian Non Governmental Organizations for the EU-Egypt Action Plan*. Cairo 2005b.

EuroMeSCo: *Barcelona Plus. Towards a Euro-Mediterranean Community of Democratic States*, EuroMeSco Report, (co-ord. Álvaro de Vasconcelos). Lisboa 2005.

European Parliament/Council of the European Union (EP/Council): "Regulation (EC) No 1638/2006 of the European Parliament and of the Council of 24 October 2006 laying down general provisions establishing a European Neighbourhood and Partnership Instrument," in *Official Journal of the European Union*, L 310. Brussels 2006.

Evans, Sara M./Nelson, Barbara J.: *Wage justice: Comparable Worth and the Paradox of Technocratic Reform*. Chicago/London 1989.

Evron, Boaz: *Jewish State or Israeli Nation?* Bloomington 1995.

Fairclough, Norman: *Language and power*. London/New York 1989.

Fairclough, Norman: *Discourse and Social Change*. Cambridge 2002.

Fay, Brian: *Critical Social Science*. Oxford 1987.

Feagin, Joe R./Orum, Anthony M./Sjoberg, Gideon (eds.): *A Case for the Case Study*. Chapel Hill 1991.

Feliu, Laura: "Global Civil Societies Across the Mediterranean: The Case of Human Rights," in *Mediterranean Politics*, Vol. 10, No 3, November 2005, pp. 365 – 383.

Ferrero-Waldner, Benita: *Bilateral relations between Israel and the European Union. The Hebrew University of Jerusalem*, Speech, 27 February 2007. SPEECH/07/108. Jerusalem 2007.

Fierro, Elena: *The EU's Approach to Human Rights Conditionality in*

Practice. The Hague/London/New York 2003.

Flick, Uwe: "Triangulation Revisited: Strategy of or Alternative to Validation of Qualitative Data," in *Journal for the Theory of Social Behavior*, Vol. 22, No. 2, 1992, pp. 175 – 197.

Flick, Uwe: *An introduction to qualitative research*, 3rd edition. London et al 2007.

Flyvbjerg, Bent: "Five Misunderstandings About Case-Study Research," in *Qualitative Inquiry*, Vol. 12, No. 2, 2006, pp. 219 – 245.

Foucault, Michel: *Die Ordnung der Dinge. Eine Archäologie der Humanwissenschaften*. Frankfurt am Main 1971.

Foucault, Michel: *Power/Knowledge: Selected Interviews & Other Writings 1972 - 1977*, 5th edition. New York/Toronto 1980.

Foucault, Michel: "Disciplinary Power and Subjection," in Lukes, Steven (ed.): *Power*. Reprint of: Foucault, Michel: Power/Knowledge: Selected Interviews and Other Writings 1972 – 1977, (ed. Gordon, Colin, 1976). New York 1986, pp. 229 – 242.

Foucault, Michel: *Discipline and Punish*, 2nd edition. New York 1995.

Frey, Frederick: "Comment: On Issues and Nonissues in the Study of Power," in *American Political Science Review*, Vol. 65, No. 4, December 1971, pp. 1081 – 1101.

Frey, Frederick: *The Location and Measurement of Power: A Critical Analysis*, Paper presented at the International Studies Association and Annual Meeting and Study Group on Power, International Political Science Association. London 1989.

Galtung, Johan: *The European Community: A Superpower in the Making*. Oslo/London 1973.

Galtung, Johan: "Violence, peace, and peace research," in Evangelista,

Matthew (ed.): *Peace Studies. Critical Concepts in Political Science.* London/New York 2005, pp. 21 – 52.

Gebauer, Gunter/Wulf, Christoph: *Mimesis: Culture, Art, Society.* Berkeley 1995.

George, Alexander L./Bennett, Andrew: *Case Studies and Theory Development in Social Sciences.* Cambridge 2005.

George, Alexander L./Smoke, Richard: *Deterrence in American Foreign Policy: Theory and Practice.* New York/London 1974.

Gerstenfeld, Manfred (ed.): *European-Israel Relations: Between Confusion and Change?* Jerusalem Center for Public Affairs/Adenauer Foundation, Jerusalem 2006.

Gerth, Hans/Mills, C. Wright: *Character and Social Structure. The Psychology of Social Institutions.* New York 1953.

Giddens, Anthony: *The Constitution of Society: Outline of the Theory of Structuration.* Berkeley 1984.

Gillespie, Richard: "Spanish Protagonismo and the Euro-Med Partnership Initiative," in *Mediterranean Politics*, Vol. 2, No. 1, Summer 1997, pp. 33 – 48.

Gillespie, Richard: "Reshaping the Agenda? The Internal Politics of the Barcelona Process in the Aftermath of September 11," in *Mediterranean Politics*, Vol. 8, No. 2-3, Summer-Autumn 2003, (Jünemann, Annette (ed.): "Euro-Mediterranean Relations After September 11. International, Regional and Domestic Dynamics"), pp. 21 – 36.

Gillespie, Richard: *A Political Agenda for Region-building? The EMP and Democracy Promotion in North Africa*, Paper 040530, Institute of European Studies. Berkeley 2004.

318

Gillespie, Richard: *Onward but not Upward: The Barcelona Conference of 2005*, in Mediterranean Politics, Vol. 11, No. 2, July 2005, pp. 271 – 278.

Gillespie, Richard/Whitehead, Laurence: "European Democracy Promotion in North Africa: Limits and Prospects," in *Democratization*, Vol. 9, No. 1, Spring 2002, (Gillespie, Richard/Youngs, Richard (eds.): "Special Issue: The European Union and Democracy Promotion: The Case of North Africa"), pp. 192—206.

Gilpin, Robert: *War and Change in World Politics*. Cambridge et al 1981.

Glaser, Barney/Strauss, Anselm L.: *The Discovery of Grounded Theory: Strategies for Qualitative Research*. New York 1967.

Glasius, Marlies/Kaldor, Mary: "Individuals first: a human security doctrine for the European Union," in *Internationale Politik und Gesellschaft*, No. 1, 2005, pp. 62 – 84.

Gochman, Charles S./Leng, Russell J.: "Militarized Disputes, Incidents, and Crisis: Identification and Classification," in *International Interactions*, Vol. 14, No. 2, May 1988 pp. 157 – 163.

Gochman, Charles S./Maoz, Zeev: "Militarized Interstate Disputes, 1816 – 1976," in *Journal of Conflict Resolution*, Vol. 28, No. 4, December 1984, pp. 585 – 615.

Goldhamer, Herbert/Shils, Edward A.: "Types of Power and Status," in *The American Journal of Sociology*, Vol. 45, No. 2, September 1939, pp. 171 – 182.

Gonzalez, Guadalupe/Haggard, Stephan: "The United States and Mexico: a pluralistic security community?" in Adler, Emanuel/Barnett, Michael (eds.): *Security Communities*. Cambridge 1998, pp. 295 – 332.

Goodman, Nelson: *Ways of Worldmaking*. Indianapolis 1978.

Gordon, Philip H.: *The Transatlantic Allies and the Changing Middle East*, Adelphi Paper 332. New York 1998.

Gramsci, Antonio: *Selections from Prison Notebooks*. New York 1971.

Grande, Edgar: "The state and interest groups in a framework of multi-level decision-making: The case of the European Union," in *Journal of European Public Policy*, Vol. 3, No. 3, September 1996, pp. 318 – 338.

Gratius, Susanne: *Lateinamerika: fragmentierter Dialog und Partnerschaft ohne Strategie*, Thesenpapier SWP-Tagung Berlin, 9.-10. Mai 2007: Die Außenpolitik der EU: zwischen interregionalem Dialog und strategischer Partnerschaft. Berlin 2007.

Green, Leslie: "Power," in *Routledge Encyclopedia of Philosophy*. London/New York 1998, pp. 610 – 613.

Grieco, Joseph M.: "Anarchy and the Limits of Cooperation: A Realist Critic of the Newes Liberal Institutionalism, in *International Organization*, Vol. 42, No. 3, 1988a, pp. 485 – 507.

Grieco Joseph M.: "Realist Theory and the Problem of International Cooperation: Analysis with an Amended Prisoner's Dilemma, in: *Journal of Politics*, Vol. 50, 1988b, pp. 600 – 624.

Grieco, Joseph M.: *Cooperation Among Nations: Europe, America, and Non-Tariff Barriers*. Ithaca/London 1990.

Grieco, Joseph M.: "The Relative-Gains Problem for International Cooperation: Comment," in *American Political Science Review*, Vol. 87, September 1993, pp. 729 – 735.

Grieco, Joseph M.: "Structural realism and the problem of polarity and war," in Berenskoetter, Felix/Williams, Michael J. (eds.): *Power in World Politics*. London/New York 2007, pp. 64 – 82.

Groeben, Norbert: "Subjective Theories and the Explanation of Human Action," in Semin, Gun R./Gergen, Kenneth J. (eds.): *Everyday Understanding: Social and Scientific Implications*. London 1990, pp. 19 – 44.

Grünert, Angela: "Loss of Guiding Values and Support: September 11 and the Isolation of Human Rights Organizations in Egypt," in *Mediterranean Politics*, Vol. 8, No. 2/3, Summer-Autumn 2003, pp. 133 – 152.

Guiza, Habib: "Proposal for a Renewed Social Dialogue in the Mediterranean Zone," publication information unavailable: *Dossier. Ten Years after the Barcelona Process: Assessment and Perspectives*. s.l. 2005, pp. 82 – 83, http://www.gencat.net/relacions_exteriors/bcn10/eng/pdf/dossier.pdf, 04/08/2007.

Gulick, Edward: *Europe's Classical Balance of Power. A Case History of the Theory and Practice of One of the Great Concepts of European Statecraft*. New York 1955.

Guttman, Louis: "An Outline of Some New Methodology for Social Research," in *The Public Opinion Quarterly*, Vol. 18, No. 4, Winter 1954/55, pp. 395 – 404.

Guzzini, Stefano: "The concept of power: a constructivist analysis," in Berenskoetter, Felix/Williams, Michael J. (eds.): *Power in World Politics*. London/New York 2007, pp. 23 – 42.

Haas, Ernst B.: "The Balance of Power: Prescription, Concept, or Propaganda?" in *World Politics*, Vol. 5, No. 4, July 1953, pp. 442 – 477.

Haas, Ernst B.: *When Knowledge is Power. Three Models of Change in International Organizations*. Berkeley/Los Angeles/Oxford 1990.

Haddadi, Said: "Political Securitization and Democratization in the Maghreb: Ambigous Discourses and Fine-Tuning Practices for a Security Partnership," in Adler, Emanuel/Bicchi, Federica/Crawford, Beverly/Del Sarto, Raffaella A. (eds.): *The Convergence of Civilizations. Constructing a Mediterranean Region.* Toronto/Buffalo/London 2006, pp. 168 – 190.

Hager, Wolfgang: "Das Mittelmeer – "Mare Nostrum" Europas?" in Kohnstamm, Max/Hager, Wolfgang (ed.): *Zivilmacht Europa – Supermacht oder Partner?* Frankfurt am Main 1973, pp. 233 - 264.

Harders, Cilja: "Gender and Security in the Mediterranean," in *Mediterranean Politics*, Vol. 8, No. 2-3, Summer-Autumn 2003, (Jünemann, Annette (ed.): "Euro-Mediterranean Relations After September 11. International, Regional and Domestic Dynamics"), pp. 54 – 72.

Harders, Cilja/Legrenzi, Matteo (eds.): *Beyond Regionalism? Regional Cooperation, Regionalism and Regionalization in the Middle East.* Hampshire/Burlington 2008.

Harper, Douglas: "Small N's and community case studies," in Ragin, Charles C./Becker, Howard Saul: *What is a Case? Exploring the Foundations of Social Inquiry.* Cambridge 1992, pp. 139 – 158.

Harsanyi, John C.: "Measurement of Social Power, Opportunity Costs, and the Theory of Two-person Bargaining Games," in *Behavioral Sciences*, Vol. 7, No. 1, January 1962, pp. 67 - 80.

Hasenclever, Andreas/Mayer, Peter/Rittberger, Volker: *Theories of International Regimes.* Cambridge 1997.

Hassdorf, Wolf: "Contested credibility: the use of symbolic power in British exchange-rate politics," in Berenskoetter, Felix/Williams, Michael J. (eds.): *Power in World Politics.* London/New York 2007, pp. 141 – 161.

Hay, Colin: "Divided by a Common Language: Political Theory and the Concept of Power," in *Politics,* Vol. 17, No. 1, February 1997, pp. 45 – 52.

Hayward, Clarissa Rile: *De-Facing Power*. New York 2000.

Hazan, Reuven Y./Rahat, Gideon: "Representation, Electoral Reform, and Democracy. Theoretical and Empirical Lessons from the 1996 Elections in Israel," in *Comparative Political Studies*, Vol. 33, No. 10, December 2000, pp. 1310 – 1336.

Henderson, Errol A.: *Democracy and War. The End of an Illusion?* Boulder/London 2002.

Herman, Lior: "An Action Plan or a Plan for Action? Israel and the European Neighbourhood Policy," in *Mediterranean Politics*, Vol. 11, No. 3, November 2006, pp. 371 – 394.

Hermann, Tamar/Yuchtman-Yaar, Ephraim (eds.): *Israeli Society and the Challenge of Transition to Co-existence*. Tel Aviv 1997.

Hettne, Björn/Söderbaum, Fredrik: "The New Regionalism Approach," in *Politeia*, Vol. 17, No. 3, 1998, pp. 6 – 21.

Higgott, Richard A./Nossal, Kim Richard: "Australia and the search for a security community in the 1990s," in Adler, Emanuel/Barnett, Michael (eds.): *Security Communities*. Cambridge 1998, pp. 265 – 294.

Hill, Christopher: "European Foreign Policy: Power Bloc, Civilian Model – or Flop?" in Rummel, Reinhardt (ed.): *The Evolution of an International Actor. Western Europe's New Assertiveness*. Boulder/San Francisco/Oxford 1990, pp. 31 – 55.

Hirst, Paul: *From statism to pluralism. Democracy, civil society and global politics*. London 1997.

Hobbes, Thomas: *Leviathan*, (ed. Tuck, Richard). Cambridge 1996.

Hofmann, Sabine: „Israel auf dem Weg in den ‚Kulturkampf'? Konfliktfelder in der Auseinandersetzung um nationale Identität und regionale Legitimation," in Pawelka, Peter/Wehling, Hans-Georg (eds.): *Der Vordere Orient an der Schwelle zum 21. Jahrhundert.* Wiesbaden 1999, pp. 173 – 196.

Hogg, Michael A./Abrams, Dominic (eds.): *Group Motivations: Social Psychological Perspectives*. London 1993.

Howell, Jude/Pearce, Jenny: *Civil Society and Development. A Critical Exploration*. Boulder et al 2001.

Hunter, Floyd: *Community Power Structure: a Study of Decision Makers*. Chapel Hill 1953.

Hurrell, Andrew: "An emerging security community in South America?" in Adler, Emanuel/Barnett, Michael (eds.): *Security Communities*. Cambridge 1998, pp. 228 – 264.

Hurrell, Andrew: "Power, institutions, and the production of inequality," in Barnett, Michael/Duvall, Raymond (eds.): *Power in Global Governance*. Cambridge 2005, pp. 33 - 58.

Huysmans, Jef: "The Question of the Limit: Desecuritisation and the Aesthetics of Horror in Political Realism," in *Millennium*, Vol. 27, No. 3, 1998, pp. 569-589.

Huysmans, Jef: "The European Union and the Securitization of Migration," in *Journal of Common Market Studies*, Vol. 38, No. 5, December 2000, pp. 751 – 777.

Hyde-Price, Adrian: "'Normative' power Europe: a realist critique," in *Journal of European Public Policy*, Vol. 13, No. 2, March 2006, pp.

217 – 234.

Hyde-Price, Adrian: "A 'tragic actor'? A realist perspective on 'ethical power Europe'," in *International Affairs*, Vol. 84, No. 1, 2008, pp. 29 – 44.

Isaac, Jeffrey C.: Power and Marxist Theory: *A Realist View.* Ithaca/London 1987a.

Isaac, Jeffrey C.: "Beyond the Three Faces of Power: A Realist Critique," in *Polity*, Vol. 20, No.1, Autumn 1987b, pp. 4 – 31.

James, Patrick: "Structural Realism and the Causes of War," in *Mershon International Studies Review*, Vol. 39, 1995, pp. 181 – 208.

Jenner, Richard A.: "Changing Patterns of Power, Chaotic Dynamics and the Emergence of a Post-modern Organizational Paradigm," in *Journal of Organizational Change Management*, Vol. 7, No. 3, 1994, pp. 8 – 21.

Jepperson, Ronald L./Wendt, Alexander/Katzenstein, Peter J.: "Norms, identity, and culture in national security," in: Katzenstein, Peter J. (ed.): *The Culture of National Security: Norms and Identity in World Politics*. New York 1996, pp- 33 - 75.

Joffé, George: "European Multilateralism and Soft Power Projection in the Mediterranean," in Tanner, Fred (ed.): *The European Union as a Security Actor in the Middle East*. Zürich 2001, pp. 31 - 56.

Johansson-Nogués, Elisabeth: "A 'Ring of Friends'? The Implications of the European Neighbourhood Policy for the Mediterranean," in *Mediterranean Politics*, Vol. 9, No. 2, Summer 2004, pp. 240 - 247.

Johansson-Nogués, Elisabeth: *Civil Society in Euro-Mediterranean relations: What success of EU`s normative promotion?* EUI Working Paper RSCAS No. 2006/40. San Domenico di Fiesole 2006.

Johnstone, Ian: "The power of interpretive communities," in Barnett, Michael/Duvall, Raymond (eds.): *Power in Global Governance*. Cambridge 2005, pp. 185 – 204.

Jünemann, Annette: "Auswärtige Politikgestaltung im EU-Mehrebenensystem. Eine Analyse der strukturellen Probleme am Beispiel der Euro-Mediterranen Partnerschaft," in Schubert, Klaus/Müller-Brandeck-Bocquet, Gisela (eds.): *Die Europäische Union als Akteur der Weltpolitik*. Opladen 2000, pp. 65 - 80.

Jünemann, Annette: "Repercussions of the Emerging European Security and Defence Policy on the Civil Character of the Euro-Mediterranean Partnership," in *Mediterranean Politics*, Vol. 8, No. 2/3, Summer 2003a, pp. 38 – 53.

Jünemann, Annette: "Security-Building in the Mediterranean After September 11," in *Mediterranean Politics*, Vol. 8, No. 2/3, Summer 2003b, pp. 1 – 20.

Jünemann, Annette/Schörnig, Niklas: "Die Europäische Sicherheits-und Verteidigungspolitik: Potenzielle Gefahren einer sich abzeichnenden Eigendynamik," in Schlotter, Peter (ed.): *Europa – Macht – Frieden? Zur Politik der "Zivilmacht Europa."* Baden-Baden 2003, pp. 101 – 133.

Kagan, Robert: *Of Paradise and Power: America and Europe in the New World Order*. New York 2002.

Kaldor, Mary: *Human security: reflections on globalization and intervention*. Cambridge/Malden 2007.

Kaldor, Mary/Martin, Mary/Selchow, Sabine: "Human security: a strategic narrative for Europe," in *International Affairs*, Vol. 83, No. 2, 2007, pp. 273 – 288.

Kaldor, Mary/Martin, Mary/Selchow, Sabine: *Human Security: A European Strategic Narrative*, International Policy Analysis,

Friedrich-Ebert-Stiftung. Bonn 2008.

Katzenstein, Peter J. (ed.): *The Culture of National Security: Norms and Identity in World Politics*. New York 1996.

Katzenstein, Peter/Keohane, Robert O./Krasner, Stephen D.: "International Organizations and the Study of World Politics," in *International Organization*, Vol. 54, No. 2, 1998, pp. 645 – 685.

Keck, Otto: "Die Bedeutung der rationalen Institutionentheorie für die Politikwissenschaft," in Göhler, Gerhard (ed.): *Die Eigenart der Institutionen. Zum Profil politischer Institutionentheorie*. Baden-Baden 1994, pp. 187 – 220.

Keohane, Robert O.: *After Hegemony. Cooperation and Discord in the World Political Economy*. Princeton 1984.

Keohane, Robert O.: *Neorealism and its Critics*. New York 1986.

Keohane, Robert O.: *International Institutions and State Power. Essays in International Relations Theory*. Boulder 1989.

Keohane, Robert O./ Nye Joseph S.: *Transnational Relations and World Politics*. Cambridge 1972.

Keohane, Robert O./Nye, Joseph S.: *Power and Interdependence*, 3rd edition. New York et al 2001.

Khader, Bichara: *État, société civile et démocratie dans le monde arabomusulman*. Louvain 1997.

Khader, Bichara: "Euro-Mediterranean Partnership or Euro-Arab Partnership?" publication information unavailable: *Dossier. Ten Years after the Barcelona Process: Assessment and Perspectives*. s.l. 2005, pp. 98 – 102, http://www.gencat.net/relacions_exteriors/bcn10/eng/pdf/dossier.pdf, 04/08/2007.

Khoury, Philip S./Kostiner, Joseph (eds.): *Tribes and State Formation in the Middle East*. Berkeley/Los Angeles/Oxford 1990.

Kimmerling, Baruch: "Between Hegemony and Dormant *Kulturkampf* in Israel," in *Israel Affairs*, Vol. 4, No. 3-4, Spring/Summer, pp. 49 – 72.

King, Gary/Keohane, Robert O./Verba, Sidney: *Designing Social Inquiry: Scientific Inference in Qualitative Research*. Princeton 1994.

Kirste, Knut/Maull, Hanns W.: "Zivilmacht und Rollentheorie," in: *Zeitschrift für Internationale Beziehungen*, Vol. 3, No. 2, December 1996, pp. 283—312.

Kiser, Edgar/Hechter, Michael: "The Role of General Theory in Comparative-historical Sociology," in *American Journal of Sociology*, Vol. 97, No. 1, July 1991, pp. 1 - 30.

Klein, Uta: „Zum Verhältnis von Nationalismus, Ethnizität, Religion und Geschlecht. Spaltungen in der israelischen Gesellschaft," in Schmidt, Renate (ed.): *Naher Osten. Politik und Gesellschaft*. Berlin 1998, pp. 109 – 134.

Knorr, Klaus: *The War Potential of Nations*. Princeton 1956.

Knorr, Klaus: *The Power of Nations. The Political Economy of International Relations*. New York 1975.

Kohler-Koch, Beate: *Regime in den internationalen Beziehungen*. Baden-Baden 1989.

Kohler-Koch, Beate: "The Evolution and Transformation of European Governance," in Kohler-Koch, Beate/Eising, Rainer (eds.): *The Transformation of Governance in the European Union*. London 1999, pp. 20 – 59.

Koopmans, Ruud/Erbe, Jessica: "Towards a European public sphere?"

in *Innovation: The European Journal of Social Sciences*, Vol. 17, No. 2, June 2004, pp. 97 – 118.

Kostiner, Joseph: *The Making of Saudi Arabia 1916 – 1936*. From Chieftaincy to Monarchical State. New York/Oxford 1993.

Kostiner, Joseph: *Conflict and Cooperation in the Gulf Region*. Wiesbaden 2008.

Krasner, Stephen D.: *Structural Conflict. The Third World Against Global Liberalism*. Berkeley/Los Angeles 1985.

Kratochwil, Friedrich V.: *Rules, Norms, and Decisions. On the conditions of practical and legal reasoning in international relations and domestic affairs*. New York et al 1989.

Krause, Keith/Williams, Michael C.: "Broadening the Agenda of Security Studies: Politics and Methods," in *Mershon International Studies Review*, Vol. 40, No. 2, October 1996, pp. 229 – 254.

Krause, Keith/Williams, Michael C. (eds.): *Critical Security Studies: Concepts and Cases*. Minneapolis 1997.

Krupnick, Charles: "Between Neorealism and Liberal Institutionalism: The CFSP and European Security Cooperation," in *Revue d'Intégration Européenne/Journal of European Integration*, Vol. XIX, No. 2-3, Winter/Spring 1996, pp. 143 – 163.

Kubba, Laith: "The Awakening of Civil Society," in Diamond, Larry/Plattner, Marc F./Brumberg, Daniel (eds.): *Islam and Democracy in the Middle East*. Baltimore/London 2003, pp. 28 – 34.

Kühnhardt, Ludger: "10 Years Euro-Mediterranean Partnership: The Human Dimension Revisited," in Marchetti, Andreas (ed.): *Ten Years Euro-Mediterranean Partnership. Defining European Interests for the Next Decade*, Discussion Paper C 154, Zentrum für Europäische Integrationsforschung. Bonn 2005, pp. 83 - 96.

Lamassoure, Alain: "L`Europe à la recherche d`une politique étrangère," in *Le Forum Franco-Allemand*. Numéro spécial 2006/07, pp. 47 – 52.

Lasswell, Harold/Kaplan, Abraham: *Power and Society. A Framework for Political Inquiry*. New Haven 1950.

Lazarsfeld, Paul/Barton, Allen H.: "Qualitative measurement in the social sciences: Classification, typologies, and indices," in Lerner, Daniel/Lasswell, Harold Dwight (eds.): *The Policy Sciences: Recent Developments in Scope and Method*. Stanford 1951, pp. 155 – 192.

Lee, Raymond M.: *Unobtrusive Methods in Social Research*. Buckingham 2000.

Leffler, Christian: "Evolution not Revolution: the Barcelona Process, ten years on," publication information unavailable: *Dossier. Ten Years after the Barcelona Process: Assessment and Perspectives*. s.l. 2005, pp. 62 – 65, http://www.gencat.net/relacions_exteriors/bcn10/eng/pdf/dossier.pdf, 04/08/2007.

Lemke, Christiane: *Internationale Beziehungen. Grundkonzepte, Theorien und Problemfelder*. München/Wien 2000.

Leng, Russell J./Singer, David J.: "Militarized Interstate Crisis: The BCOW Typology and Its Applications," in *International Studies Quarterly*, Vol. 32, No. 2, June 1988, pp. 155-173.

Lennon, David: "The European Union: A Leader in Humanitarian and Development Assistance," in Guttman, Robert J. (ed.): *Europe in the new Century – Visions of and Emerging Superpower*. Boulder 2001, pp. 127 - 138.

Levy, Jack S.: "War and Peace," in Carlsnaes, Walter/Risse, Thomas/Simmons, Beth A. (eds.): *Handbook of International Relations*. London/Thousand Oaks/New Delhi 2002, pp. 350 - 368.

330

Levy, Jack S.: "Case Studies: Types, Designs, and Logics of Inference," in *Conflict Management and Peace Science*, Vol. 25, No. 1, March 2008, pp. 1 – 18.

Lewis, Bernard: "The Roots of Muslim Rage," in *Atlantic Monthly*, Vol. 266, No. 3, September 1990, pp. 47 – 60.

Lightfoot, Simon/Burchell, Jon: "The European Union and the World Summit on Sustainable Development: Normative Power Europe in Action?" in *Journal of Common Market Studies*, Vol. 43, No. 1, 2005, pp. 74 – 95.

Lijphart, Arend: "Comparative Politics and the Comparative Method," in *American Political Science Review*, Vol. 65, No. 3, September 1971, pp. 682 – 693.

Lijphart, Arend: "The Comparable-Case Strategy in Comparative Research," in *Comparative Political Studies*, Vol. 8, No. 2, July 1975, pp. 158 – 177.

Lincoln, Bruce: *Authority. Construction and Corrosion*. Chicago/London 1994.

Lipschutz, Ronnie D.: "Global civil society and global governmentality: or, the search for politics and the state amidst the capillaries of social power," in Barnett, Michael/Duvall, Raymond (eds.): *Power in Global Governance*. Cambridge 2005, pp. 229 – 248.

Lipschutz, Ronnie D.: "On the transformational potential of global civil society," in Berenskoetter, Felix/Williams, Michael J. (eds.): *Power in World Politics*. London/New York 2007, pp. 225 – 243.

Lister, Sarah: "Power in partnership? An analysis of an NGO's relationships with its partners," in *Journal of International Development*, Vol. 12, No. 2, March 2000, pp. 227 – 239.

Lofthouse, Alexander/Long, David: "The European Union and the

Civilian Model of Foreign Policy," in: *Revue d'Intégration Européenne/Journal of European Integration*, Vol. 19, No. 2-3, Winter/Spring 1996, pp. 181—196.

Luciani, Giacomo: "The Economic Basket of the Barcelona Process: Outcomes and Perspectives," publication information unavailable: *Dossier. Ten Years after the Barcelona Process: Assessment and Perspectives.* s.l. 2005, pp. 71 – 77, http://www.gencat.net/relacions_exteriors/bcn10/eng/pdf/dossier.pdf, 04/08/2007.

Luhmann, Niklas: *Soziale Systeme. Grundriß einer allgemeinen Theorie.* Frankfurt am Main 1984.

Luhmann, Niklas: *Die Gesellschaft der Gesellschaft.* Frankfurt am Main 1997.

Lukes, Steven: *Power. A Radical View.* Houndmills et al 1974.

Lukes, Steven: "Power and the battle for hears and minds: on the bluntness of soft power," in Berenskoetter, Felix/Williams, Michael J. (eds.): *Power in World Politics.* London/New York 2007, pp. 83 – 97.

Machiavelli, Niccolò: *Discourses on Livy*, (trans. Mansfield, Harvey/ Tarcov, Nathan). Chicago 1996.

Manners, Ian: "Normative Power Europe: A Contradiction in Terms?" in *Journal of Common Market Studies*, Vol. 40, No. 2, June 2002, pp. 235 – 258.

Manners, Ian: "Normative power Europe reconsidered: beyond the crossroads," in *Journal of European Public Policy*, Vol. 13, No. 2, March 2006, pp. 182 – 199.

Manners, Ian: "The normative thics of the European Union," in *International Affairs*, Vol. 84,

No. 1, 2008, pp. 45 – 60.

Maoz, Zeev: *Paths to Conflict: International Dispute Initiation, 1816 – 1976*. Boulder 1982.

March, James G./Olsen, Johan P.: *Rediscovering Institutions. The Organizational Basis of Politics*. New York/London 1989.

Marchetti, Andreas: "Introduction," in Marchetti, Andreas (ed.): *Ten Years Euro-Mediterranean Partnership. Defining European Interests for the Next Decade*, Discussion Paper C 154, Zentrum für Europäische Integrationsforschung. Bonn 2005a, pp. 5 - 6.

Marchetti, Andreas: "Promoting Good Governance. The Keystone to a Sustainable Mediterranean Policy," in Marchetti, Andreas (ed): *Ten Years Euro-Mediterranean Partnership. Defining European Interests for the Next Decade*, Discussion Paper C 154, Zentrum für Europäische Integrationsforschung. Bonn 2005b, pp. 47 - 58.

Matlary, Janne Haaland: "Much ado about little: the EU and human security," in *International Affairs*, Vol. 84, No. 1, 2008, pp. 131 – 143.

Maull, Hanns W.: "Germany and Japan: The New Civilian Powers," in *Foreign Affairs*, Vol. 69, No. 5 Winter 1990/91, pp. 91 – 106.

Maull, Hanns W.: "Europa und Japan: Perspektiven für die Zukunft einer Beziehung," in Maull, Hanns W. (ed.): *Japan und Europa: Getrennte Welten?* Frankfurt am Main/New York 1993.

Maull, Hanns W.: "Deutschland als Zivilmacht," in Schmidt, Siegmar/Hellmann, Gunther/Wolf, Reinhard (eds.): *Handbuch zur deutschen Außenpolitik*. Wiesbaden 2007, pp. 73 – 84.

Mawdsley, Jocelyn: "On the way to a European Armaments Policy?" in Schlotter, Peter (ed.): *Europa – Macht – Frieden? Zur Politik der "Zivilmacht Europa."* Baden-Baden 2003, pp. 134 – 158.

Maxwell, Joseph A.: "Understanding and Validity in Qualitative Research," in Miles, Matthew B./Huberman, A. Michael: *The Qualitative Researcher's Companion*. London 2002, pp. 37 - 64.

Mayer, Hartmut: "Is it still called 'Chinese Whispers'? The EU's rhetoric and action as a responsible global institution," in *International Affairs*, Vol. 84, No. 1, 2008, pp. 61 – 79.

Mayring, Philipp: *Qualitative Inhaltsanalyse. Grundlagen und Techniken*, 10th edition. Weinheim 2008.

Mearsheimer, John J.: "The False Promise of International Institutions," in *International Security*, Vol. 19, No. 3, Winter 1994/95, pp. 5 – 49.

Menéndez, Irene/Youngs, Richard: *The Euro-Mediterranean Partnership Turns Ten: Democracy's Halting Advance?* Instituto Português de Relações Internacionais 2006, http://www.ipri.pt/artigos/artigo.php?ida=109, 18/08/2007.

Merrit, Richard L./Zinnes, Dina A.: "Validity of Power Indices," in *International Interactions*, Vol. 14, No. 2, May 1988 pp. 141 – 151.

Michalek, Jan J.: "Economics in the Mediterranean. Common Challenges," in Marchetti, Andreas (ed.): *Ten Years Euro-Mediterranean Partnership. Defining European Interests for the Next Decade*, Discussion Paper C 154, Zentrum für Europäische Integrationsforschung. Bonn 2005, pp. 59 - 81.

Miles, Matthew B./Huberman, A. Michael: *Qualitative data analysis: a sourcebook of new methods*. Beverly Hills 1984.

Miles, Matthew B./Huberman, A. Michael: "Reflections and Advice," in Miles, Matthew B./Huberman, A. Michael: *The Qualitative Researcher's Companion*. London 2002, pp. 393 - 398.

Miliband, Ralph: *The State in Capitalist Society*. London 1969.

Miliband, Ralph: "The Capitalist State: Reply to Nicos Poulantzas," in *New Left Review*, Vol. 59, January/February 1970, pp. 53 – 60.

Mill, John Stuart: *A System of Logic, Ratiocinative and Inductive.* Honolulu 2002.

Mills, C. Wright: *The Power Elite.* New York 1956.

Mitchell, David: *Making Foreign Policy: Presidential Management of the Decision-making Process.* Burlington 2005.

Mitrany, David: *The Functional Theory of Politics.* New York 1975.

Morgenthau, Hans J.: *Politics Among Nations. The Struggle for Power and Peace*, 3rd edition. New York 1960.

Müller, Harald: "Internationale Regime und ihr Beitrag zur Weltordnung," in Kaiser, Karl/Schwarz, Hans-Peter (eds.): *Die neue Weltpolitik.* Bonn 1995, pp. 384 – 395.

Müller-Brandeck-Bocquet, Gisela: "Die Mehrdimensionalität der EU-Außenbeziehungen," in Schubert, Klaus/Müller-Brandeck-Bocquet, Gisela (eds.): *Die Europäische Union als Akteur der Weltpolitik.* Opladen 2000, pp. 29 – 44.

Musu, Constanza: "Two Years of EU-Israel Action Plan: An Assessment of the Political Dimension from a European Perspective," in Nathanson, Roby/Stetter, Stephan (eds.): *The Middle East under Fire? EU-Israel Relations in a Region Between War and Conflict Resolution.* Friedrich-Ebert-Stiftung. Herzliya 2007, 37 – 46.

Nagel, Jack: *The Descriptive Analysis of Power.* New Haven 1975.

Nathanson, Roby/Stetter, Stephan (eds.): *The Israeli European Policy Network. The Monitor of the EU-Israel Action Plan. Friedrich-Ebert-Stiftung.* Tel Aviv/Vienna 2006.

Nathanson, Roby/Stetter, Stephan (eds.): *The Middle East under Fire?*

EU-Israel Relations in a Region Between War and Conflict Resolution. Friedrich-Ebert-Stiftung. Herzliya 2007.

Newman, David: "Conflicting Israeli Peace Discourses," in *Peace Review*, Vol. 9, No. 3, September 1997, pp. 417 – 424.

NGO Monitor: *Promoting critical debate and accountability of human rights NGOs in the Arab-Israeli conflict*, http://ngo-monitor.org/issues/eu.htm, 30/05/2007.

Nicolaïdis, Kalypso/Nicolaïdis, Dimitri: „The EuroMed beyond Civilizational Paradigms," in Adler, Emanuel/Bicchi, Federica/Crawford, Beverly/Del Sarto, Raffaella A. (eds.): *The Convergence of Civilizations. Constructing a Mediterranean Region*. Toronto/Buffalo/London 2006, pp. 338 - 377.

Norton, Anne: *Reflections on Political Identity*. Baltimore 1988.

Nye, Joseph S. Jnr.: *Soft Power. The Means to Success in World Politics*. New York 2004.

Nye, Joseph S. Jnr.: "Notes for a soft-power research agenda," in Berenskoetter, Felix/Williams, Michael J. (eds.): *Power in World Politics*. London/New York 2007, pp. 162 – 172.

Oppenheim, Felix E.: *Political Concepts: A Reconstruction*. Chicago 1981.

Organski, Abramo F.K.: *World Politics*. New York 1958.

Organski, Abramo F.K./Kugler, Jacek: *The War Ledger*. Chicago 1980.

Ortega, Martin: "The Euro-Mediterranean Dialogue and the EU's Common Security and Defence Policy," in Marchetti, Andreas (ed.): *Ten Years Euro-Mediterranean Partnership. Defining European Interests for the Next Decade*, Discussion Paper C 154, Zentrum für

Europäische Integrationsforschung. Bonn 2005, pp. 25 - 45.

Osgood, Robert E./Tucker, Robert W.: *Force, Order, and Justice.* Baltimore 1967.

Parsons, Talcott: *Sociological Theory and Modern Society.* New York 1967.

Patton, Michael Quinn: *Qualitative Evaluation and Research Methods*, 3rd edition. London 2002.

Peretz, Don/Doron, Gideon: "Sectarian Politics and the Peace Process: The 1999 Israel Elections," in *Middle East Journal*, Vol. 54, No. 2, Spring 2000, pp. 259 – 273.

Peters, Joel: "Practice and Their Failures: Arab-Israeli Relations and the Barcelona Process," in Adler, Emanuel/Bicchi, Federica/Crawford, Beverly/Del Sarto, Raffaella A. (eds.): *The Convergence of Civilizations. Constructing a Mediterranean Region.* Toronto/Buffalo/London 2006, pp. 212 - 235.

Piscatori, James L.: "Democratization and Islam," in *Middle Eastern Journal*, Vol. 45, No. 3, Summer 1991, pp. 427 – 440.

Platt, Jennifer: "Cases of cases…of cases," in Ragin, Charles C./Becker, Howard Saul: *What is a Case? Exploring the Foundations of Social Inquiry.* Cambridge 1992, pp. 21 – 52.

Pollack, Mark A.: "Delegation, agency, and agenda setting in the European Community," in *International Organization*, Vol. 51, No. 1, Winter 1997, pp. 99 – 134.

Poulantzas, Nicos: *State, Power, Socialism*, 3rd edition. London/New York 2000.

Prat y Coll, Juan: "Ten Years of the Barcelona Process," publication information unavailable: *Dossier. Ten Years after the Barcelona*

Process: Assessment and Perspectives. s.l. 2005, p. 6, http://www.gencat.net/relacions_exteriors/bcn10/eng/pdf/dossier.pdf, 04/08/2007.

Prior, Lindsay: *Using Documents in Social Research*. London 2003.

Radwan, Samir: "Assessment of the Barcelona Process from the Mediterranean Partners` Perspective," publication information unavailable: *Dossier. Ten Years after the Barcelona Process: Assessment and Perspectives*. s.l. 2005, pp. 78 – 84, http://www.gencat.net/relacions_exteriors/bcn10/eng/pdf/dossier.pdf, 04/08/2007.

Ragin, Charles C.: *The Comparative Method. Moving Beyond Qualitative and Quantitative Strategies*. Berkeley/Los Angeles/London 1987.

Ragin, Charles C.: "Introduction. Cases of ‚What is a case?',“ in Ragin, Charles C./Becker, Howard Saul: *What is a Case? Exploring the Foundations of Social Inquiry*. Cambridge 1992, pp. 1 - 18.

Ray, James Lee: *Democracy and International Conflict. An Evolution of the Democratic Peace Proposition*. Columbia 1995.

Ray, James Lee: "Democracy. On the Level(s), Does Democracy Correlate with Peace?" in Vasequez, John A. (ed.): *What Do We Know About War?* Boulder 2000, pp. 299 – 316.

Ray, James Lee/Vural, Ayse: "Power Disparities and Pardoxical Conflict Outcomes," in *International Interactions*, Vol. 12, No. 4, June 1986, pp. 315 – 342.

Reiter, Dan/Stam, Allan C.: *Democracies at War*. Princeton 2002.

Ricci, David: "Receiving Ideas in Political Analysis: the Case of the Community Power Studies," in *Western Political Quarterly*, Vol. 33, No. 4, December 1980, pp. 451 – 475.

Ringmar, Erik: "Empowerment among nations: a sociological perspective," in Berenskoetter, Felix/Williams, Michael J. (eds.): *Power in World Politics*. London/New York 2007, pp. 189 – 203.

Risse, Thomas: "Deutsche Identität und Außenpolitik," in Schmidt, Siegmar/Hellmann, Gunther/Wolf, Reinhard (eds.): *Handbuch zur deutschen Außenpolitik*. Wiesbaden 2007, pp. 49 – 61.

Risse-Kappen, Thomas: "Democratic Peace – Warlike Democracies? A Social Constructivist Interpretation of the Liberal Argument," in *European Journal of International Relations*, Vol. 1, No. 4, 1995, pp. 491 – 517.

Ritchie, Jane/Spencer, Liz: "Qualitative Data Analysis for Applied Policy Research," in Miles, Matthew B./Huberman, A. Michael: *The Qualitative Researcher's Companion*. London 2002, pp. 305 - 330.

Rittberger, Volker (ed.): *International Regimes in East-West Politics*. London 1990.

Roe, Paul: "Securitization and Minority Rights: Conditions of Desecuritization," in *Security Dialogue*, Vol. 35, No. 3, 2004, pp. 279 – 294.

Romilly, Jacqueline de: "Les valeurs de l`Europe," in *Le Forum Franco-Allemand*, Numéro spécial 2006/07, pp. 141 – 154.

Rosecrance, Richard: "The European Union: A New Type of International Actor," in Zielonka, Jan (ed.): *Paradoxes of European Foreign Policy*. The Hague 1998, pp. 15 – 23.

Ruggie, John: *Constructing the World Polity: Essays on International Institutionalization*. London 1998.

Rummel, Reinhardt/Wiedemann, Jörg: *Paradoxes of European Foreign Policy. Identifying Institutional Paradoxes of CFSP*, EUI Working Paper RSC No. 1997/67. San Domenico 1997.

Rupert, Mark: "Class powers and the politics of global governance," in Barnett, Michael/Duvall, Raymond (eds.): *Power in Global Governance*. Cambridge 2005, pp. 205 – 228.

Russell, Bertrand: *Power. A New Social Analysis*, 7th edition. London/New York 1995.

Russett, Bruce: *Grasping the Democratic Peace. Principles for a Post-Cold-War World*. Princeton 1993.

Russett, Bruce: "A neo-Kantian perspective: democracy, interdependence and international organizations in building security communities," in Adler, Emanuel/Barnett, Michael (eds.): *Security Communities*. Cambridge 1998, pp. 368 – 394.

Sade, Tal: "Taking Stock of the Action Plan: An Israeli Perspective," in Nathanson, Roby/Stetter, Stephan (eds.): *The Middle East under Fire? EU-Israel Relations in a Region Between War and Conflict Resolution*. Friedrich-Ebert-Stiftung. Herzliya 2007, pp. 29 – 36.

Salamé, Ghassan (ed.): *Démocraties sans democrats: Politiques d'ouverture dans le monde arabe et islamique*. Paris 1994.

Sandler, Shmuel: *The State of Israel, the Land of Israel: The Statist and Ethnonational Dimensions of Foreign Policy*. London 1993.

Scharpf, Fritz W.: *Interationsformen – Akteurszentrierter Institutionalismus in der Politikforschung*. Opladen 2000.

Schattschneider, Elmer Eric: *The Semisovereign People: A Realist's view of Democracy in America*. New York 1960.

Schäfer, Isabel: "Die EU, der Mittelmeerraum und der Nahe Osten: vom Multilateralismus zurück zum Bilateralismus," in Thesenpapier SWP Tagung Berlin, 9. – 10.5.2007: *Die Außenpolitik der Europäischen Union: Zwischen interregionalem Dialog und strategischer Partnerschaft*. Berlin 2007.

Scheele, Brigitte/Groeben, Norbert: *Dialog-Konsens-Methoden zur Rekonstruktion subjektiver Theorien*. Tübingen 1988.

Schlotter, Peter: "Die Europäische Union: eine 'Zivilmacht'? – Zur Einführung," in Schlotter, Peter (ed.): *Europa – Macht – Frieden? Zur Politik der "Zivilmacht Europa."* Baden-Baden 2003, pp. 7 – 17.

Schmid, Dorothée: "The Use of Conditionality in Support of Political, Economic and Social Rights: Unveiling the Euro-Mediterranean Partnership's True Hierarchy of Objectives," in *Mediterranean Politics*, Vol. 9, No. 3, Autumn 2004, pp. 396 – 421.

Schmid, Dorothée: "European Views of the Israeli-Palestinian Conflict: The Contribution of Member States to Framing EU Policies" in Nathanson, Roby/Stetter, Stephan (eds.): *The Middle East under Fire? EU-Israel Relations in a Region Between War and Conflict Resolution*. Friedrich-Ebert-Stiftung. Herzliya 2007, pp. 99 – 125.

Schmidt, Brian C.: "Realist conceptions of power," in Berenskoetter, Felix/Williams, Michael J. (eds.): *Power in World Politics*. London/New York 2007, pp. 43 – 63.

Schmidt, Manfred G.: "Der konsoziative Staat – Hypothesen zur politischen Struktur und zum politischen Leistungsprofil der Europäischen Union," in Grande, Edgar/Jachtenfuß, Markus (eds.): *Wie problemlösungsfähig ist die EU? Regieren im europäischen Mehrebenensystem*. Baden-Baden 2000, pp. 33 – 57.

Schmitt, Carl: *The Concept of the Political*. Chicago 1996.

Schmitz, Hans Peter/Sikkink, Kathryn: "International Human Rights," in Carlsnaes, Walter/Risse, Thomas/Simmons, Beth A. (eds.): *Handbook of International Relations*. London/Thousand Oaks/New Delhi 2002, pp. 517 - 537.

Schölderle, Thomas: *Das Prinzip der Macht. Neuzeitliches Politik- und Staatsdenken bei Thomas Hobbes und Niccolò Machiavelli*.

Berlin/Cambridge 2002.

Schubert, Gunter: "China und die Europäische Union im Kontext der GASP," in *Aus Politik und Zeitgeschichte*, B 19 – 20, 2002, pp. 21 – 28.

Scott, John: *A Matter of Record: Documentary Sources in Social Research.* Cambridge 1990.

Searle, John R.: *The Construction of Social Reality.* New York 1995.

Seligman, Adam B.: *The Idea of Civil Society.* Princeton 1995.

Sen, Amartya: *Identity and Violence. The Illusion of Destiny.* New York 2006.

Sfeir, Antoine: "L`Europe – monde arabe et musulman, regards croisés," in *Le Forum Franco-Allemand*, Numéro spécial 2006/07, pp. 88 – 96.

Sherif, Muzafer: *In Common Predicament: Social Psychology of Intergroup Conflict and Cooperation.* Boston 1966.

Shore, Sean M.: "No fences make good neighbors: the development of the US-Canadian security community, 1871-1940," in Adler, Emanuel/Barnett, Michael (eds.): *Security Communities.* Cambridge 1998, pp. 333 – 367.

Simon, Herbert: *Models of Man.* New York 1957.

Simonds, Frank H./Emeny, Brooks: *The Great Powers in World Politics. International Relations and Economic Nationalism.* New York 1935.

Simoni, Marcella: "The Role of Civil Society in EU/Israeli-Palestinian Cooperation," in Nathanson, Roby/Stetter, Stephan (eds.): *The Middle East under Fire? EU-Israel Relations in a Region Between War and Conflict Resolution.* Friedrich-Ebert-Stiftung. Herzliya 2007, 146 –

165.

Singer, David J.: "Inter-nation influence: a formal model," in *The American Political Science Review*, Vol. 57, No. 2, June 1963, pp. 420 – 431.

Singer, David J.: "Variables, Indicators, and Data: The Measurement Problem in Marco-Political Research," in *Social Science History*, Vol. 6, No. 2, Spring 1982, pp. 181 – 217.

Singer, David J.: "Reconstructing the Correlates of War Dataset on Material Capabilities of States, 1816 – 1985," in *International Interactions*, Vol. 14, No. 2, May 1988, pp. 115 – 132.

Singer, David J./Diehl, Paul F.: *Measuring the Correlates of War*. Ann Arbor 1990.

Singer, David J./Small, Melvin: *The Wages of War, 1816 – 1965: A Statistical Handbook*. New York 1972.

Skocpol, Theda: *States and Social Revolutions*. Cambridge/New York/Melbourne 1979.

Small, Melvin/Singer, David J.: *Resort to Arms: International and Civil Wars, 1816 – 1980*. Beverly Hills 1982.

Smith, Karen Elisabeth: *The Use of Political Conditionality in the EU's Relations with Third Countries: How Effective?* EUI Working Paper SPS No. 97/7. Badia Fiesolana/San Domenico 1997a.

Smith, Karen Elisabeth: *Paradoxes of European Foreign Policy. The Instruments of European Foreign Policy*. EUI Working Paper RSC No. 97/68. Badia Fiesolana/San Domenico 1997b.

Solana, Javier: Speech delivered by the Secretary General of NATO at CE.Mi.S.S/RAND International Conference on The Future of NATO`s Mediterranean Initiative. Rome, 10 November 1997, http://www.nato.int/docu/speech/1997/s971110a.htm, 07.07.2007.

Solingen, Etel: *Regional Orders at Century's Dawn. Global and Domestic Influences on Grand Strategy*. Princeton 1998.

Solingen, Etel/Ozyurt, Saba Şenses: "Mare Nostrum? The Sources, Logic, and Dilemmas of the Euro-Mediterranean Partnership," in Adler, Emanuel/Bicchi, Federica/Crawford, Beverly/Del Sarto, Raffaella A. (eds.): *The Convergence of Civilizations. Constructing a Mediterranean Region*. Toronto/Buffalo/London 2006, pp. 51 – 82.

Spinoza, Baruch de: *Tractatus Politicus*, (trans. Samuel, Shirley). Leiden 1989.

Sprinzak, Ehud/Diamond, Larry: *Israeli Democracy under Stress*. Boulder 1993.

Sprout, Harold/Sprout, Margaret (eds.): *Foundations of National Power*. Princeton 1945.

Sprout, Harold/Sprout, Margaret: *Foundations of International Politics*. Princeton 1962.

Sprout, Harold/Sprout Margaret: *The Ecological Perspective on Human Affairs: With Special Reference to International Politics*. Princeton 1965.

Spykman, Nicholas John: *America's Strategy in World Politics. The United States and the Balance of Power*. New York 1942.

Stanley, Bruce: *People to People: An Evaluation and Future Prospects*, Jerusalem Conference Initiated by Canadian, Norwegian and EU Delegations, 5 April 2005. Jerusalem 2005.

Steeg, Marianne van de: "Rethinking the Conditions for a Public Sphere in the European Union," in *European Journal of Social Theory*, Vol. 5, No. 4, 2002, pp. 499 – 519.

Sterling-Folker, Jennifer/Shinko, Rosemary E.: "Discourses of power: traversing the realist-postmodern divide," in Berenskoetter, Felix/Williams, Michael J. (eds.): *Power in World Politics*. London/New York 2007, pp. 244 – 264.

Stevenson, William D./Sebo, Stephen A.: "Elements of Power System Analysis," in IEEE Transactions on Systems, Man and Cybernetics, Vol. 6, No. 7, July 1976, p. 512.

Stinchcombe, Arthur L.: *Constructing Social Theories*. New York 1968.

Stone, Clarence N.: "Systematic Power in Community Decision Making: A Restatement of Stratification Theory," in *The American Political Science Review*, Vol. 74, No. 4, December 1980, pp. 978 – 990.

Strauss, Anselm L./Corbin, Juliet M.: *Basics of Qualitative Research*, 2nd edition. London 1998.

Tawney, Richard Henry: *Equality*. London 1971.

Tedeschi, James T./Bonoma, Thomas V.: "Power and Influence. An Introduction." in Tedeschi, James T. (ed.): *The Social Influence Processes*. Chicago 1972, pp. 1 – 49.

Telò, Mario: *Europe: a Civilian Power? European Union, Global Governance, World Order*. Chippenham/Eastbourne 2006.

Tetlock, Philip E./Belkin, Aaron (eds.): *Counterfactual Thought Experiments in World Politics*. Princeton 1996.

Tewes, Henning: *Germany, Civilian Power and the New Europe. Enlarging Nato and the European Union*. New York 2002.

Thucydides: *History of the Peleponnesian War,* (trans. Warner, R.). New York 1972.

Tilly, Charles: "International communities, secure or otherwise," in Adler, Emanuel/Barnett, Michael (eds.): *Security Communities.* Cambridge 1998, pp. 397 – 412.

Toumi, Khalida: "Culture Lies at the Heart of the Mediterranean Construction," publication information unavailable: *Dossier. Ten Years after the Barcelona Process: Assessment and Perspectives.* s.l. 2005, pp. 92 – 98, http://www.gencat.net/relacions_exteriors/bcn10/eng/pdf/dossier.pdf, 04/08/2007.

Tovias, Alfred: "Israeli Policy Perspectives on the Euro-Mediterranean Partnership in the Context of EU Enlargement," in *Mediterranean Politics*, Vol. 8, No. 2, Summer 2003, pp. 214 – 232.

Tovias, Alfred: "Economic Liberalism between Theory and Practice," in Adler, Emanuel/Bicchi, Federica/Crawford, Beverly/Del Sarto, Raffaella A. (eds.): *The Convergence of Civilizations. Constructing a Mediterranean Region.* Toronto/Buffalo/London 2006, pp. 191 - 211.

Trenz, Hans-Jörg: "Media Coverage on European Governance," in *European Journal of Communication*, Vol. 19, No. 3, 2004, pp. 291 – 319.

Tzifakis, Nikolaos: "EU`s region-building and boundary-drawing policies: the European approach to the Southern Mediterranean and the Western Balkans," in *Journal of Southern Europe and the Balkans*, Vol. 9, No. 1, April 2007, pp. 47 – 64.

United Nations Development Programme/Regional Bureau for Arab States (UNDP): *The Arab Human Development Report 2002.* New York 2002.

Vasconcelos, Álvaro: "Barcelona Plus: Towards a Euro-Mediterranean Community of Democratic States," publication information unavailable: *Dossier. Ten Years after the Barcelona*

Process: Assessment and Perspectives. s.l. 2005, pp. 66 – 69, http://www.gencat.net/relacions_exteriors/bcn10/eng/pdf/dossier.pdf, 04/08/2007.

Vasconcelos, Álvaro/Joffé, George: "Political Transition in the Middle East," in *Mediterranean Politics*, Vol. 5, No. 1, Spring 2000, (Vasconcelos, Álvaro/Joffé, George (eds.): "Special Issue on the Barcelona Process. Building a Euro-Mediterranean Regional Community"), pp. 3 – 6.

Vasquez, John A.: *The Power of Power Politics. From Classical Realism to Neotraditionalism.* Cambridge 1998.

Vaughan, Diane: "Theory elaboration: the heuristics of case analysis," in Ragin, Charles C./Becker, Howard Saul: *What is a Case? Exploring the Foundations of Social Inquiry.* Cambridge 1992, pp. 173 – 202.

Védrine, Hubert: "L`Union européenne sur la scène internationale," in *Le Forum Franco-Allemand*, Numéro spécial 2006/07, pp. 44 – 46.

Verba, Sidney: "Some Dilemmas in Comparative Research," in *World Politics*, Vol. 20, No. 1, October 1967, p. 111 – 127.

Volpi, Frédéric: "Regional Community Building and the Transformation of International Relations: The Case of the Euro-Mediterranean Partnership," in *Mediterranean Politics*, Vol. 9, No. 2, Summer 2004, pp. 145 - 164.

Volpi, Frédéric: "Introduction: Strategies for Regional Cooperation in the Mediterranean: Rethinking the Parameters of the Debate," in *Mediterranean Politics*, Vol. 11, No. 2, July 2006, pp. 119 - 135.

Wæver, Ole: "Securization and Desecurization," in Lipschutz, Ronnie D. (ed.): *On Security.* New York 1995, pp. 46—86.

Wæver, Ole: " European Security Identities," in *Journal of Common Market Studies*, Vol. 34, No. 1, March 1996, pp. 103 – 132.

Wæver, Ole: "Insecurity, security, and asecurity in the West European non-war community," in Adler, Emanuel/Barnett, Michael (eds.): *Security Communities*. Cambridge 1998, pp. 69 – 118.

Wæver, Ole/Buzan, Barry/Kelstrup, Morten/Lemaitre, Pierre: *Identity, Migration and the New Security Agenda in Europe*. London 1993.

Waltz, Kenneth W.: *Theory of International Politics*. Boston et al 1979.

Waltz, Kenneth W.: "Reflections on Theory of International Relations: A Response to My Critics," in Keohane, Robert O. (ed.): *Neoliberalism and Its Critics*. Cambridge 1986, pp. 322 – 345.

Wartenberg, Thomas E.: *The Forms of Power: From Domination to Transformation*. Philadelphia 1990.

Wartenberg, Thomas E: "Situated Social Power," in Wartenberg, Thomas (ed.): *Rethinking Power*. New York 1992, pp. 79 – 101.

Webb, Michael: "Die Mittelmeerpolitik der EU," in Meyer, Berthold (ed.): *Unruhezone Mittelmeer – Westeuropa und seine südlichen Nachbarn*, Dokumentation der Frühjahrsakademie 1996 der Hessischen Stiftung Friedens- und Konfliktforschung und Bericht über das Akademieprogramm 1990 - 1996. Frankfurt am Main 1996, pp. 148 – 154.

Weber, Max: *Politik als Beruf*. München 1958.

Weber, Max: *Economy and Society. An Outline of Interpretive Sociology*, (eds. Roth, Guenther/Wittich, Claus). New York 1968.

Weber, Max: *Essays in Economic Sociology*, (ed. Swedberg, Richard). Princeton/New York 1999.

Weissbrod, Lilly: "Israeli Identity in Transition" in *Israel Affairs*, Vol. 3, No.3 – 4, Spring/Summer 1997, pp. 47 – 65.

Wendt, Alexander: "The Agent-Structure Problem in International Relations Theory," in *International Organization*, Vol. 41, No. 3, Summer 1987, pp. 335 – 370.

Wendt, Alexander: "Anarchy is What States Make of it: The Social Construction of Power Politics," in *International Organization,* Vol. 46, No. 2, Spring 1992, pp. 391 – 425.

Wendt, Alexander: "Collective Identity Formation and the International State," in *The American Political Science Review*, Vol. 88, No. 2, June 1994, pp. 384 – 396.

Wendt, Alexander: *Social Theory of International Politics*. Cambridge 1999.

White, Gordon: "Civil society, democratization and development," in Luckman, Robin/White, Gordon (eds.): *Democratization in the South. The jagged wave*. Manchester et al 1996, pp. 178 – 219.

Whitman, Richard G.: "The International Identity of the EU: Instruments as Identity," in Landau, Alice/Whitman, Richard G. (eds.): *Rethinking the European Union: Institutions, Interests and Identities*. Basingstoke 1997, pp. 54 – 71.

Whitman, Richard G.: *From Civilian Power to Superpower? The International Identity of the European Union*. London/New York 1998.

Wieviorka, Michel: "Case studies: history or sociology?" in Ragin, Charles C./Becker, Howard Saul: *What is a Case? Exploring the Foundations of Social Inquiry*. Cambridge 1992, pp. 159 – 172.

Wight, Martin: *Power Politics*. London 1946.

Williams, Michael C.: "Hobbes and international relations: a reconsideration," in *International Organization*, Vol. 50, No. 2, Spring 1996, pp. 213 – 236.

Williams, Michael C.: "Words, Images, Enemies: Securitization and International Politics," in *International Studies Quarterly*, Vol. 47, No. 4, 2003, pp. 511 – 531.

Wintle, Michael (ed.): *Culture and Identity in Europe: Perceptions of Divergence and Unity in Past and Present*. Aldershot 1996.

Wolff, Stephan: "Analysis of Documents and Records," in Flick, Uwe/Kardorff, Ernst von/Steinke, Ines (eds.): *A Companion to Qualitative Research*. London 2004, pp. 284-290.

Wolfinger, Raymond: "Nondecisions and the Study of Local Politics," in *American Political Science Review*, Vol. 65, No. 4, December 1971a, pp. 1063 – 1080.

Wolfinger, Raymond: "Rejoinder to Frey's Comment," in *American Political Science Review*, Vol. 65, No. 4, December 1971b, pp. 1102 – 1104.

Wright, Quincy: *The Study of International Relations*. New York 1955.

Wrong, Dennis H.: *Power: Its Forms, Bases, and Uses*. New York et al 1980.

Yin, Robert K: "The Case Study as a Serious Research Strategy," in *Science Communication*, Vol. 3, No. 1, 1981, pp. 97 – 114.

Yin, Robert K.: *Case Study Research: Design and Methods*, 3rd edition. London 2003.

Yolles, Maurice: "Revisiting the political cybernetics of organizations," in *Kybernetes*, Vol. 34, No. 5, 2005, pp. 617 – 636.

Young, Oran: "International Regimes: Towards a New Theory of Institutions," in *World Politics*, Vol. 39, 1986, pp. 104 – 122.

Youngs, Richard: *Democracy Promotion: The Case of the European*

Union Strategy, CEPS Working Document 167, Center for European Policy Studies. Brussels 2001.

Youngs, Richard: "The European Union and Democracy Promotion in the Mediterranean: A New or Disingenuous Strategy?" in *Democratization*, Vol. 9, No. 1, Spring 2002, (Gillespie, Richard/Youngs, Richard (eds.): "Special Issue: The European Union and Democracy Promotion: The Case of North Africa"), pp. 40—62.

Youngs, Richard (ed.): *Survey of European Democracy Promotion Policies 2000 – 2006*, Fundación par alas Relaciones Internacionales y el Diálogo Exterior (FRIDE). Madrid 2006.

Youngs, Richard: *Is European Democracy Promotion on the Wane?* CEPS Working Document No. 292, May 2008, http://www.ceps.eu, 21/05/08.

Zapata-Barrero, Ricard/González, Elisabet: "The Euro-Mediterranean Non-discourse on Political Participation of 'Mediterranean immigrants' in the EU," in *Mediterranean Yearbook*, 2006, pp. 86 – 90.

Zimmermann, Moshe:„Festungsmentalität und Verfolgungswahn. Die israelische Gesellschaft und der Friedensprozess," in *Internationale Politik*, Vol. 53, No. 4, April 1998, pp. 47 – 56.

Zorob, Anja: *Europäische Nachbarschaftspolitik: Eine erste Bilanz*, German Institute of Global and Area Studies, Institut für Nahoststudien, GIGA Focus Nahost No. 1, 2007, pp. 1 - 8.

Zürn, Michael: "Regimeanalyse," in Albrecht, Ulrich/Volger, Hartmut (eds.): *Lexikon der internationalen Politik*. München 1997, pp. 434 – 436.

Politikwissenschaft

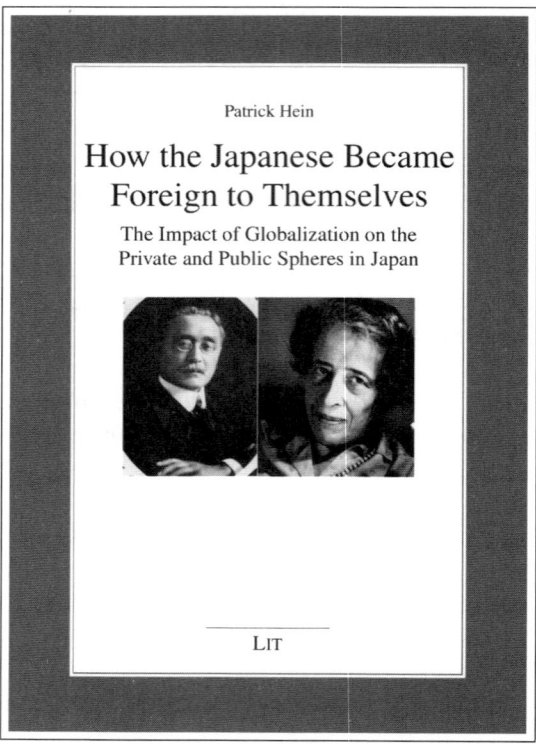

Patrick Hein
How the Japanese Became Foreign to Themselves
The Impact of Globalization on the Private and Public Spheres in Japan
The question whether Arendt's distinction of the 'private, public and society' can be applied to the Japanese cultural context will be examined. It will be argued that repressed needs for equality, plurality and independence have made their way back through increased civil political participation and that this process is driven by the renaissance of the pre Meiji Samurai principle of ethical individualism.
Bd. 164, 2009, 240 S., 34,90 €, br., ISBN 3-643-10085-6

LIT Verlag Berlin – Münster – Wien – Zürich – London
Auslieferung Deutschland / Österreich / Schweiz: siehe Impressumsseite

David Wineroither

KANZLERMACHT – MACHTKANZLER?

Die Regierung Schüssel im
historischen und internationalen Vergleich

LIT

David Wineroither
Kanzlermacht – Machtkanzler?
Die Regierung Schüssel im historischen und internationalen Vergleich
„Kanzlermacht – Machtkanzler?" beleuchtet eines der jüngsten Kapitel der österreichischen Politikge-
schichte: die Kanzlerschaft Wolfgang Schüssels, die Regierungsjahre von Schwarz-Blau und Schwarz-
Orange 2000 – 2007. Kaum ein Kanzler vor ihm hat die Gesellschaft mehr bewegt, sie drastisch pola-
risiert. Im Zentrum dieser politikwissenschaftlichen Analyse steht die politisch-kulturelle, die „mehr-
heitsdemokratische" Wende des Jahres 2000. Das Buch stellt und beantwortet auch die „Machtfrage":
Schüssel selbst war der einflussreichste *political leader* seit Bruno Kreisky, aber dabei alles andere als ein
Alleinentscheider.
Bd. 165, 2009, 424 S., 29,90 €, br., ISBN-AT 978-3-643-50051-9

LIT Verlag Berlin – Münster – Wien – Zürich – London
Auslieferung Deutschland / Österreich / Schweiz: siehe Impressumsseite

Christoph Doktor

Die Aussen- und Sicherheitspolitik
Sicherheitspolitik
Österreichs und der Schweiz
gegenüber der GASP der
Europäischen Union

Eine diskurstheoretische Analyse

Politikwissenschaft

LIT

Christoph Doktor

**Die Aussen- und Sicherheitspolitik Österreichs und der Schweiz gegenüber der GASP
der Europäischen Union**

Eine diskurstheoretische Analyse

Die vorliegende Arbeit untersucht aus diskurstheoretischer Perspektive die sehr unterschiedlichen Politiken der beiden mitteleuropäischen Kleinstaaten Österreich und Schweiz gegenüber der europäischen Integration und insbesondere ihrer aussen- und sicherheitspolitischen Dimension, der GASP. Die in den politischen Debatten reproduzierten diskursiven Konstruktionen der nationalen Identitäten stehen im Mittelpunkt der Analyse. Die Untersuchung zeigt auf, wie die unterschiedlichen historisch überlieferten und in den nationalen Identitäten fest verankerten Inhalte der Konzepte von „Staat und Nation", „Europa" und „Sicherheit" die jeweiligen Reaktionen der beiden Staaten gegenüber der Europäischen Union beeinflussen und damit als ein struktureller Rahmen der nationalen Aussen- und Sicherheitspolitiken fungieren.

Bd. 166, 2009, 272 S., 25,90 €, br., ISBN-CH 978-3-643-80009-1

LIT Verlag Berlin – Münster – Wien – Zürich – London
Auslieferung Deutschland / Österreich / Schweiz: siehe Impressumsseite

Sven S. Kasper

Politikwissenschaft

LIT

Sven S. Kasper

Systemtheoretische Analyse des Einflusses der deutschen Wirtschaft auf die deutsche Außenpolitik

Wirtschaft und Politik sind eng verflochtene gesellschaftliche Subsysteme. Ihr Verhältnis ist geprägt durch Austausch und Kooperation sowohl in der Innen- als auch der Außenpolitik. Letztere steht im Zentrum der Untersuchung. Dabei wird mit Hilfe von Gabriel Almonds systemtheoretischem Modell der außenpolitische Prozess Deutschlands betrachtet und analysiert. Hauptgegenstand der Untersuchung ist die Einflussnahme der Wirtschaft auf die deutsche Außenpolitik. Darüber hinaus wird Almonds Ansatz hinsichtlich seiner Anwendbarkeit auf die Untersuchung außenpolitischer Prozesse und Abläufe beurteilt.

Bd. 169, 2009, 288 S., 31,90 €, br., ISBN-CH 978-3-643-90025-8

LIT Verlag Berlin – Münster – Wien – Zürich – London
Auslieferung Deutschland / Österreich / Schweiz: siehe Impressumsseite

Die Neutralitätsfalle

Österreichs Sicherheitspolitik in der Sackgasse?

Mit einem Vorwort von Benita Ferrero-Waldner
und Werner Fasslabend

Markus Krottmayer

LIT

Markus Krottmayer
Die Neutralitätsfalle
Österreichs Sicherheitspolitik in der Sackgasse?
Der Autor plädiert anhand von acht Argumenten für die Abkehr Österreichs von der Neutralität im Rahmen der europäischen Integration.
Der wichtigen Frage nach der Aktualität der Neutralität in Europa, insbesondere Österreichs Status als Neutraler innerhalb der europäischen GASP/ESVP wird in diesem Buch nachgegangen.
Im Europa des Lissabon-Reformvertrages ist die Frage der Zeitmäßigkeit der Neutralität Österreichs akut.
Bd. 170, 2009, 280 S., 19,90 €, br., ISBN 978-3-643-50083-0

LIT Verlag Berlin – Münster – Wien – Zürich – London
Auslieferung Deutschland / Österreich / Schweiz: siehe Impressumsseite